# A CASTLE
IN THE BACKYARD

# A CASTLE
# IN THE BACKYARD

## The Dream of a House in France

*Betsy Draine*
*Michael Hinden*

THE UNIVERSITY OF WISCONSIN PRESS

The University of Wisconsin Press
1930 Monroe Street
Madison, Wisconsin 53711

www.wisc.edu/wisconsinpress/

3 Henrietta Street
London WC2E 8LU, England

5        4        3        2        1

Printed in the United States of America


Library of Congress Cataloging-in-Publication Data

Draine, Betsy, 1945–
A castle in the backyard : the dream of a house in France / Betsy
Draine and Michael Hinden.
p. cm.
ISBN 0-299-17940-0 (cloth : alk. paper)
1. Dordogne (France)—Social life and customs. 2. Draine, Betsy,
1945—Homes and haunts—France—Dordogne. 3. Vacation
homes—France—Dordogne. I. Hinden, Michael. II. Title.
DC611.D7 D73 2002
944'.72—dc21
2002001362

*à vos désirs*

# CONTENTS

# PREFACE

In 1985, for what it costs these days to buy a midsized car, we bought an old stone house in the hilltop village of Castelnaud-la-Chapelle in the Dordogne Valley of southwest France. The ancient name of this province is Périgord, but after the Revolution, it was renamed the Department of the Dordogne, in honor of the gently winding river that shaped its landscape. This verdant region lies one hundred miles inland from Bordeaux, bordered by the wine country of Bergerac to the west and Cahors to the southeast. It used to be that when Americans thought of France, they thought of Paris, or the Riviera, or perhaps Normandy. With the popularity of Peter Mayle's charming books, everyone now seems to know Provence as well. But few Americans know the Dordogne. In France, the department is renowned for its walnuts, truffles, *foie gras*, prehistoric cave paintings, and natural beauty.

In many ways this is still *la France profonde*, remote and slow to change, despite the influx of Parisians who come camping on their summer holidays. Périgord remains a poet's inspiration—the Frenchman's Paradise, Henry Miller called it on a visit between the wars. Flanked by ocher cliffs and unmarred by major highways, the Dordogne Valley glows with the gold of sunflowers set against green swaths of corn and tobacco. The river, wide and sparkling, is constantly visible, flowing through planted fields, by castle keeps, past towns perched on bluffs or ranged along its banks, and on to enter thin poplar woods lying between settlements.

Périgord rose to prominence in the Middle Ages during the Hundred Years War, when the Dordogne River marked the battle line between France and England. It was then that most of its great castles were built, churches fortified, and walled villages established, some of them strategic garrisons called *bastides*, planned around central market places with their streets radiating out from a central grid. The English finally were expelled from the area at the Battle of Castillon in 1453, but the Wars of Religion in the sixteenth century between Catholics and Huguenots roiled the valley again with savage fighting. In the following century, agriculture expanded, as did river trade, with barges plying the route between Bergerac and Bordeaux. Yet the Industrial Revolution left Périgord untouched, and the province was poor in the eighteenth and nineteenth centuries, remaining heavily wooded and divided into small tracts and farms. Much of the region's charm today derives from its rural character.

In the medieval village of Castelnaud-la-Chapelle, a minor building boom occurred after the Revolution, when the castle that gives the town its name was nearly demolished. Emboldened farmers and workers seized the castle's dressed limestone blocks for the construction of their own homes. Perhaps that accounts for the harmonious ensemble of the village today, as it appears to have been built all of a piece out of golden stone.

There are 409 inhabitants in Castelnaud, including us. Our cottage fits snugly between its neighbors, perched at the foot of the fortress that used to provide the town's defense. Over fifteen summers, we have settled in, making friends, exploring the countryside, and learning the local history and cuisine. During that time we have witnessed the transformation of our village from a picturesque cluster of half-deserted houses to a thriving attraction centered on its well-publicized château, which has been converted to a museum of medieval warfare. We recognize that we ourselves are part of the town's transformation: *"les américains,"* who (for reasons inexplicable to old-time residents) purchased a home in a country where we have no relatives and who travel thousands of miles each summer to take up housekeeping next to the castle walls.

No one in town speaks English, but our French is serviceable, and the richest part of our experience has grown from ties with our neighbors, among them the daughters of the electrician who knock on our door excitedly as soon as we arrive each summer, the local real-estate agent who sold us our house and who continues to besot us with homemade wine, and the elderly widow who lived in the village all her life, never saw Paris, and would tell us the tale of her life's tragedy over and over again, forgetting that we already knew it by heart.

Their stories are part of ours, although we have changed the names of individuals to protect their privacy and occasionally modified details for the same reason. Along the way we have supplied information that might interest others who have been stirred by the romance of living in France. How we found and bought our house in Castelnaud is part of the story. But this is not a how-to book; neither is it a tourist guide, although we could not write about the Dordogne without describing its beautiful walking trails, cave paintings, and mouth-watering food. Simply, this is an account of our experience of establishing a second home in France. It is also a story of transformations—of a house, a village, and a way of life.

Of course, Castelnaud has changed our way of life too. We were closing in on middle age when we began our adventure. As academics (we met while teaching in the English Department at the University of Wisconsin–Madison), we had our summers available for travel and research. With no children, we were able to dream of spending part of each year overseas. What we did not anticipate was the extent to which our relationships in the village would bind us to Castelnaud the year round. We have translated a cookbook of regional walnut specialties written by one of our neighbors; three children and one set of parents from the village have visited us in Madison; and our production of international greeting cards at Christmastime is now considerable.

Creating a life for ourselves in a French provincial village has been an experiment as well as a collaboration. The same may be said of this book. We have pooled our memories and shared the writing. Friends who learned we were working on a manuscript together were always curious as to how the process worked. Eventually it was like walking: when one foot takes a step, the other has to go in the same direction. Sometimes we divided responsibilities for the first drafts of chapters, but more often, one of us would write several pages and the other would pick things up wherever the previous day's work came to a halt. We constantly traded places at the computer. To avoid confusion on the part of the reader, we have limited the focus to Betsy's perspective, but when Betsy is speaking, it may be Michael who's writing: in other words, "Betsy" is us.

We have tried to remain faithful to our shared experience, though our friends in the village who find their lives twined with ours may wish we had been more reticent. We ask their indulgence. This book would not have been possible without their warmth and generosity in making room for us in their lives. We will always be grateful for their friendship.

We owe a note of thanks to Raphael Kadushin at the University of Wisconsin Press for his suggestion that we might shape our experiences into a memoir and for his helpful comments on the manuscript in its various stages.

We also thank our American friends, families, and colleagues, who took a lively interest in our adventure as it was unfolding and who encouraged us to follow our hearts.

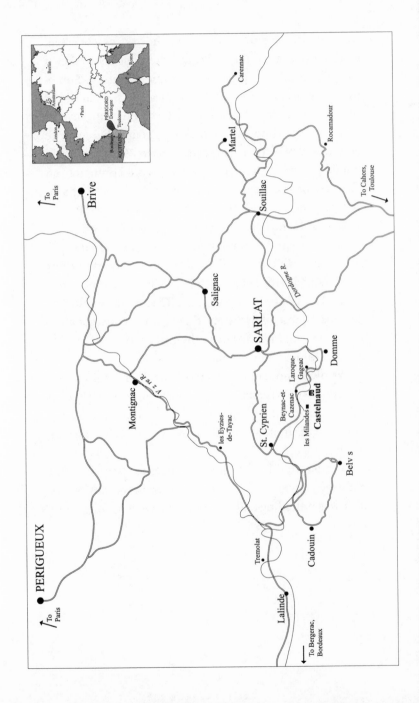

# I

# HOUSE HUNTING

## A CHANGE OF PLANS

As we drove into Sarlat on a hot July afternoon, buying a house was not on the agenda. We were simply looking for a place to spend the night. Sarlat is the gem of Périgord, a golden maze of medieval streets and alleyways, but it was not designed for modern traffic. In 1837, to ease congestion, the city fathers decided to cut a thoroughfare—they called it a *traverse*—through the center of town, splitting the city into two gnarled hemispheres. As a result, the street map of Sarlat looks like an open walnut shell. On one side of the *traverse*, now called la rue de la République, there are steep, twisting lanes with old limestone houses, adorned with hanging flower pots. On the other side lie the town's more public spaces: Saint Sacerdos Cathedral, with its strange onion-shaped belfry, the old cemetery and its mysterious tower known as the Lantern of the Dead, the stately

Hôtel de Ville, and a cluster of Renaissance *manoirs,* with Gothic bays and mullioned windows. There are pruned public gardens and a broad cobblestone square, where a bustling open-air market is held on Saturdays. On either side of la rue de la République, the amber-colored buildings of the city gleam with pride.

But these delights are invisible from the traffic-clogged *traverse.* Cramped shops and cafés with cheap plastic chairs line both sides of the street. There isn't a leaf of shade, and in summer cars and trucks spouting diesel exhaust nudge along, baking in the heat. If your first introduction to Sarlat is a traffic jam on la rue de la République, you'll wonder why the *Guide Michelin* devotes five pages to the town. Yet that is just how we saw Sarlat on a scorching summer's day in 1984, and looking back on it, that is where our story begins.

We were nearing the end of a rambling automobile tour that began in Paris, led us south through the flat Loire Valley and the mountainous Auvergne, and in the last week had brought us to the rolling hills of the Dordogne. We had several days left to the trip before we were due in Nice to catch our returning charter flight to the States. The route was circuitous, but Michael had driven through the Dordogne years before and wanted me to see a little of the countryside before we linked up again with the *autoroute* to the Côte d'Azur.

A travel writer once observed that the Dordogne, with its picturesque byways and narrow country roads, is pre-eminently a land for dawdlers, but even on that blistering day, speeding through on our way to make a plane connection, with the car windows rolled down and the scenery going by in a warm blur, we caught its allure. What I remember are rows of poplars along a river bank leaning in the breeze, their feathery V-shaped branches like quills casting lean reflections in the water as we rounded a bend; newly mown hay rolled up like yellow carpets, with nearby farm buildings nestling companionably together like a litter of kittens; a ruined manor with pepper pot towers deserted in a meadow; sunlight gleaming on a village at the crest of a hill, its houses stacked almost on top of one another; shady passages through forests alternating with hot stretches of open road and the smell of tar; a sharp blue, cloudless sky.

Even the meanest farmhouse looked inviting, thanks to the cheerful cast of the local stone, which seemed so different from the gloomy gray of the row houses farther north. In the Dordogne the houses are built with limestone, often in uneven blocks that soften edges and give the rural buildings an affable air of nonchalance. Depending on the hour, the color of the stone can take on a variety of hues, from pinkish gold in the morning to blazing white in the afternoon, to yellow, amber, ocher, and dark rust as the sun goes down. I remember thinking to myself as we drove along that these must be the loveliest houses in the world.

For lunch we had stopped in Brantôme, a lazy old town at the fork of two branches of the river Dronne, the site of a massive Benedictine abbey founded by Charlemagne in 769. We picnicked in the park under a cool pavilion and gazed across the water at the stately monastery. Then in the afternoon, our luck changed. We became snarled in traffic as we tried to negotiate the regional capital, Périgueux, which can be a bottleneck in summer for trucks on the way south. Michael's temper grew shorter as the heat built up, and he was in no mood for more traffic when we finally reached Sarlat. We were looking forward to a shower and a good meal after a cramped afternoon in our rented Renault 5.

We were following a wonderful hotel guide called *Les Logis de France,* which features only small, family-run hotel-restaurants. At the typical *logis,* the husband serves as chef, the wife runs the hotel, and the older children wait on tables. Each *logis* has its own personality and appeal, unlike the newer motel chains, which try to imitate American efficiency. Once, after a blazing day on the road, we decided to splurge on one of those modern wonders in order to get an air-conditioned room—only to find that the system was turned off every night because the French guests found the air too cold. In the morning we were baffled by the automated breakfast buffet, which presented a row of glistening machines to dispense orange juice, coffee, and dry cereal. We watched as an elderly Frenchman came into the breakfast room wearing a béret and smoking a *Gauloise.* He tried the coffee machine, wagged his head back and forth in incomprehension, muttered, banged his cane on the floor to summon a human being, and demanded a glass of red wine and a baguette. We saluted him with our un-French glasses of orange juice and after that steered clear of the motels.

According to our *Logis* guide, there was a venerable family-run hotel in Sarlat called the Saint Albert, and that was where we were headed for the evening. It was now about five in the afternoon with the sun still almost directly overhead and beating down on the hood as we crept along Sarlat's rue de la République, inhaling exhaust fumes and looking for a turnoff to the little side street on which the hotel was located. The little street was easy to miss, and we had to circle round and come down the traverse a second time to find it. Then parking took a long time. When we finally found a space, Michael trotted up the block and then returned disconsolately with the news that the Saint Albert was fully booked.

Heat waves rose from the pavement, making me light-headed; tourists hustled by. Michael, impatient, was for pushing on. It would still be light for hours, he reasoned, and the breeze of a country road seemed preferable to walking the hot streets of the city, looking for a second-choice hotel. According to the guide, there was a rural *logis* at Labastide-Murat, about an hour or so's drive along back roads, and there was another at Cabrerets, which perhaps might take two hours. As a backup, there was still another listing in a place called Najac farther on to the south, although the village was not on our itinerary and did seem remote when we finally found it on the map. In all likelihood, though, we would be settled in an hour, enjoying a good dinner at a quiet country hotel.

We have a running argument when we travel. One of us believes in reservations; one of us does not. According to Michael, the advantage of traveling by car is that you can always find another hotel if your first choice isn't available, whereas if you book ahead sight unseen, you may regret your choice. I say that only a masochist would travel without reservations at the height of the tourist season and risk having to sleep in the car. We rehashed this discussion each morning as we reviewed the day's itinerary.

"What about booking ahead at the Hotel Saint Albert in Sarlat?" I had asked over breakfast.

"Sounds OK, but let's just go there. We'll get there early and see what it looks like."

Now we were there. It looked fine.

"Maybe we should call Labastide-Murat."

"It's early yet."

"If the Saint Albert is full, they may be full there too," I pointed out.

"This is the city. We're headed off the beaten track; we'll be fine."

Well, it *was* still early, and so far we had always ended the day with a roof over our heads. Michael was confident that our luck would hold at the next stop, and I didn't protest. In fact, as we edged back into traffic and out of the city, it felt good to be moving again.

Sarlat lies in a glen at the heart of Périgord Noir, or Black Périgord, so named for its dense forests of oak and walnut. A few miles south of town, beyond a series of ridges, the road dips and enters the broad basin of the Dordogne Valley. Green fields of leafy tobacco, corn, beans, and lettuce spread across the flats. Here the Dordogne is a queenly river with soft meanders, for it is tamed by controlling dams upstream. Elsewhere it is a powerful river, one of France's longest, originating high in the mountains of the massif Central and flowing westward for three hundred miles to Bordeaux, where it joins the Gironde and empties into the sea. But here the river takes its ease, flowing gracefully between tree-lined banks that afford open vistas, looping around cliffs topped by castles, and curving across the plain.

At the hamlet of Carsac we rested briefly and stopped to admire an exquisite twelfth-century country church built in the yellow stone that so attracted us. Rounded and low, it was gracefully placed on its green lawn by the side of the road. The porched doorway was simply carved with modest, bare columns, leading the eye into the dark of the interior. Inside, the church was small yet felt expansive. High above our heads, the stone roof arched comfortingly, while to the sides and beyond the altar, Gothic chapels multiplied space. Standing before the linen-draped altar with its one vigil candle, we were surrounded by a bubble of golden light. Only the need to find a room for the night prevented us from lingering.

Leaving the Sarladais (the old diocese of Sarlat), we crossed the river, and soon the landscape began to change from lush to rugged. Only twenty miles to the southeast, the contrast was striking. For this is the beginning of *causse* country, defined by dry, whitish limestone plateaus. Water drains through the porous stone, carving wind-swept, arid basins and escarpments. Sheep and goats graze on scrubby plots demarcated by gray stone walls. The tree cover is juniper, the vegetation thin, though near Cahors there are ancient vineyards from which a dark, tangy red wine is produced. Here the building stone, like the cliffs, is pinkish gray or white, and the châteaus look more foreboding than those made with the homey yellow stone of the Dordogne. The region is riddled with caves and ravines and is sparsely settled.

After a twisting, bumpy drive that took us longer than expected, we arrived at Labastide-Murat. This lonely village stands at a high point on the *causse* and boasts few attractions. One is a museum dedicated to Joachim Murat, one of Napoleon's best generals and a favorite son (in honor of whom the town was renamed). The other is a perfectly charming *logis*—which, like the Saint Albert, turned out to be booked full. As we pulled away from the hotel, I gazed with envy at a group of cheerful guests congregating on the terrace for their apéritifs and reading over the posted menus. There was no need to say anything. Michael threw up his hands. A good hour later we met a similar fate in Cabrerets: no rooms to be had. Now only Najac stood between us and the abyss. Capitulating, Michael pulled up at a roadside phone booth, rang the Hotel Belle Rive in Najac, and reported that the *patron* would hold his last remaining room for us, provided we arrived in time for dinner.

*"Mais, oui, Monsieur, on arrive!"* "We're on our way!"

We were expected by nine. It was already almost eight, and the drive ahead of us looked difficult. By now we had traversed the departments of the Dordogne and the Lot and were headed into the Aveyron, a semi-deserted region of wild gorges and cataracts. Here the road winds through dense thickets, up steep hills, and down the sides of ravines. As the shadows lengthened and the settlements grew farther apart, we seemed to be leaving the France of graceful living for the rough country of another era. The smaller roads felt no wider than paved trails. Below Villefranche-de-Rouergue, the main road branches off and twists through the Gorges de l'Aveyron above a roaring river, dipping up and down with dangerous switchbacks as it tracks the Aveyron through its canyon. The terrain is tortuous, the driving perilous and slow, so that by the time we approached Najac, it was pitch dark. In the last hour we had passed no other villages, no hotels. Just before entering the town, we crossed a bridge over a black ravine and followed signs to the Hotel Belle Rive. The thickly wooded road plunged lower and lower, finally dead-ending at the doorstep of a long, low-lying, white-stoned inn.

Without unpacking, and barely aware of our surroundings, we checked in and rushed straight to dinner.

It was nearly ten. Only a few guests still lingered in the rustic dining room. Two tired-looking waiters were clearing the tables of debris: empty wine bottles, crusty bread crumbs on the pink tablecloths, plates of cleanly picked bones piled on what remained of a dark sauce. We ordered what the other guests apparently had devoured, the plat du jour, a delectable rabbit ragout, and of course a bottle of local red wine to go with it. Perhaps it was the novelty of rabbit stew; perhaps it was the table set with crude oversized cutlery in front of a huge hearth straight out of the Middle Ages; or perhaps it was the late hour, the long drive, and the profound relief of having dinner at all after facing the prospect of a night without shelter—but we were enchanted.

Our spirits continued to rise as we wound through the stone halls hung with tapestries, found our room, used a five-inch-long iron key to spring the lock, and swung open the heavy door to see bright white linens turned down over a flowery duvet, dark furniture sized for a couple of woodland giants, and lace-curtained French windows that promised to give onto a romantic terrace. Too tired to peer out the windows, we notched them open a bit (an infraction of French protocol for healthy sleeping, we later found) and dropped asleep to the faint sound of water gurgling over pebbles.

The next morning, prying ourselves out from under the sheets, we stepped out to see our terrace. There was no terrace at all—instead, several yards of ivy slanted down to the edge of a clear-running brook, backed by a wood of stunted oaks and evergreens. The air was crisp, with a sharp taste of pine. We took a deliciously deep breath and stood together, gazing into the tangled wild. I thought for some reason of Hansel and Gretel on their first morning in the forest. Luckily, we were not banished or lost, just happily waylaid.

Once fully awake and breakfasted, we planned to visit the town's ruined castle and then undo this detour, however magical, and regain our itinerary toward Nice. We had in hand a faded guide to the castle that the hotelier had given us. The black-and-white pamphlet looked like a relic from the prewar period and led us to expect a musty attraction. Instead, we fell deeper under Najac's spell.

The weathered-gray walls of Najac Castle rise high above a steep hill surrounded on three sides by a loop of the Aveyron. Though crumbling, the crenellated towers dominate the heights; their gloomy massiveness must have struck terror in the hearts of attackers in the days of feudal wars. The guidebook told of others who had dared this same approach: crusaders against the heretical Cathars in 1216, the English in the Hundred Years War, Huguenot brigands in 1572, and, as a last insult, ten thousand rebellious peasants in the 1643 revolt of the Croquants. They must have been mad, I thought, to go up against this fortress. It firmly possesses its summit, surveying the sides of the hill that drop precipitously to the gorge of the Aveyron and guarding the side on which the castle is most vulnerable, the causeway leading to the village.

Imagining the flight of otherworldly heretics seeking refuge from the Pope's battalions, we climbed the towers, peered into the dungeon, and mounted the battlements to gaze out at the rugged hills. The view from the heights of the castle seemed unchanged from the thirteenth century. The town may have added buildings here and there, but the architecture would have been the same, and the dramatic shape of the village on its spit of rock must have defined it since its settlement. In a circle as far as the eye could see, the scruffy woods and rocky hills were still largely uninhabited, with just a glimpse of a stone cabin here and there.

We scrambled down from the castle and set out to visit the town. Najac clings to its ridge with talons of limestone, each building perched at a perilous angle. The ridge itself drops and rises again, creating the impression of two separate towns like the humps of a camel linked by a narrow street of uneven paving stones. At the top of that ridge looms the *château fort.* On the first level below the castle, a blocklike church straddles a rocky point and gathers the little village around it. Farther along the road, the ridge rises, opening into a broad square framed by ancient half-timbered houses supported by stone pillars. This, I thought, must be the public market that the hotel keeper had told us not to miss. With no one else in sight, we stood in the central open square, imagining the Saturday markets that since the 1300s were famed for Najac cheese and ham. We walked back up the main street, admiring the mossy stone houses with gray slate roofs, the odd bits of Renaissance masonry, and the huge fourteenth-century fountain carved from a single block of local stone. Strangely, the town seemed deserted. Except for open doorways in a few shops on the central square, there was little sign of life. Here was an isolated medieval village that had yet to be discovered, and we had it to ourselves.

"We should really get on our way," Michael said reluctantly. I waited. "But this place is terrific. Let's see the rest of it."

We started by circling the church, looking up for gargoyles and finding none. Instead, as we reached the back of the massive stone edifice, we found a tiny graveyard with a frightening view of the gorge. Rounding a corner, we were face to face again with the fortress castle—secular power staring down spiritual power. The secular apparently had won, for the church had been forced to fortify itself to the point of ugliness. When Najac Castle was held by enemies of the Pope, this prisonlike church was a refuge for holy warriors and those they protected, and when the castle was taken again by friends of the Church, this sanctified fortress stood by as a second site of the town's defense. Today the old wooden door was locked, without the customary sign telling visitors to apply to this or that house for the guardian. Far from feeling put off, we felt ever more strongly the appeal of this town that had fought over time and under different regimes for its right to hold onto one craggy ridge in the wilderness.

Slowly, as we continued exploring the town, we began to notice how many of the old stone houses stood empty and bore a simple notice: *À Vendre*—For Sale. Not just one house here or there, but a dozen scattered along the main street alone. At first our thoughts were philosophical, not acquisitive. Why were residents willing to abandon this enchanting village, and where had they gone? What was the mystery of Najac? Michael, caught up in the adventure of discovery, recited lines from one of his favorite poems, Keats's "Ode on a Grecian Urn":

> And little town, thy streets for evermore
> Will silent be; and not a soul to tell
> Why thou art desolate, can e'er return.

The baker in the central square offered a prosaic answer to the puzzle while we chatted at his counter, eating slices of cold quiche for lunch. Like many such towns in the Aveyron, he told us, Najac could not provide jobs for its young. The town slowly was being depopulated as older residents died and their grown children left for the larger cities. Houses that had been in the same family for generations were glutting the market. Who would buy them? Parisians, he sniffed, who would use them as summer homes, leaving the town deserted the remainder of the year. But unlike some of the towns to the north (nearer Paris), Najac had not yet become chic, and the houses, however low the asking price, were not being snapped up. The town was dying, he pronounced, and he did not know whether his shop would survive.

After lunch, with rising excitement, we continued our exploration, only now we paused in front of each stone house that was for sale, peering through windows and circling the property. They looked so cozy, with their low front stoops leading into a small living room, with lace-curtained windows placed to catch views of the church, the castle, or neighbors walking by. Gradually the tendrils of a dream began winding their way into our conversation. We had tumbled upon a secret village preserved, it seemed in amber, since the Middle Ages, with rows of alluring houses standing empty and available, according to the baker, at bargain prices.

Michael gave me a conspiratorial glance. "What do you think it would take to own one?" he asked slyly.

Once voiced, the question multiplied and gathered an irresistible momentum. As professors of English, we had limited means, but we did have our summers to travel, and the idea of a vacation getaway had crossed our minds before. We often talked about finding a little place in the country where we could relax and enjoy a change of scene. But in remotest France? Could we picture ourselves here every summer? How would we spend our days and nights? Would we prize the eerie feeling of living among the ghosts of a noble and yet savage history? Would the rough beauty of the rugged landscape retain its appeal, or would we, in a few years, feel dashed by its bleakness? Would we become part of village life—and, indeed, would village life revive, or would we become the last inhabitants of a dead town? In any case, could we afford to buy one of the smaller places?

The same questions would be repeated over the coming year. Michael had spent his happiest college days at the Sorbonne on his junior year abroad; I had won a high-school prize for French, then lazily dropped the language in college, though remaining a Francophile. In our twenties, long before we met in Madison, we each had developed friendships with couples in France—Michael's friends were in Bordeaux and mine in the Loire and Paris. In truth, we both had a long-standing love of France. Nonetheless, we had no French relatives, no professional connections, no clear rationale for choosing France— never mind a remote village in the Aveyron—over the more sensible candidates for a vacation home, such as northern Wisconsin (an easy drive from Madison, where we live and work) or Cape Cod (near our East Coast families). But didn't we feel a sense of heightened energy being here? Wasn't it exciting to try to communicate in a second language and to negotiate the quirks of cultural difference? Wasn't this countryside the most beautiful in Europe, and French cuisine the best in the world? Maybe so, but how long would such feelings stand up against the realities of a lonely town like Najac? And in any case, the prices probably were beyond our reach.

I put the case for caution. "It's true we have almost three months in the summer, but we can't spend that much time away from our work. How could we do our research and writing in a place like this?"

"Well, what better way to ensure you write than to plunk yourself down in a spot so desolate that you have nothing to do there *but* write?"

I pointed out the lack of a library, never mind an English library. Michael countered that we could ship over whatever books and materials we might need for a summer's worth of writing.

He had a point, but I still had reservations. I got a lonely feeling when I thought of buying a house so far away, coming to France to be on our own, far from friends and family for months at a time. Feeling a bit of a coward, I divulged this misgiving.

"Believe me, we'll get visitors," Michael replied.

Despite my doubts, I was drawn to the idea. I don't know whether it was the stones, or the hills, or the castle, or the isolation, or the connection to the past, but I felt the attraction as strongly as he did.

I thought about how Michael and I had met, well into our thirties, each with already established friendships and careers. When we married, I moved into the house that Michael had bought some years before, a comfortable 1920s bungalow on Madison's funky east side. I had become fond of the house, with its Prairie-style leaded windows and oak floors and paneling. One of the early cues that we were compatible was that he had made every decorating choice just as I would have, right down to the round oak table in the dining room, with its matching high-backed chairs. Although I liked every-thing about the house, I regretted that there had been little room left for mutual adventures in homemaking.

For shared projects, we turned to vacation planning. Together we had mapped trips over semester break to Mexico and several other warm-weather destinations. This summer trip had been a joint project, too, with each of us taking responsibility for half the itinerary. I decided what we would do in Paris and planned a visit for us to friends I had known since college days who now lived near Chinon, in the Loire Valley. Michael had added a drive through the Auvergne and the Dordogne. We had enjoyed the trip as much for its surprises as for its intrinsic delights. Now Michael's luck-of-the-road style of travel had brought us to Najac, where we both felt the lure of a romantic hideaway. The idea of ex-tending the adventure by buying a little house here might well be foolish, but at the same time it offered us the chance to share the experience of creating a home together. That was appealing.

At just this point in my musings—in front of a Re-naissance house across from the church, to be exact—I spotted this sign:

---

Maisons à vendre

M. Castagnet, Notaire

150,000–400,000 f.

---

Looking over at Michael, I saw that his eyes had fol-lowed my stare. Until now we had seen no prices on the discreet For Sale signs posted on houses. Now we had some hard information. At that moment in international finance, the exchange rate for the U.S. dollar was nearing an unprecedented high. At ten francs to the dollar, which was where the rate was hovering, M. Castagnet was advertising houses for sale at between fifteen thousand and forty thousand dollars apiece. Perhaps the idea wasn't so impractical, after all. Yet could these be the charming stone houses we had been circling all day, or was the notary hawking some starter hovels on the outskirts of town? Although it was well past time to get on the road toward Nice, we agreed we had to find out. Without further conversation, we noted M. Castagnet's address and phone number and got in the car.

In rural France, the notary is an important official, and often his house is the finest around. No property can be bought or sold without his services. It is the notary who checks the legal status of the property, draws up the contract, registers the deed, and holds the buyer's deposit. When the final papers are signed, the notary disburses the purchase money to the seller, after deducting the seller's capital-gains taxes on behalf of the state. It is also the notary who relays whatever commission is due to the real-estate agent. For each service, naturally, the notary charges a fee, and these add up: hence the perception that notaries are well-to-do. Sometimes the notary doubles as the real-estate agent, giving him a monopoly in the area, and that was the case in Najac.

M. Castagnet's office was in his house, a rather modest one, though it did boast a gleaming gilt notary's shield over the door. The house was suspiciously far from the town center, which supported our fear that the properties advertised were in distant locales. But a short talk with M. Castagnet and a glance at the photos he had pinned to a bulletin board confirmed that he represented five of the houses we had seen that day. Castagnet was a smooth, well-fed man of about fifty, with sleek skin and hair, and he wore a three-piece suit, which seemed oddly urban for the provinces in July. He was restrained, though responsive to our questions, and we had many. Ratcheting our French up from the tourist level we had been using on vacation, we quizzed him about the history of the town, the economy of the region, the availability of services. If we were to become serious about buying a house in Najac, could we get a loan in France? Were there any laws prohibiting Americans from buying French property? What if we became stranded in the middle of negotiations and had to leave for the States. Could business be completed by mail?

*"Pas de problème, pas de problème!"* he assured us, warming to our visit. "And would *monsieur et madame* care to visit some properties today?"

That offer was more than we had bargained for. Until this proposition, we had been in the realm of whimsical conjecture. With a glance at our watches, we indicated that we had a plane to catch. Our flight was scheduled to depart from Nice in forty-eight hours, hundreds of miles away, and the route was going to be mountainous. However, we assured him that we would return next summer. We promised to describe our interests by mail and left with a handful of photos and specification sheets.

We returned to the car, consulted the maps, and started the engine. Suddenly, Michael cut the motor and said, "Wait a minute. I'll be back." As he hiked up the street and disappeared into a building with a flag in front of it, I pondered the possibilities: A quick phone call to tell M. Castagnet we would take the two-bedroom next to the bakery? An international call to home, canvassing the family for help with a down payment? The call of nature, perhaps? None of the above. Eventually Michael returned with a long handwritten list of real-estate agents in the Aveyron, Lot, and Dordogne. The French post office is a marvelous institution. No matter how small the town, the post-office phone booth has beside it a complete set of phone books for all the departments of France. In a half hour, a determined romantic can copy down what he needs to know about real-estate services in three river valleys.

And that was how the search began: by chance. Either you find a hotel room in Sarlat or you plunge into the wilds of the Aveyron and come back with a dream.

On the drive to Nice there was only one topic of conversation. In a bookshop at the airport, Michael found a paperback called *Achetez Votre Maison Sans Surprises* (Buy your house without surprises). Excited as a boy with a magazine for a new hobby, he read to me from it on the flight home, relating the peculiarities of the French home-buying system. We learned about the notary's role, the several legal steps and contracts to be negotiated, the various fees and percentages to be added to the cost. We were startled to discover that in the part of France we were interested in, the buyer pays the agent's commission, the notary's fee, a survey fee, and a transaction tax, which combined can add a whopping 18 percent to the purchase price! More appealing were the home-inspection tips: how to spot a "lizard," or jagged crack, in a seventeenth-century wall, how to test for insects in ancient ceiling beams, what might be the cost of replacing a tile roof, and what to consider before renovating a grange.

"We're getting ahead of ourselves," I cautioned, as our plastic dinner trays arrived. Michael mumbled agreement, but I noticed that after eating, he read the book over again, cover to cover.

Back in Madison, we busied ourselves preparing for the school year, and soon we were involved in the familiar routine of teaching, grading, meetings, and research. But checking the mail each day as the leaves began to turn colors was exciting, as one by one, the real-estate agents to whom we wrote began to reply. They begged us to accept their most distinguished sentiments, offered encouragement, and put themselves entirely at our disposal. Best of all, they sent pictures and descriptions of properties for sale. As real-estate agents everywhere have purred since time immemorial, they added: "these prices won't last."

Every night at the end of dinner, we examined the most recent photos and spun fancies of living in cottages, farmhouses, townhouses—and even a windmill. We sipped many a cup of tea plotting our adventure next summer. We would go to the southwest of France for two months and focus on the Aveyron, in or near Najac. If we were swept away, then so be it. But I, at least, was prepared for the possibility that "our house" would not present itself or fall within our budget. Michael's hopes had no such conditions. Instead, he had plans to meet every contingency.

In order to preserve the advantage of a favorable exchange rate (which could plummet at any time), he set up a bank account in Paris where he stashed francs bought at nine-plus to the dollar. That part was easy enough: a call to Crédit Lyonnais in Chicago, relayed to New York, took care of things. As the year went on, with an eye on upward and downward ticks in the currency market, he began to wire money to our new account, cashing in some certificates of deposit and drawing on other savings. By spring he had wired enough for a down payment and had established a budget for our search.

In correspondence with the agents, Michael relayed our specifications: a stone house typical of the region, with at least one bedroom, running water, and just enough land for a few flowers and herbs. We found it hard to explain what kind of situation we wanted. It wasn't isolation itself, or a historic town, or being on the heights that we wanted, but rather that feeling of sharing a daring adventure that Najac had conjured.

Were we on a lark? I suppose so. Responsible voices might argue that a couple in our position should have been salting away money for retirement, investing in the stock market, or choosing some practical fling like kitchen remodeling. But where was the fun in that? Compare striding the ramparts of a fog-misted castle to evaluating stock prospectuses or countertops. When you are bent on romance, you have no patience for objections. And yet the tepid enthusiasm of others may give you pause.

One cold winter's night—one of those nights that give Wisconsin its deep-freeze reputation—we prepared to welcome friends in for dinner. As the guests came to the door, they stamped on the wooden landing, creating that distinctive crunch of subzero snow. They unwrapped, shucked their boots, thawed out, and were duly warmed and fed. After dinner, in the glow of the gas-log fire (a real hearth fire would let in the freezing air), we laid out the real-estate ads and exposed our summer dreams.

But the tiny black-and-white photos didn't convey the poetic allure of abandoned Najac. Our friends couldn't feel the warm sun of the southwest on the mossy stone houses or visualize the integrity of their placement on the pencil-thin ridge. How could they imagine choosing one of these far-away properties as a second home? We touted one of our favorite listings, an ancient stone house with a stone-slab roof that is the local sign of authenticity. No one seemed thrilled by the idea of a stone roof. Someone pointed out the church belfry looming over the street, casting the house in perennial shadow and threatening an hourly clang of bells from dawn to twilight. And where was this town located exactly? The Aveyron—where was that? How far from Paris? What was it near? What's there to do? How about restaurants? Was this the only area we were considering?

Michael looked pained, but then the conversation turned. Though unimpressed by the ruins of Najac and a number of other similarly desolate locales, our company quite liked the photo of a white-stone two-story near the Quercy city of Souillac, which we had dismissed as too modern looking. Then they saw the possibilities in a medieval tower, once the bishop's treasury, in Puy-l'Évêque, on the river Lot. They fussed over the charm of a town house in the castle-crowned village of Beynac, in the Dordogne. In minutes, the group had us practically moved into the tiny one-bedroom yellow-stone house and were pointing out the real-estate agent's notations about charming hotels and restaurants nearby. They could all come to visit at once, laying siege to a hotel right down the street.

After more wine, the talk grew playful, gliding from mock panegyrics on the region into sham estate names for some of the bargains in the brochures: Pigsty in Périgord, Dump of the Dordogne, Lean-To on the Lot. But as our friends said goodbye, still needling us, each caught one of us to beg, *sotto voce*, that we ignore the jibes and follow our dream.

Over the dishes, we discussed the evening's conversation. Our friends had reawakened some of my original doubts. Maybe it was a mistake to prefer the rustic to the urban and the crude to the comfortable. If we were to buy a summer home, we needed to picture how we would go about leading a normal life there, a life with friends to entertain and laundry to wash and meals to fix. Where would we shop for food? Was a really good farmers market a must, or would we make do with a limited choice of local produce? Would we feel it a waste to be in France but far from restaurants? Najac, as far as we could recall, had only the hotel for dining out.

I tried to imagine what our relationship to neighbors would be. Did we really want to be off by ourselves, or would we prefer a location in a lively village with people who could develop into friends? If so, what kind of place would be most welcoming to a pair of Americans getting their rusty French back into practice? We continued this discussion over the next few weeks and gradually came to a decision to widen our search. We would return to the Aveyron but would look also in the more populated valleys of the Lot and the Dordogne, even though prices there might be higher. They offered more villages, restaurants, markets, services. Tourism in the Dordogne and wine in the Lot, as well as robust agriculture in both valleys, promised that their beautiful old towns would not die, but prosper. I remembered

Bérénice, my French friend who restored a stone complex in the Loire, frowning as she spoke of a dying town, and sighing *"Triste, triste . . . "* Perhaps the charm of a melancholy village would wane, and the solitude would come to feel depressing. We decided we had better test the ambiance of a range of locations before saying, "This is the place!"

This turn of events sent Michael back to his maps, to replot our itinerary for the following summer. We agreed to begin the search in Najac and to visit all the houses M. Castagnet could show us. Then we would look elsewhere as well, to form a basis for comparison.

And so, we did return to Najac that next summer and spent a long day with M. Castagnet inspecting houses that we had entered a hundred times in our imagination. But a year's interval had undermined our resolve. This time we were sensitive to the eerie solitude of empty houses and the town's craggy isolation. Amenities were few, and restaurants scarce compared to the Dordogne. We hadn't been deceived in our impression of the town's unspoiled beauty and dramatic setting. And we were still delighted by our romantic hotel. But I think that in our minds we had decided to move on before ever stepping over the threshold of M. Castagnet's first property, the little house near the church. Charming it was, though instead of a septic system, it had a dry holding tank in the basement for the storage of human waste, which would have to be pumped out every year—and it was a fact that the church bells next door could deafen you. We took notes and feigned interest, but the notary probably could tell we were backing out of Najac as we backed out the door.

Sometimes we still moon over Najac, for it was there that we first had the dream of living in France. Years later, when the bustle of tourism in the Dordogne was getting us down, we revisited the town and found it unchanged. It was like seeing an old lover on the street.

# THE FALL OF A HUNDRED STARS

During the rest of that summer, we scoured the valleys of the Dordogne and the Lot, eventually inspecting forty houses. I was the one who kept saying no. Michael stalked each house the way a lion stalks a zebra. If it could be had, he wanted it, no matter its condition. As far as he was concerned, the more *typique* the better. *Typique* means typical, but applied to regional houses, it means true to the local style. To be *typique* is to have authenticity; it does not ensure that the house will have the essentials. For instance, one of his favorite finds had no roof. Another lacked a floor (you just walked on the beams, peering warily at the story below). Most lacked heat but for a fireplace. One had no electricity, another no potable water. One had water but no plumbing. One, a converted chapel, lacked windows. Sometimes a ceiling, sometimes a wall, was missing. Michael kept reasoning that we were shopping the low end of the market and should expect a few defects. I wanted walls and a roof.

Many of the homes we saw remain a blur. There were a few memorable exceptions: a cottage so deep in the woods that no road could reach it, shown to us by a dapper agent with slicked-back hair who reeked of cologne; a little house by the side of the road that had been converted to a Buddhist shrine by Vietnamese monks, shown by a nervous agent who wore house slippers and a business suit; an old half-restored manse with no water supply and a pig farmer for a neighbor, shown by a chirpy British woman, the only female agent we encountered.

The whole of that summer, the quality of our days was determined by the real-estate agents into whose hands we entrusted our search. The clever ones got the sense of our taste after one showing and then led us to properties of ever-increasing interest, so that we ended the day with serious prospects to discuss over dinner. The dimmer ones dragged us from one dismal dwelling to the next, leaving us with the sense of a day wasted. A few of these agents were exasperating. We met the strangest one of all through an inadvertent introduction by the landlord whose house we were renting in Temniac, a quiet suburb of Sarlat that once served as the palatial residence of Sarlat's bishops.

Our landlord, Yves Bouter, was a gruff bear of a man who drove a huge machine for tearing up streets—the mechanical monster was parked in front of the house. Excavation was his business, politics his meat. Bouter was aggressively proud of his membership in the Communist Party, and we could hardly get a word in edgewise to finalize our rental agreement as he rattled on about his battles on behalf of progress and against the witless blockers of development. For an avowed communist, though, Bouter maintained an odd assortment of opinions. He was all for private property—he was, in fact, a private contractor, proud of his house, land, and digging machine—but he railed against the value-added tax (as every Frenchman does regardless of political party). He enjoyed being called a communist mostly for the label's revolutionary cachet. The subject that really riled Bouter was religion—he was an atheist—and his nemesis in this debate was a hated next-door neighbor, a lunatic (according to Bouter) named Vidal (he spat out his name). It was only when we mentioned that we were thinking of buying a house that Bouter warned us about Vidal, a part-time real-estate agent who presided over an archaic religious cult whose members dunked themselves in so-called holy springs and mumbled strange incantations in the woods.

"*Méfiez-vous!*" Watch out for him, Bouter insisted, his face coloring with pique.

Well, this was news. A real-estate agent next door? Could we resist? We waited a day before approaching the neighbor (and made sure that when we did, Bouter was not in sight). There was no sign in front of M. Vidal's house to indicate that he was an *agent immobilier*, but next to the doorbell was a little card announcing that such was his profession, so we rang. A portly young man in his thirties, with disheveled hair, opened the door halfway, keeping his foot against it, to see who had disturbed his afternoon. Suspiciously, he asked who we were and how we had found him. When we revealed that M. Bouter had mentioned his name, the *agent* strengthened his grip on the doorjamb, cursed his neighbor, and even peered over our shoulders to see whether the devil himself might be bearing down on him in his infernal earth-moving machine. But no, birds chirped, the sun shone, the couple at his door looked pleasantly blank, rather innocent, yes, foreign—in fact, by their accents American (so probably not communist)—and possibly therefore potential clients. Such were the changing perceptions we tracked on his face as we patiently smiled and waited for the storm to subside. Recovering, he asked us in and led us through a maze of smoky rooms to a little makeshift office toward the back of the house.

"*Raymond, qui est là?*" a sharp, authoritative voice called out.

"*Rien, maman, c'est des clients,*" he replied, shutting the office door firmly against mother and all other intruders on his domain.

We stated our business, and he brooded for a while, stroking his chin like a ham actor affecting thought.

Yes, he said with some hesitation, it might be that he had some properties at his disposal, but first he must ask us some questions. They came in a barrage. What was our religion, our national background, our motives for wanting to buy property in Périgord, our knowledge of the history of the region, our political sympathies, might he ask? We remained polite and vague, astounded at this peculiar way to begin a relationship with new clients. Gradually, as the interrogation progressed, we began to plumb the mystery.

Vidal professed allegiance to the vanished kingdom of Languedoc (the southern tier of the country that now calls itself France), with its ancient language, customs, fiefdoms, and religion. His mornings, he told us, were spent studying *Occitan,* the local dialect that had been nearly lost when *les parisiens* imposed their version of French on the whole nation. His afternoons were spent dabbling in real estate. But Vidal had chosen a paradoxical profession. A self-appointed guardian of the region's *patrimoine,* he was reluctant to sell off chunks of it to foreigners, or Parisians for that matter; yet those were the prospective buyers of old properties in Périgord. We silently wondered how he made a living. Perhaps *maman* provided, and he didn't have to. For an hour he rambled on, telling tales of counts and troubadours, battles won and castles lost, and holy springs in the vicinity that still maintained their healing powers. Our house hunting seemed derailed, but his monologue was intriguing, especially when Vidal turned to the subject of religion.

He was, he disclosed, a Cathar, which came as a surprise, since the sect had died out in the fourteenth century. We knew a bit about the Cathars. The heresy had caused one of the great stirs of the Middle Ages. The Cathars considered themselves untainted Christians and attacked the Church for its corruption. Their doctrine was dualistic, pitting the goodness of pure spirit against the evil of the body and the material world. Their practice insisted on a distinction between the elites of the sect, called "perfects," who abstained from meat and sex, and those tempted by the world, a category that encompassed everyone else. In 1208, Pope Innocent III launched a crusade against the heretics and sent a brutal fanatic named Simon de Montfort to wipe them out. During the years of crusade that followed, thousands of Cathars were massacred, including many in Najac (we had read about the Cathars while studying the town's history). The chief Cathar stronghold, Montségur Castle, fell in 1244, and the inhabitants were cruelly executed. The movement surfaced again in the village of Montaillou but was suppressed by an inquisition in 1320. These martyrs were among the last of the Cathars—until M. Vidal, that is. Whether he was "perfect" enough to abstain from meat and sex was a question we did not pursue.

We must have passed his interrogation, or else we were just good listeners, for Vidal agreed to show us a selection of properties *dans le style.* From Vidal we learned that the style of the true Périgordian house is based on practical considerations. The ground floor (originally just packed earth) is reserved for storage or even animal quarters. A staircase leads to the *séjour,* the main living area, centered around a hearth, often with room in the chimney for little seats at the sides for sitting close to the cooking pot on winter evenings after the embers have died down. Exposed wooden beams (*poutres*) support the ceilings. Tables, chairs, benches, and wood-framed beds round out the main living space, with pegs on the wall for hanging clothes. For dry storage, there might be an attic, reached by a ladder, under a sharply pitched roof. Nowadays these *greniers* are often converted to bedrooms; but in the old days, family life—cooking, eating, conversing, sleeping—was crowded into the *séjour.* Outside there would be a well and outhouse and perhaps a dovecote or *pigeonnier:* pigeons were kept for food and for their droppings, which make good fertilizer. The real glory of an old house can be the roof if it is still original, made of angled limestone slabs (called *lauzes*) inserted without mortar or cement into a steep lattice frame. A house possessing all these virtues is a house with character, *une maison de caractère.*

Vidal's informative lectures were punctuated by intemperate rants. For our agent, the impure of spirit in the modern age were those who purchased a house *dans le style* and then defiled it through careless restoration. The gravest sins included covering the natural stones of the exterior with stucco (*crépis*), hiding exposed beams with particle-board ceilings, wallpapering over natural stone walls, replacing a stone roof with cheap, mass-produced tiles, blocking up a fireplace in the kitchen to make room for modern appliances, or erasing original features like an old stone sink built right into the wall with a drainage spout to the outside. Vidal was eccentric, all right, but he knew his architecture. Over the next few weeks we saw many jarring examples of intended home improvements that had ruined the charm or simplicity of an original structure.

However, the properties that our tutor showed us were authentic to a fault. Some were mossy ruins. They grew progressively less habitable as we moved from site to site until at last we stood before his proudest offering, which was little more than a pile of rubble oxidizing in a field. The roof had caved in, and the earthen floor was littered with debris, including an ancient wheelbarrow, wooden down to its broken-off wheels. The house, or what was left of it, had no running water or electricity. Daylight gaped through chinks in the walls. There were no windows or sign that there had ever been any. Termites had bored deep rivulets through the old beams. But not a pebble had been harmed by restoration. Such houses can fetch their price in the Dordogne, for there are buyers who love nothing better than to renovate a ruin from the bottom up. But such an undertaking was not for us.

We tried explaining our preferences to Vidal, but since he remained perpetually in the teaching mode, nothing got through. Eventually we framed an excuse to pry ourselves from his grip, pretending that we wanted to devote the remainder of our time in the area to sight-seeing. In actuality, we scouted several agents in Sarlat and systematically toured the properties in their portfolios. Nothing panned out. The properties we liked were too expensive, and the ones that were reasonable in price had too many flaws. We joked about Vidal but had to acknowledge the training he had given us on the desirable characteristics of regional homes. As a result, we had become particular in our tastes.

The last time we saw Vidal, he was glowering across his hedge at our landlord, M. Bouter. They were apparently in the midst of one of their frequent spats, jousting with raised voices. Recalling that moment, I imagine that our landlord and his neighbor might have been locked in symbolic combat over the future of Périgord. On one side was a developer who earned his living bulldozing the past and on the other a fanatical preservationist clinging to tradition: a communist and a Cathar.

Vidal's opposite in personality was a mild-mannered agent named Georges Rossignol, who had written to us during the year about some properties in the old market town of Puy-l'Évêque. By the time we headed there, we had been searching fruitlessly for nearly a month, all the while growing more attached to the beauty of the surrounding countryside.

Occupying a bend in the Lot River, the heart of the old town of Puy-l'Évêque is serene and sleepy on a summer's afternoon. Its thirteenth-century houses huddle by the river's edge soaking up sun, the intense light etching lines in old walls and casting an inverted reflection of towers in the muddy water. There are two main squares, one across from the hotel, with a great open space that houses the weekly market, and another one hidden higher up among the shops on the hill leading up to the church. In a corner of that smaller commercial square, we found M. Rossignol's office.

There was something pleasing about the way the building looked. It was half-timbered, and authentically so; the timbers were dusty gray with age. The old shop looked put upon, listing a bit under the pressure of the more solid stone store to its left. Pasted all over the windows were sun-faded pictures of properties in the Lot, the region crossed by the river whose lazy meander forms the site of Puy-l'Évêque. Just then the shop door opened and a gentle voice inquired if we would like to come in and look through the catalogs. The kindly eyes of an elderly man who might have been a schoolmaster looked out at us from behind rimless glasses. His well-brushed brown suit and courtly manner seemed suited for another *métier* altogether, but here indeed was the *agent immobilier* who had sent us such a polite letter last October. Sitting in front of his littered desk, I found myself expressing our hopes and divulging our means, as he puffed quietly on his pipe and spoke hardly a word. He smiled benevolently and suggested that we leave the catalogs for the next day and instead profit from the beautiful afternoon by going to see a few properties.

By now we were accustomed to the familiar routine of regional house hunting: the agent proposes a house, you get into his car and he drives you there (always by the most picturesque route, even if it is miles out of the way). The ride back gives the agent time to press home the sale. There's no escaping the pitch, since you need the ride home to your car, parked at the agency.

We piled into M. Rossignol's bouncing Peugeot and sat back as it lurched into gear. As usual, first we were shown the least attractive properties, the principle being to start the client's tour with hovels that couldn't be sold to a wrecking crew and then to progress to the plausible listings, displaying them to comparative advantage. We began in town with several gloomy structures that needed major work and then moved out into the country. Noting the hour as the sun began to drift a little lower in the sky, M. Rossignol worked up to his move.

"Now I am going to show you a house that would be perfect for summer vacations. This one has been completely restored and has all the modern conveniences."

And so we were taken to the odd place we remember as the filmmaker's house. By Rossignol's route, we crossed the Lot twice, passing neat vineyards, each with its manor house boasting to be Château de Something Grand, and rising at last from the river valley to the height of a steep wooded hill. The sides of the road were marked by crumbling stone walls, beyond which skinny black goats were grazing. As we mounted, the views to our left grew ever more striking—ending in a blanket of gold and green plots cut by the curling ribbon of the Lot. We parked in the small square of an attractive hamlet, where every house had been carefully restored. Roofs were tiled neatly with factory-fresh curves of clay tile. New doors were made of thick planks of wood, stained dark and nailed with medieval-looking hardware. The stonework was flawless, free of *chaux*, the quicklime used as a joiner; in a "house of character," the *chaux* is placed deep in the stonework and does not appear at the surface. Taking this in at a glance, we wondered how any of these meticulously reconstructed homes could be in our price range.

With an indicative thrust of his chin, M. Rossignol guided our eyes to a one-story building opposite the church. Since it had no windows (and instead two doors), the building looked like it might have been a barn for small animals or a wine cellar for the grand house next to it. Entering through the larger of the building's two doors, we were surprised to see a white stucco foyer, lit from above through a skylight, giving onto a huge stone-walled *séjour* centered round a raised hearth, over which hung a pair of hunting rifles. Another skylight threw a circle of light on the tile flooring. The kitchen to the left beyond a dividing half-wall was brand new, with appliances scaled perfectly to the setting. Everything was as if installed yesterday: up-to-code electrical outlets, efficient water heater run on butane gas kept in a tank in the garden, which was visible through glass doors in the dining area. Someone had been an expert gardener, and someone was keeping up the property in impeccable style.

We asked about the owner. A rising filmmaker, we were told. He had bought the whole village five years ago and had renovated every building in it, including the church. There were no local inhabitants. Most had been killed in the last war, and the few remaining had died or moved away. The only true local was the farmer whose goats we had seen, and his place was up the road away from the village. The filmmaker lived in this house and rented the big house next door to an English woman, a professor at Cahors. We would have a companion, then, urged M. Rossignol—imagine, three English professors in the same little village! Yes, I thought to myself, the only three residents, all foreign residents in fact, in a perfect imitation of a traditional French hamlet.

Meanwhile, Michael plunged on, examining every joist and beam (exposed of course, and recently stained) and asking more questions. Where was the filmmaker? (In Asia, on location. He expected to be in the East a long time.) What would happen, then, to the other buildings and the church, even? Would they be up for sale soon? (Oh, who knows—only time would tell. But with such a beautiful complex, there would not be a problem. Some person of taste would snatch them up and cherish them, without doubt.)

What was it that felt wrong? Without being able to locate a single inauthentic detail, I felt the whole ensemble to be false. Reluctantly, Michael agreed. The restoration might be faithful, but the ambiance was counterfeit. The village was not meant to *be* lived in. It was meant to *look* lived in—through the eyes of a camera. True to his *métier*, unconsciously perhaps, the filmmaker had created a film set. It was difficult trying to convey to M. Rossignol that we did not want the house because it was inauthentic, but it was important that he understand our views. In our house hunting we had run the gamut between rubble and a movie set, and I was beginning to wonder if we would ever find something that we could buy.

"*Alors,*" he said. "So you want a house that is genuine but not primitive—well equipped but, on the other hand, not too polished. And at a small price, too. *Eh, bien.*" There was one more house to show us on the other side of the ridge. He would take us there.

It would be the house that broke our hearts.

Once more into the agent's beat-up Peugeot. The suspension got a workout as we traversed the hills above Puy-l'Évêque, puttering along twisting, picturesque roads that ended on a plateau. There the car slowed, turning into a dirt lane. We bumped our way by a run-down farmhouse with equipment rusting outside. Then, after skirting abandoned fields, we passed a half-built house that had been left standing with bare cinder blocks for at least several years. This bit of squalor produced a sense of unease, but it was soon behind us, as the car pushed forward through uncut grass.

About a quarter mile up the dirt road we came to a low-lying limestone building, apparently restored within the last decade, its roof tiles modern but weathered and its stonework neatly pointed. The building was authentic in the style of the Lot country: beige-toned stone, white mortar, long lines, red-clay tile for the roof in Spanish style. The look was simple and satisfying, but it was the site that was breathtaking. Directly ahead of us and the house was a wide sweep of knee-deep grass, providing the platform for a panoramic view of the valley below. From left to right and for miles into the blue distance, there was nothing but fields, farms, and woodlands. As he struggled to open the shutters on the door and insert the proper key to enter, M. Rossignol told us with an expansive sweep of his hand that the site had six acres of land, five of them in the long slope that dropped to that astounding view. There was room on the side for enlarging the house, if we wished. Right now, we were focused on more basic matters. What was it like inside?

The door opened into a kitchen that brightened immediately, as the pale stone walls reflected the light from the doorway. A second wedge of light widened across the room, as M. Rossignol opened the side door of the kitchen. The new light revealed, set in the back right corner, a passageway into the other room. In one corner of that room, to the left of the fireplace, was the *évier*, the traditional stone wash basin, draining directly outside through the front wall of the house. Once all the windows were open, a warm light fell on walls that were an attractive patchwork of plaster and stone.

Now, where was the bedroom? A loft, M. Rossignol indicated, pointing up. A wooden ladder hung next to the back door, and it led up to a narrow gallery, just wide enough for two single beds. The view from there down to the main room was appealing, but backing down a ladder at night to go to the bathroom might be difficult.

By the way, where was the bathroom? Rossignol coughed nervously and pointed to the corner of the loft, where there stood a pink plastic potty, a larger version of the kind you train baby on.

"*Qu'est-ce que c'est?*" we asked.

A chemical toilet, he admitted circumspectly. "*Très pratique.*"

What was chemical about the potty was a receptacle for the waste into which you could spoon stuff that looked like cat litter, to muffle the smell. Rossignol suggested getting a duplicate and putting it out in the open-air ruin off the kitchen, for privacy and ventilation. The pink one could stay aloft for use at night and on rainy days.

"*Très pratique,*" he repeated, stretching a smile.

So, we had arrived at the sticking point. The house had no bathroom.

"We could build an outhouse," Michael ventured.

That astounded me. Michael's only carpentry project to date had been a wooden paper towel holder he built in junior-high shop class. His mother still kept it—but for sentimental reasons, not craftsmanship. My highest accomplishment was a planks-and-bricks bookcase for my first apartment. More importantly, we are not a camping couple. Nothing in our history suggested we would take well to the outhouse lifestyle.

M. Rossignol seemed to sense the problem. To make this house really work for us, he advised, we should restore the ruined half, adding a bedroom and a bath. There were excellent craftsmen in the region who could do the job well. Moreover, there was an architect in Puy-l'Évêque who was a good friend. Scrupulous, honest, *un homme sérieux,* he could design the project and supervise it in our absence; we could rely on his rectitude. And since he was M. Rossignol's *copain,* his bid would be *raisonnable.* The work could be completed in time for our return next summer. He even was prepared to call his colleague in for a consultation at no charge. What did we have to lose?

Calling in an architect was an unsettling development. Was it right to ask for a professional's time if we were not serious about both the house and the prospect of adding to it? It would be like going to the jeweler's to try on engagement rings before you decided to marry. I nonetheless nodded to Michael, a gesture that did not escape Rossignol's attention. He cheerily packed us back into the Peugeot and gave us a little tour of the two tiny villages that would be our nearest neighbors. Both were lovely ensembles, one with a Romanesque chapel and the other with a communal oven. Back at the office, we waited while he called his architect friend, and we parted with a date to meet at eleven the next day.

At three in the morning, we were shaken awake by thunder so resounding that it rattled our rented room. Nerves set on edge, we stayed alert for hours, rehearsing the problems and possibilities of the house on the hill. The rainy morning found us sober and purposeful. We were going to determine if an addition were feasible, and if so whether we could afford it.

We were nervous as we negotiated the rain-washed hills and splashed through sudden streams crossing the road. Our Renault 5 arrived safely at the heights, but it struggled down the dirt lane, slithery with mud and pocked with puddles. We slid to a stop and waited for the Peugeot to arrive. In only a few minutes, it pulled up, bearing two passengers. Dependable M. Rossignol took his time getting out, lifting a black umbrella to the sky. His architect friend was a younger man, athletic and wiry. He darted out of the car, threw up the hood of his slicker, and charged over to greet us. A bearded, laugh-lined face gave a rueful grin. We should wait in the car while he and Georges opened the house—no need for us all to drown on the doorstep. He bounded back to the Peugeot, withdrew his briefcase, and sprinted over to the house door, which he unlocked for his friend in a flash. A flick of the light switch, and he was waving us in.

From that point, Martin—for he insisted on first names, American style—was in charge. Throwing off his rain gear and indicating we should do the same, he motioned us over to the kitchen table.

"Georges and I talked this over last night," he said in the lilting southwest accent that I was beginning to understand with relative ease. (I still greatly appreciate the fact that in the Lot and Dordogne, people pronounce their consonants distinctly, and they like to savor a sentence, giving the novice time to work out unfamiliar phrases.) "I must tell you," he warned, "there are only two alternatives. I know, because I did the original restoration work ten years ago. Georges told you what I proposed that the owners do back then—rebuild the ruin, with a bedroom and bathroom. That's one option. Look." And he unfurled a complicated blueprint, nearly covering the table. We knew at a glance that this was too much for us.

Plan Two was more modest. It would add only what we needed for immediate occupation, a toilet and a shower. To keep the costs down, we would not touch the ruin—too many structural problems. Instead, we would build a little hang-to off the back of the existing house, placing the plumbing and water heater just behind the kitchen, so that both bathroom and kitchen could be served by the same pipes.

Flipping back and forth between the two blueprints, we liked the simplicity of the second plan. All right, what would it cost? It was a good thing we were still sitting down. The estimate was one-fourth the asking price of the entire property. When we blanched at the price, Martin gave a chagrined smile and said, regretfully, that standards were standards. He had outlined a stark but solid plan; anything less would compromise all the previous work that had made this restoration admirable.

Martin was not about to damage a *maison de caractère*. If that meant he would lose a potential client, so be it. For him and for us, the choice was between a quality job or no job at all. We told him forthrightly that, though we liked his second plan, we feared we could not afford it, but we would review our finances. If our calculations showed we could both buy the house and do the addition, we would put in a bid. Shaking both men's hands, we promised to get back to them quickly. They stayed behind in the house as we tromped through the soaked grass to our car.

This decisive interchange had taken less than an hour. Now what? Go home and add up the numbers?

"No," Michael said, "It's noon. Let's find out what the best hotel in Puy-l'Évêque can do for a weekday lunch."

The Hotel Bellevue occupies a site high above the Lot and offers a panoramic view of the winding river from its snug dining room. Its kitchen is as satisfying as the setting. A classic meal from the Lot unrolled effortlessly: pork pâté crunchy with walnuts, local salmon trout in butter sauce, lamb chops grilled with Provence herbs and halved tomatoes, then the tray of Cantal, and cinder-coated goat cheese. After choosing our tarts (strawberry for me, apple for Michael), we got down to business. We didn't have the money for both house and addition, and we were reluctant to incur additional debt. If we bought this house, we would have to follow Rossignol's first suggestion—live without a bathroom until we could afford one.

Coffee came, and we stared out the window in the drizzling rain at the river swirling below. We waited for the rain to stop, but when we got in the car, we did not head north toward Sarlat. Instead, we turned south, to revisit the house one more time. The road was still muddy and the grass soggy, but our shoes were already fit for the wastebasket, so we squished around the property, discovering the rubble of more foundations. A long time ago there must have been a complex of buildings here in the form of an L. These remnants provided the basis for many a fanciful scheme of reconstruction. And a scramble down the hillside revealed a long area on the flat, which some day would be perfect for a swimming pool. As we turned and tramped back up the hill, we faced a house that tugged at our hearts.

It was then that we noticed an inscription of some kind in the lintel above the door. It looked like a date but had faded to near illegibility. The last two digits appeared to be 00, but the numbers preceding them, if that's what they were, were effaced. No, wait—there was a 7, or maybe a 9, or then again, a 1. Was the date 1900? 1700? There appeared to be only a single digit preceding the zeroes, which made no sense for a date. Just after the date was a design in the form of a star. What could it mean? We puzzled for a long time, then Michael cried:

"I've got it! It's not a date at all. It's a name: One Hundred, One Hundred Stars, *Cent Étoiles.*"

Yes, it was a perfect name for a home on this magnificent site, which would be dazzled by stars on a cloudless night. From that moment on, the house became *"Cent Étoiles."* That was a dangerous step, like giving a name to a puppy in a pet store. Once we had named it, we wanted it and assumed it was ours.

M. Rossignol was pleased when we appeared at his office the next morning with the prospect of a bid, but he masked his excitement. No seller should be insulted by an honest bid, he opined. And with that he reached into his drawer and pulled out a wire ending with a round disk—the *écouteur*, he called it—which sat in the palm of one's hand and functioned as a second earpiece for the old-fashioned stand-up telephone. As soon as M. Rossignol attached the wire, Michael took the *écouteur* in hand and braced for the ordeal of bargaining in French by telephone. The trial was not prolonged. The smooth Parisian voice on the other end of the line politely refused to consider an offer under the asking price. Michael leaned over to the mouthpiece and outlined our financial dilemma, which met with no sympathy. Now Rossignol interposed to mention that the lack of a bathroom would necessitate a substantial investment in the property, which the client felt might justify a slightly lower bid. There was a chill in the owner's voice. Even lacking a bathroom, the property was magnificent; had there been a bathroom, the price would be much higher. Indeed, the property was underpriced (the implication being that M. Rossignol had undervalued it—at this, Rossignol flapped his arms in exasperation and expelled air through pursed lips). As a favor to the client, the owner would hold the asking price where it was for a week. After that, he intended to raise it. The client would be advised to give the matter some reflection.

The conversation ended with hollow niceties between agent and owner, and M. Rossignol turned to us apologetically. He had not expected the owner to be so adamant. He would have warned us if he had thought the offer was without hope. Now, however, the will of the owner was clear, and one had to admit he was not unreasonable. We should think about raising our offer. We could see that he was worried not only about losing our bid but also about losing his contract to list the property. We had just given our highest bid, yet we did not want to say we were finished. So we said a simple thank-you, shook hands, and took our leave.

For the next two weeks we tried to whip up an interest in nearby properties shown to us by other agents. We traipsed in and out of town houses, examined many a rural cottage, and even considered an abandoned hotel for a rock bottom price in a hamlet few tourists could find. The summer sun had returned, and we found ourselves exhausted by our forays in the midday heat. In actuality we were sulking, and our thoughts kept returning to *Cent Étoiles*. One night, after a second glass of wine, we toyed with the idea of putting down the bulk of the asking price with the promise of the remainder within a short time—say, a year. In the morning we thought better of it. For another day or two we brooded. It had become too hot for house hunting anyway, so we lounged around trying to read. Finally, we got in the car and headed toward Puy-l'Évêque for a final visit to help make up our minds. It was three when we reached the turnoff to the property. In the mid-July heat, the dirt road kicked up clouds of dust. Our plan was that Michael would pace out the property, mapping the spaces available for future building and landscaping, while I would sketch the ruin and develop options for how we would use it in the near and long term.

The afternoon sun beat down on my head as I walked to the center of the yard to get the best view of the house and the ruin. The house had lost none of its beauty, but in the strong light it did have a different aura—a harsh severity. Well, that was its power; its rugged stone would provide shelter both from rain and from heat. Or would it? Facing west, the house took the full brunt of the sun in the afternoon, when the heat would be worst. Was there a shade tree for respite? Not a one in sight. We hadn't noticed on our rainy visits that the hill was completely open to the sky, without a bush or a sapling disrupting its lines. With forehead dripping sweat, I looked out at that view and saw it differently from weeks ago. Then, the moist emerald of the high grass had formed the foreground for a panorama of deep greens and foggy blues. Now the dry grass, burned gold by just two weeks of summer sun, gave way to a vista of olive, tan, and dusky brown. On blazing afternoons, no umbrella on a terrace could offer sufficient relief from the sense of overexposure to sun and heat.

I have always been sensitive to the sun. My Irish skin is of the "never tans" variety; the only color it takes is murderous magenta. Even with all surfaces protected (sunblock, straw hat, long sleeves), I have never been able to reset an internal thermostat that sounds the alarm at ninety degrees. What would I do next year at this time, when the hot spell came? I imagined long, stuffy afternoons locked behind closed doors reading or napping, when it was too hot to emerge even into the shaded ruin. I reminded myself that summer was only one season, and the house was perfectly situated to remain dry and well preserved through the winters. But summer was when we would be here. Perhaps this house was just too exposed for our particular use of it. Given my Celtic predilection for the cool and the green, perhaps we should be looking in the more northerly and lush Dordogne, not here in the dry and sparse Lot.

Michael took the news like an oblivious parent receiving a call from the police saying that Junior is under arrest. First, it can't be true. Then, there must be some misunderstanding. He had just spent an hour happily pacing the property, finding alternative locations for an outhouse, siting a future swimming pool (he relishes a good baking at poolside), and planning a lifetime's worth of construction projects. Sure it was hot, but that's what summer is all about. You don't reject a perfectly good house because it would be hot in July. But as we stood there I was turning from pink to pale, a warning of incipient heatstroke. Now genuinely concerned, Michael led me to a nook of shade in a corner of the ruin, and the serious talk began.

We reviewed the virtues of *Cent Étoiles*—the authenticity of the simple house, its flawless restoration, its ruins and room for expansion, its grand spread of land, its exquisite views. Then we revisited its faults. The house was isolated. It lacked hot water, a toilet, a shower, a real bedroom. The bareness of the hill exposed it too much to the summer sun. Remedying these ills would take an enormous investment—much more money and time than we had. It was a house that bred dreams, but for us they were fantasies. Disheartened, we stood in the shadow of the ruin and agreed to abandon our bid.

That was the fall of a hundred stars.

**3**

A CASTLE IN THE BACKYARD

Our spirits were at their lowest ebb when, with only one week remaining in our search, we found ourselves back on Sarlat's rue de la République, exactly where our journey had begun the year before. On previous visits to Sarlat, we had noted a shop with a faded awning bearing the words "Agence Agis," but when we looked in the windows we saw no photos of properties for sale and thought the place looked abandoned. So we passed it by. Now, though, we had exhausted every other possibility.

"We may as well go in," Michael grumbled. (I had gotten over *Cent Étoiles,* but he was still sulking.) "We've tried everyone else."

As we entered, a frail, elderly man looked up in surprise. He was hunched over a stack of papers at a desk, but the rest of the office was bare of furniture or equipment. When we explained our business, he smiled and corrected our misunderstanding. No, this was not a real-estate agency but his insurance agency, and in fact it was now being closed because he was retiring. He was just sorting out his files. *"Mais attendez"*—this offered in response to our downcast expressions—it just so happened he had a good friend who was a real-estate agent, though semiretired, who, as chance would have it, had stopped in that very afternoon to collect his old insurance records.

"Paul," he called to an unseen person in the back room, "would you come out here for an instant?"

The muffled rumble of a slowly closing file drawer preceded the entry of a squat, sinewy old-timer with a penguin gait. He was encumbered by a white sling over his left arm.

"Excuse me for being clumsy," he grumbled in his chewy country accent, glancing up to catch the onlookers with a rueful grin. *"Ça* [waving his injured wing] *me fait mal."*

There was something immediately likeable about this fellow, a natural energy undimmed by age. With his furrowed brown skin, tanned right up over the balding pate, he looked like a farmer. He was dressed in work pants and a checkered short-sleeve shirt. Informed that *monsieur et madame* were looking for a house, he introduced himself as Paul Meunier and offered the local handshake that would in future be so familiar to us— right hand extended but twisted on its side, so the contact is a faint brushing of thumbs. He broke into a snaggle-toothed grin, so we assumed this odd gesture of greeting must be due to the injury that put the other arm in a sling. Years later, when we knew him well enough to ask questions about manners, M. Meunier explained that workers' hands are half the time soiled and the other half sore, so the kindly way to greet is this gentle touch. The gesture says "at the moment, I'm not quite in form for a handshake—but you understand."

Although retired, Meunier divulged with a wink that he still had his real-estate license and a network of sources throughout the valley, former colleagues like M. Agis. From them he knew what properties would be up for sale, long before they showed up in the windows of the Sarlat agents. He himself was from a little village nearby, and he had a *copain* in every hamlet. No house changed hands around here without his knowing it. He kept his eye on things—this said as he bobbed and weaved like an old boxer, glancing left, glancing right, into an imaginary distance. His dimply grin undercut the self-promotion and gave him an air of friendly self-mockery. Soon we were laughing with him and hoping that, underneath the raillery, he actually knew of a property or two.

By now we were expert in laying out our specifications. Meunier squinted and nodded sagely as he listened.

"Do you have time to accompany me home for an apéritif?" he queried. "I know of something that might interest you. Just give me a half hour to finish my business here."

This was an unorthodox tactic, but at this point we were refusing no offers. For the next thirty minutes, we strolled Sarlat's lovely side streets, speculating on M. Meunier's professional qualifications. Had he ever been a full-time house agent, or was he really a farmer who dabbled in real estate? Was he right now calling up old contacts and hunting up a property, or did that shrewd squint say he had one selected already? No way to find out but to follow him home.

Wandering the cobblestone byways that branched off the *traverse*, we regretted the impression of Sarlat we had formed the previous summer. With the exception of the traffic flow on la rue de la République, it really was a gorgeous old city, brimming with character. We followed one serpentine alley and came to an exquisite fountain standing opposite the Hôtel Plamon, an elegantly restored house from the Gothic period, connected by a series of arcades to a lovely covered market. There were similar architectural pleasures waiting around every turn. Yes, we had been mistaken about Sarlat—but then again, it was that very mistake that put us on our quest for a house in France. Now we were afraid that search would end without result.

We rendezvoused at Agence Agis, expecting to take M. Meunier to his car and then follow behind him.

"*Mais non,*" he explained, "*comme ça* [lifting his injured arm] I can't drive; my nephew brought me here this afternoon. It is you who will drive me home."

We were parked in the square just steps away and were soon on the road, with M. Meunier directing and providing guided commentary. Playfully he pointed at the Renaissance manor we were passing, winking that we should be staying there—it had recently opened as a hotel and had romantic rooms for couples like us. When we reached the crossroads village of Vézac, he urged us to visit its old church, a little jewel, in spite of recent restoration (we later learned that for Meunier "recent" meant seventeenth century). There, in a field of erect corn, nestled a plump little Romanesque chapel, all rounds and arches. It begged for a visit at more leisure.

As we motored on, M. Meunier's chatter formed the background for our entry into the most beautiful stretch of the Valley of the Dordogne.

A sharp turn after the church at Vézac brought us to a plain blooming with yellow sunflowers and flanked by limestone escarpments, each topped by a storybook castle towering above the low-banked winding river. This was the very heart of the valley, and somehow we had missed it in our previous explorations. We were so struck that we asked to stop the car, and our guide advised a safe spot to pull in. We stepped out at the foot of the Château of Marqueyssac, which rose high on our left—a broad, *lauze*-roofed manor house from the sixteenth century, guarding behind it luxurious parks extending a mile along its cliff. In the far distance, M. Meunier pointed out another landmark, the elegant Château of Lacoste, decorating its wooded ridge with eighteenth-century poise. It was dwarfed, however, by the nearby ruin of the huge medieval Château of Castelnaud, looming a thousand feet above a steep ocher cliff. The castle's partially restored walls seemed fused into a golden mass glinting in the sun. Far below and to the west, we could see the graceful towers of Fayrac, a miniature *château fort* looking like a fairy's castle, nestled on the far bank of the river along a shaded road. From there our eyes swept the plain past fields and pastures to a promontory equal to Castelnaud's in height and menace. On its summit stood Beynac, Castelnaud's rival during the Hundred Years War, its machicolated towers soaring toward the clouds. The entire valley, broad and verdant, was encircled by castles. In years to come we often would return to this vantage point with guests to enjoy a visual symphony of landscape and architecture that has few counterparts any-where in the world.

Excited now, we continued on across the planted plain toward Castelnaud, its fortifications growing ever larger and more complex as we approached the cliff. Crossing the wide and blue-silk Dordogne on a narrow stone bridge, we came to the tangled intersection of five roads. M. Meunier gave the order to turn left and then abruptly right, onto a steep lane that forced Michael back into first gear. As we mentally urged the car up the hill, we wondered what mountain eyrie we were being led to. Suddenly the roadside foliage fell away, and above us, across a veritable gorge, the Château of Castel-naud emerged, massive and now almost burnt orange in the late afternoon light. From this side we saw a magnificent fortress built on four levels—at the base a belt of rounded defenses, then a high straight wall that must shelter the castle entrance, next huge blocks and towers forming the castle itself, topped by a high rec-tangular turret with a dark stone roof. We had thought we had seen, in the ruins of Najac, the castle of our childhood dreams. Here was a ruin more massive, more complex, more dominant, and yet just as mysterious as Najac, though, under this warm afternoon sky with its amber coloring, much sunnier. It projected an aura of triumph and pride.

With every turn, it became more evident that we were headed around the perimeter of the gorge and straight up to the towering castle and the cluster of houses beneath its walls. Just as we were about to enter the village, our host signaled us to stop. We were then no more than twenty yards from the end of the "route du Château," with the monumental castle rising directly ahead. To the right was a gated lane leading shortly to a house so steeply perched on the side of the hill that its second story was at street level and its first on a terrace below. This was his home, M. Meunier announced proudly, and he would be honored if we would come in and meet his wife. It took all our effort to shift attention from the huge castle above to the small domestic scene at our level, but in politeness we accepted the invitation and entered by a stone porch shaded by a flourishing arbor laden with grapes.

"My other *métier*," our host confided, giving one of the bunches a testing flick of the fingers. "My vines are over the hill. That's how my arm got in such bad shape. Tending vines is pitiable work." But he looked wonderfully happy as he said it.

We entered a dark hall lined with work boots. At her husband's call, Mme. Meunier appeared with a delighted smile, as if unexpected strangers were the greatest treat life offered. Madame was, if possible, even more energetic than monsieur but a good deal more self-effacing. She was agile, short, and squat like her husband, with a frizzy head of hair dyed carrot red. Her small, curvaceous face was a study in mirth, all dimpled cheeks, crinkled eyes, and laughter lines. To match her husband in age, she must have been in her seventies, but she looked much younger, with only a stoop indicating her years. Giving no sign of being inconvenienced by our visit, she scurried to set out bottles, glasses, and crackers. As we were American, she offered us whisky, then scotch. Declining, we were teased for letting our country down. At last we settled on selections, the two men clouding glasses of water with dollops of Ricard and the women drinking orange soda. (In truth, neither one of us can bear the licorice taste of *pastis,* and I would have loved some cold white wine, but our observations in cafés confirmed the typical male and female choices, which indeed monsieur and madame approved, taking the same.)

Sipping and smiling, we waited for the talk of real estate to begin, but instead we faced a strangely familiar barrage of questions. Why did we want a home in Périgord? Where were our families from? Were our fathers in the War, and if so where did they serve? And what about ourselves? Did we have children? Did we expect to have many visitors? We puzzled at this interrogation, wondering if there were some secret compact of real-estate agents in Périgord and fearing that we had tumbled into the clutches of yet another Cathar. We were becoming edgy when M. Meunier rose and said it was time for a little excursion. He had something to show us.

We were too far into the game to give up now, so we followed him out his door, across his yard, and through the gate to the road. We had expected to get in the car, as usual, for a drive to some far-off property; instead, we followed M. Meunier on foot up the route du Château. With the castle directly ahead, occupying much of the skyline with its ocher curves and angles, we had to force ourselves to attend to the knee-high stone fences and beflowered roadside at our level. Within a score of steps, we were at the crossroads of the original *bourg* of Castlenaud. The way to the left led by quaintly porticoed homes and mounted up and around a bend. The lane to the right descended past little shops to a café, and from there to a gathering of stone houses. In front of us, the *Mairie,* or town hall, welcomed visitors with an open door, a flying flag, and a huge pot of hanging geraniums matching the red of the French tricolor. Just to the left of the *Mairie*'s porch, a square archway cut tunnel-like under the building's upper story, which was connected in turn to a large private house to the left.

Our escort led us through the shadowed archway, then halted—for breath, we thought, since the ascent of the path was steep. But no, he had stopped to turn our attention to the left. M. Meunier raised his free arm to point up a little side path that held just four houses built steeply against the hillside. The first two were separated by a high wall, which supported a narrow terrace overlooking the path. He indicated the second of the two houses, which, nested high on the slope, looked taller than its two stories.

"*C'est là.* I call it the little birdcage," said our friend. "It sits on its perch, and it is just right for housing two love birds."

He gave us a mischievous wink and then looked up again, as proudly as if the house were his own. Attached to the heavy front door, just under the iron knocker in the form of a salamander, was a sign: *À Vendre.* It was now clear why we had been subjected to interrogation. Our agent was no closet Cathar but simply a careful villager, particular about his neighbors-to-be. If we purchased this house, we would be living almost next door. Not only for his own sake but for the sake of the village, he felt a responsibility to vet us. And, somehow, we had passed the test. I realized suddenly that he had passed our test, too. We had found our agent.

The little house was narrow but solid, designed vertically like a tower. The tawny gold stonework was even and finely pointed, the roof steeply pitched and newly tiled. A window hidden by dark-stained shutters looked out above the massive front door, which had antique wrought-iron fittings and outsized nail heads. But it was difficult to concentrate on the exterior of the house, because rising behind and above it was the stupendous Château of Castelnaud, cast in the same color of stone. As I looked up, the chimney of the house was framed by the great oval of the castle's artillery tower, still half in ruin. It appeared that the diminutive house was sitting in the castle's lap.

While Michael walked ahead with M. Meunier, I stayed put to get a better sense of the house in its surroundings. Standing in the pathway facing the castle, I could touch the low wall of a miniature garden patio that the house on the right had fashioned out of a triangle of space maybe five feet on each side. There thrived a potted pink mimosa, tropical grasses, deep purple fuchsias, mauve gladioli, and a blanket of striped petunias. Sheltered under the mimosa was a white wire cage, housing a canary, who trilled at me on cue. With a smile, I looked up the castle path, past two small attractive houses. To the left, beyond the house for sale, were two further houses, at angles to "ours" and blending nicely with it in shape and color to form an attractive little *quartier.*

I quickly climbed up the path to join the men in front of the house. We stepped up three stairs onto a stone stoop that ran across the whole front. On its right end stood a huge stone flower basin, as big as a sink; I could just picture it full of crimson geraniums like the ones by the *Mairie.* Then we were through the doorway, following Meunier, who had produced a heavy iron key to open the dungeon-like lock. We found ourselves entering a small but attractive kitchen, the kind you cook, eat, chat, and lounge in. At the center was a square pine table, surrounded by four cane-seated chairs (as is typical of the region). We saw them better when M. Meunier opened the shutters to reveal a view that since has become dear to us—not a scenic landscape but a little corner of a dry-stone retaining wall leading back to the wine-cellar entrance of the house across the path. On the wall, in the sun, slept a calico cat. There was a trellis of old-fashioned red roses against the wall and a pot of petunias next to the cellar door, but what captured the eye was the beauty of the ocher stones—their cut, their angles, the way the light caught them, and the way they formed several depths and levels in the small scene framed by the kitchen window. This view would sweeten a cup of tea sipped at the kitchen table. In fact, the recessed window sill, being more than a foot deep (as deep as the stone wall of the house), would be the perfect place for a cutting board. I could see myself chopping onions or pounding meat while looking out at this little sliver of village life.

The rest of the kitchen was simplicity itself—a curtained closet for storing food, a sink and stove on one whitewashed wall, refrigerator and wooden dish cabinet on another, and just enough room for four people to take their places at the table. M. Meunier pointed out the butane-gas water heater over the sink:

"Very efficient," he promised. "The same tank supplies the kitchen and the water closet. And you can get a fresh tank any time day or night from the café next to the *Mairie*. The Daniels have the concession there."

A dividing wall separated the kitchen from the bathroom, which was even more compact but decorated in cheerful blue and white tiles. It offered all that was needed: sink, commode, shower stall, even a gleaming bidet.

A winding wrought-iron staircase led up to the next level, which was the principal room, or *séjour*. The interior walls were left with the original stone exposed, matching the exterior of the building. With the electric lights on, the stones glowed warmly, making a golden cocoon. A wooden floor and new ceiling beams had been recently installed; their raw wood called out for finishing with stain and wax. The room boasted a nicely proportioned stone fireplace and, opposite it, one large window, which looked out on the flourishing garden of the house below, the one connected by the archway to the *Mairie*.

We stood a long while at the open window, taking in the fullness of the view. We surveyed the village—the back of the *Mairie* and the shops to the left, the schoolhouse on the hill to the right, a neighbor's back garden and kitchen window straight ahead, and in the distance a high rim of wooded hills—a lovely view, with its harmonious blend of village animation and natural peace.

Then we followed M. Meunier up the winding stairway to the upper floor, which had been converted from an attic to a sleeping loft. Here the original beams supporting the roof had been retained; they looked ancient and gave the little room with its sharply pitched ceiling a romantic air, despite the fact that you had to walk crouching like a troglodyte or risk banging your head. (Since neither one of us is tall, that wouldn't be a major drawback.) The walls of the loft, like the room below, exposed the original stone. While a mustard yellow carpet blended nicely with the walls, an awful wallpaper with a pattern of tumescent flowers covered the slanted ceiling and promised florid nightmares, but wallpaper could be stripped. A window at floor level (there wasn't room for a higher placement) looked out over the grassy terrace and onto the tiled roof of the house next door. If you put your head out the window, you had a grand view of the castle ramparts. Just a glimpse round the room made it clear why the house was for sale: four narrow single beds were crammed into a space that would be tight for a double bed. As a vacation house, this "birdcage" had grown too small for a pair with two chicks, a boy and a girl.

The house was charming and ready to live in, and when we learned the asking price, we exchanged an exclamatory glance. And that was before we returned to the main room and stepped out onto the hillside terrace, which sat directly below the walls of the castle and looked up toward the splendid stonework of its barbican and keep. The small yard was overgrown with brambles and waist-high grass, growing in thick tufts. But even with nettles sticking to our jeans, we were stirred by the beauty of the stones surrounding us. This little patch of terrace could be our private domain. We could establish a summer garden against the stone walls, set up a table with umbrella, and eat outside on pleasant summer afternoons or evenings, with the castle as a backdrop. The situation of the terrace sheltered it from view of the houses below, creating a feeling of seclusion even though we would be in the middle of the village.

We stood in the deep grass and pelted Meunier with questions. How old was the house? He couldn't say for sure. Certainly from the nineteenth century, maybe late

eighteenth. It had been there as long as he could remember, and he had been born in the castle tower just
above (thereby hung another story for another day). The
house had been nearly a ruin fifteen years ago, when the
present owners, Parisians, began restoring it for summer use. Before them, the village postmistress had lived
in the house, and it had been in a primitive state. Poor
woman, she lived in the main room and cooked in the
kitchen below, which had a fireplace that now was covered up. According to Meunier, there had been no stairwell joining the floors, so to get to the kitchen, she had
been obliged to go out onto the terrace and walk down
the stone stairs behind the house and around to the
front door. Of course there had been no running water
in those days; an outhouse had stood in a corner of the
terrace, backed against the dry stone wall that marked
the boundary between the house and the castle grounds.
The Parisians (M. Meunier never referred to the owners
by name) had bought the place for a pittance, but they
had restored it from top to bottom: repointed the walls,
replaced the roof, redid the floors and ceilings, installed
an interior stairwell, added electricity, water and a bathroom. *Impeccable.* And now, to accommodate the children that had come along, they wanted to buy a bigger
apartment in Paris. To make that happen, the little
summer house would have to be sacrificed.

"*C'est une bonne affaire*"—it's a bargain. "Think it
over," advised our agent, "stay a while, walk around the
village, and when you are done, meet me back at my
house and let me know if you are interested."

We disguised our mounting enthusiasm and cau-
tiously agreed that since we hadn't yet explored the cas-

tle grounds, we should do so. We sought out the short, steep path to the castle and its overlook. By now it was late afternoon, and no one else was in sight. The castle itself was silent, closed. At the edge of its grounds we stood at a knee-high wall and looked out over a superb panorama. Beneath our gaze the green valley spread from east to west with the Dordogne River winding gracefully through the flats. In the distance, tiny cattle grazed beside round, golden haystacks in neatly laid out fields. Directly across the plain stood the Château of Marqueyssac (where we had parked earlier in the day), with its myriad windows open, suggesting summer hospitality. To the east, the cliffside village of la Roque-Gageac basked in the orange rays of the afternoon sun. And to the west, beyond a wide bend in the river, Castelnaud's enemy, the stronghold of Beynac, glowered from atop its rocky escarpment. We fantasized looking out on this vista as often as we liked if we were home owners here. We could carry up a bottle of wine, dangle our legs over the wall, and have an apéritif before dinner, gazing down on the valley below. We stood in silence for a long time.

"Well?" Michael asked.

This was house number 41. It had a castle like Najac, a view surpassing that of *Cent Étoiles*, and this time a bathroom. It was beautiful and in the style of the region. It nestled in a sweet little neighborhood, promising a connection to village life. And it just felt right.

"Yes," I said, "Yes I will Yes" (quoting Molly Bloom's soliloquy, which I had been saving for just such an occasion).

But there wasn't much time. We had to reach the owners, make a bid, arrange for all of us to sign papers before a notary, and catch our return flight to Chicago in six days. M. Meunier proved his mettle, tracking down the Parisians at work and conveying our bid. With his penchant for drama, Meunier had us come back to his house next day to hear the verdict. Avoiding our eyes, he shuffled us down his darkened hall and into the dining room, seated us, and called in his wife to join us at the table before he lifted his chin and announced, "Well, my children—we are neighbors!" Then it was all embraces and kissed cheeks, pats on the back, and celebration. Mme. Meunier brought out her best *muscat* (a wine sweet enough to be shared by the ladies) and wished us *la jouissance de la maison*—the enjoyment of possessing the house. Our excitement was so overwhelming that we fumbled for words, and the Meuniers had to carry on chatting without us. Eventually, the wine slowed our pulses to a calmer beat, and we managed to thank M. Meunier for his good offices and set about making the arrangements for the closing.

It was now Wednesday. The Parisians were due to depart on Sunday for vacation in Corsica, and monsieur *le parisien* had been having trouble getting his printing business ready for his departure. He could not close the business until Friday night—so he and his wife would drive down to Sarlat overnight, execute the papers by Saturday noon, drive seven hours back to Paris, get a few hours sleep, and put themselves and the children on the plane on Sunday morning. We would depart on their tails, leaving Sunday for an overnight in Paris before our Monday flight back to the States. And in between, what was there to be done?

Michael had looked it all up again in *Achetez Votre Maison Sans Surprises*, but in the excitement of an accepted bid, the steps had flown out of his mind. Old hand and raconteur that he was, M. Meunier delighted in reviewing the routine. On Saturday we would sign the *avant-contrat*, the preliminary contract, which amounts to a promise by the seller to sell and the buyer to buy at the agreed price. Luckily, it was only fifteen years since the last sale of the house, so the necessary documents would be easily found at the Sarlat notary's office and could be used as the model for the sale to us. If there had been surveys to run or deeds to research, the three days between now and Saturday would not have been enough for drawing up the contract. Since we were not premising the purchase on obtaining a loan, the notary was willing to waive our presence at the second step, the signing of the final contract of sale. On Saturday, he would take into escrow our check for 10 percent of the price. This would act as our down payment and would be retained by the seller if we did not come through with the remainder by the date of final contract, in three months.

We were prepared for this contingency. The francs for a down payment were already sitting in a Paris bank, and our French checkbook was awaiting its first use. When the notary received full payment, plus fees for himself, he would act as our agent in signing the final contract. The sellers would come back down from Paris, sign the papers, witness the notary's signature, and receive the purchase price of the house. Meanwhile, our friend Meunier reminded us with his by now familiar grin, he would take his agent's fee on the side—no need to involve the notary in all that—and he would represent us at the signing and collect the keys. Why not? We were in the hands of our neighbor-to-be, and we trusted him on instinct.

In the days that followed, we made several trips up the footpath to the castle, checked the tiles of our roof from the castle ramparts, tried the wine at the local café, picked up a warm baguette at the *dépôt de pain* and ate it with cheese we bought from the grocery van that pulled up at noon in front of the *Mairie*, became nervous about the sign for a woodcarver's shop that we noticed on a near neighbor's door (would there be the whine of an electric saw at all hours?), and quelled our fears by a chat with M. Meunier, who said the young man had his studio elsewhere and was as quiet as a monk, though not so celibate. Mostly we gazed in wonder at the golden birdcage under the castle walls, finding it hard to believe that it soon would be ours. We concentrated so intently on our future home that we scanted the rest of the village and found when we returned to Madison that we retained only a hazy picture of it in our minds.

The morning of the *avant-contrat* dawned grayly, with a drizzle that was bound to put a damper on the usually bustling Saturday market at Sarlat. Michael, never at his best before breakfast, pulled the pillow over his head, unexpectedly out of sorts. While I warmed croissants in the oven, he suddenly worried that this contract was a folly. What sense did it make to *buy* a house in France, when perfectly charming cottages were there for the renting? What was this mania for possession, and why, for pity's sake, in a tiny village where we would never have a moment's privacy? Was it too late to call the whole thing off? Queasiness brought Michael to his feet and into the bathroom, from which he emerged only shortly before time to depart. I chalked his slowness up to his habitual dislike of morning deadlines and left him to breakfast alone while I got the car started. We were due at the notary's at ten. If we left by nine-fifteen, we would have time for traffic jams, full parking lots, and any trouble locating the office. At nine-twenty, I checked on Michael and found him half-dressed. At a quarter to ten, he emerged from the house, with *Achetez Votre Maison Sans Surprises* clutched to his chest.

"Can you hide this in your purse?" he asked, while pulling out of the driveway. "But first, read the paragraph on page 93 about conditions that would negate the sale. They say that if the *certificat d'urbanisme* contains reservations, the sale will be annulled. We better find out about that before we sign the papers."

I was shocked to find him looking so jittery. What had happened to the house-hunting *chevalier* who, having laid siege to forty houses without success, had finally taken the forty-first as his prize? The thrill of conquest seemed to have given way to premature buyer's remorse. He was worrying about the possibility of damp walls and rotting timbers, while I, who had blocked action on all previous sales, felt as serene as an *escargot* in her shell.

The drive to Sarlat was therefore quiet, marked only by a few words of gratitude for the rain that had kept the crowds away and left us a parking spot just opposite our destination, the public library on la rue de la République. For the notary had his chambers on the top floor of the library, which, conveniently, housed the deeds of all properties in the region. The venerable old building had charms of its own, mullioned windows and beautifully carved *boiseries,* but we passed these by on our way up two flights of creaking wooden stairs to the notary's office. Though the grandfather clock in the waiting room showed us ten minutes late, the notary was still preparing papers and M. Meunier had not arrived. But there sat "the Parisians," to whom the notary's secretary introduced us. The secret of their anonymity revealed itself— the family name was not French and therefore unpronounceable to M. Meunier. Mme. Gulesserian—tiny and pretty as a ballerina—told us that her family came from Saint-Cybranet, the next town to Castelnaud, and her grandmother had crocheted the living-room curtains that we were about to inherit. Her dark, wiry husband reached for her hand and explained that giving up "the little house" was painful for them both. He was the son of Armenian immigrants who had settled in France. The couple had bought the little house in the first year of their marriage, so that Françoise could keep a toehold in the valley where she was born, while they built their printing business in Paris. Here the conversation halted with the simultaneous entrance of M. Meunier from the outer door and the notary from his inner room. With handshakes all round, we were ushered into love seats facing the notary's desk.

M. Meunier stood off to the side, while the notary handed one copy of the contract to the Gulesserians and the other to us. He began by asking the Gulesserians to verify the description of the house, the date of the previous sale, the encumbrances (pathway held in common with the neighbors, back wall of the terrace owned by the castle), and the price agreed. He then turned to us to ask if we understood and agreed to the same. I waited for Michael to speak, since he usually took the lead in conducting business in French, but for the moment he was struck dumb. When he did not budge, I answered, "*Oui, Monsieur.*" Michael was pale.

"Even the encumbrances, Madame, you have understood their significance?" Yes, I thought so. This would mean that any repairs or changes to the pathway would have to be agreed to by the neighbors, with costs shared, and as for the terrace wall, it meant that we could not repair or change that either, as the wall would be the responsibility and the property of the owner of the castle. My accent wasn't the best, but the content satisfied the notary, and he looked toward Michael for assent. But panic had washed clean the part of his brain that had taken *les cours de Civilisation Française* at the Sorbonne and seen him through this summer's negotiations. For the time being, we might as well have been speaking Chinese.

Within minutes all the questions were answered, even one that I remembered to put, about what would happen if the *certificat d'urbanisme* contained reservations, and what sort of reservations those might be. The notary gave examples and assured us that it was his business to guarantee the integrity of the sale; we could count on him to be exigent about any problems that might develop. With that, he presented the pen to Michael, who was wary enough in his moment of temporary disability to ask me in English if this was really a good idea.

"Yes," I said, indicating where he should sign. "And I'll sign after you"—which I did, followed by the Gulesserians. Like an automaton, Michael pulled out his check for the down payment and handed it to the notary. Color then slowly returned to his cheeks.

*"Félicitations!"* The notary shook our hands, M. Meunier clapped us on the back, and the Gulesserians invited us to share a bottle of champagne at their favorite café. Though they were due back on the highway in an hour, they would not fail to carry on the tradition of hospitality by former owner to new. The wet streets were thronged with marketers, out for fresh vegetables now that rain had lessened to a mist. We dodged folded umbrellas and full food baskets and found shelter in the Café du Théâtre, where the order for champagne was taken with pleasure. The three men (for M. Meunier was included in the invitation) discussed encumbrances, while Mme. Gulesserian gave me some advice that made all the difference in the coming years. First, buy locally. Don't purchase out of town what you can purchase in town, and if you must buy something from out of the region, keep it quiet. Second, get all your services from townspeople and their relatives: the roofer is M. Meunier's nephew, the electrician is the husband of Mme. Laval who runs the gift shop, the plumber is the mayor's cousin. When you need anything, walk down to Mme. Laval's shop and ask her advice—and follow it rigorously. Third, call everyone monsieur and madame and *vous,* not *tu;* no first names unless invited, and don't expect to be invited. If we followed these rules, we would avoid the mistakes that had kept the Gulesserians outsiders in the village despite fifteen years of habitation and the wife's lineage in a neighboring town. Tears welled in her eyes, but the champagne cork was popping, and the flurry of pouring soon lifted all our spirits. The Gulesserians toasted our pleasure in our new house; we lifted a glass to their safe route home and their coming vacation; new and old owners raised a

glass in tribute to M. Meunier, who had brought us together.

By now Michael was himself again and chatting away. Whatever doubts had seized him in the notary's office were brushed aside. In a burst of magnanimity, he offered to treat everyone to lunch. No one objecting, the party moved to an outdoor table under an awning and set to work on a bountiful meal served family style, with large platters of country pâté, steak with *sauce Périgueux*, *pommes frites*, salad, and *tarte aux pommes*, washed down by several bottles of the local red. Over dessert we looked at each other, both tipsy, and beamed.

We were the owners of a house in France! And it had a castle in the backyard.

# II

## DORDOGNE DAYS

# WE ARRIVE WITH A KEY

By October the entire transaction was complete. In Madison we received a thick sheaf of documents from the notary confirming that our wire transfer had been received, our account credited, the papers signed and stamped *comme il faut*, the monies dispersed in accordance with the *avant-contrat*, our title and deed recorded. Included in the packet was a photocopy of an ancient survey map depicting our little plot of land in relation to the castle grounds. Delighted, we examined the glossy paper with a magnifying glass. There was our little rectangle of property located diagonally below the outline of the round artillery tower. The entire area was designated a classified historic site.

From M. Meunier we received a note of congratulations and a large, dungeon-sized key taped to a piece of cardboard. All joys (and any problems) of the house were now ours. From the Gulessarians we received forwarded bills, for by mutual agreement they had transferred the home's utility and insurance accounts to our name. We had water and electric bills to cover, a home owners policy, and the expectation of a property tax bill, which did not arrive that year. Even when the tax rolls caught up with us, our annual expenses would be light. However, that first summer we did have an empty house to fill. The only article that came with the house was its key. There were three rooms to furnish—bedroom, living room, and kitchen—not to mention garden furniture, dishes, utensils, tools, and fix-up materials to buy.

We spent the Wisconsin winter obsessively going over room measurements and fomenting projects for our first summer in the house. There would be the new wood floor and ceiling beams to finish in the *séjour*, unwanted wallpaper (the maddening floral pattern) to strip from the peaked ceiling of the bedroom, doors and shutters to stain, the kitchen and bathroom to whitewash, window screens to buy or make (make, it turned out, because no one sold them), a garden wild with nettles to tame, and those empty rooms to fill with furniture. For the *séjour* we would look for a couch, a chair, a small wardrobe, and a pair of little tables (antiques if we could find them) that could serve as desks and fit just so into the corners. We would need a bed for the attic *chambre*, and we wanted a double mattress. But how could we get something that size up the winding wrought-iron staircase? Faced with the same problem, the previous owners had settled for single beds narrow enough to fit through the bedroom window. Obviously, any furniture would have to go in that way or come disassembled. A flexible foam rubber mattress might be just the thing, if we could find one. There was a modern furniture store in Bordeaux that seemed promising for some of these items, and we had located a giant IKEA outlet next to the Bordeaux airport that was sure to carry disassembled furniture. Naturally we couldn't do everything at once. We would start with the basics: a table to eat on, a few chairs, a stove, a refrigerator, and a bed.

On the trip over in June we looked like refugees carrying their worldly possessions on their backs. We were encumbered by duffle bags stuffed with pillows, sheets and towels, blankets, a small woven rug for the living-room floor, cushions for a sofa we hoped to buy, clothes to take and clothes to leave, pots and pans and kitchen implements, hand tools and sundries, not to mention a portable computer and dual-current household gadgets. A month earlier we had shipped books and school supplies ahead, for we both had writing projects we planned to work on while we were setting up the house. In one of the duffles were two inflatable rubber mattresses designed for pool use, which could serve as temporary bedding for our first night or two, in case we had trouble finding a real bed. (This plan proved unnecessary, but the mattresses did serve as great river rafts. Later that summer Michael logged four hours on one, starting up-river and floating down the Dordogne until reaching the beach landing at Castelnaud, sunburned but sporting a triumphant smile.) Like the conscientious students we had always been, we were overprepared—and more than a little nervous. After all, once we opened our door, we would no longer be scouting but adjusting. What if we had made a mistake?

Arriving groggy-eyed at the Bordeaux airport on a humid gray morning, we flipped down the back seat of our rented Renault 5 (transforming the car into a minivan) piled in our possessions, and headed directly to IKEA with our shopping list. The store was a wonderland of economical European design, and we quickly filled two shopping carts with must-haves. We entered the cashier's line with carts laden with neat, flat boxes containing the elements of two chests of drawers, two book shelves, several lamps, a parasol and the round top of an outdoor garden table, its frame with legs, and matching chairs, all of which, said the clerk, could be assembled using simple tools. Those we had. While Michael was standing in line with the shopping carts, I found a bargain on a set of white dishes with glassware included. A fine haul for two hours of shopping—all we needed now for our arrival was a bed. For that we nosed into the narrow lanes of old Bordeaux, where we located the compact Habitat store.

The many-storied Habitat specializes in modern home furnishings, a rarity in this region of France, where massive, overstuffed pieces with velour fabrics and heavy walnut frames are still the fashion. On the top floor, we found what we wanted, a simple Scandinavian-style bed with a double-sized foam rubber mattress and light wooden sides and slats for support, which could be taken apart and easily reassembled. On the floor below, we found our couch, a foam-rubber flip-out sofa bed in creamy white, simple but comfortable enough to stretch out on with a book. It would serve as our principal piece of furniture in the *séjour* and as a guest bed for overnight visitors. We were able to squeeze the bed into the car, with the mattress rolled up and the slats and sides shoved into whatever space remained, but the sofa would have to be sent by truck. (Delivering it a few weeks later would prove a trial; twice the truck driver had to turn back at the narrow entrance to our village because his vehicle was too large to negotiate the turn. He returned at weekly intervals in progressively smaller vans; finally on the third try he succeeded—but delivered the wrong sofa. Exasperated, we kept it. The driver nodded knowingly and whispered a relieved *"Merci, Madame."*)

With our little car cram-packed on arrival day, we set out from Bordeaux and stopped at the first inn for a midday meal. We were a bit late for the lunch sitting, but this was our first day as home owners in France, and we wanted to do things right. No skipping lunch. We shared hopes and apprehensions over beef stew and crusty bread. Michael took the time for *un petit café*, following custom to the letter.

Back on our route, we relished every detail of the passing scene. The drive from Bordeaux to Bergerac is flat, with vineyards flanking both sides of the road. You can see the difference between the old-growth vineyards, with thick, stunted black trunks, and the newly planted vines, looking thin, green and vulnerable, propped up by wooden stakes. We called out the names of the most famous vineyards as we passed them. We tried to put into words what made the ordinary roadside houses so appealing—the warmth of the color of the stone, the simplicity of their shapes, the way they looked fully decorated by just one blue hortensia bush on the side or a grape arbor over the door. As we approached our region, we left vineyards behind and began moving through flat little one-street towns. Suddenly the road widened and we were skirting Bergerac, a substantial city that we would want to return to (if only to see where love-sick Cyrano came from). A few kilometers of commercial streets without a glimpse of the medieval inner city led us out of Bergerac, back toward the river, and along a charming canal, where old men sat on chairs, fishing.

Somewhere between the towns of Lalinde and Trémolat, we both said at once, "Now we're here—this is the Dordogne." It happens every year at the same spot. The river that the road follows all the way from the sea suddenly becomes *our* Dordogne—wider, smoother, clearer than in its stretches closer to Bordeaux and Bergerac. The first signal of a difference are the regal swans that glide in pairs under the bridge at Lalinde. Once we cross the bridge, the car swings slowly to the left, to hug the wooded riverbank, and the landscape becomes gentler—the greens are greener, and the blue of the river softens the summer light.

We passed fields thick with scarlet poppies, clovered pastures rising up to a grand white manor house, and the first groves of walnut trees. Though the road was open to the sun, there was a feeling of access to cooling shade in those groves, or among the poplars by the river, or within the walls of the stone churches we passed by. We wanted to stop at every turn in the road, but we were increasingly anxious to reach Castelnaud.

We knew we were near when after a sharp curve, the castle of Beynac suddenly rose up above us. It was a menacing sight, after all that soft scenery. We continued along the river into the village of Beynac, with its cobblestoned streets and stone-roofed houses. On our right was the riverbank, where old-fashioned wooden barges moored alongside modern canoes and kayaks. To the left was the village, built along the cliff face. The footpaths between the houses looked inviting, and I was about to propose that we take a day in the next week to go sight-seeing here, when Michael boomed out, "Castelnaud!" My head swiveled back in the direction his was pointing, and across the river I sighted the distinct outline of the castle's keep. Its effect was totally unlike Beynac's. Instead of awe, it incited anticipation. It looked magnificent—and desirable—in the distance.

With our focus on the ocher towers of our castle, we paid little attention to the outskirts of Beynac, the stone overpass for the train bridge, or the tobacco barns and fields on the way to the bridge over the river to Castelnaud. Instead, we scanned the castle's rounded towers, its strong, straight parapets, and the impressive mass of cliff that forms its base. All was a fiery orange, as the stone caught the afternoon sun slantwise. My eyes followed the line of the stronghold's structures from the highest roofed turret to the lowest ruined dungeon, and down from there past stone houses hugging the hillside to the belfry of the church.

We crossed the ancient stone bridge, with its three massive columns and its wide, sturdy arches. Now the Castelnaud cliff was above us, too close for its heights to be visible. At the end of the bridge, we negotiated a sharp left turn, then a quick right, and started up the narrow road winding to the town. We concentrated on the steep road until a sudden break in the foliage opened on a dramatic side view of the castle. From this distance, we could see the different hues of towers signaling the several periods of its construction, the evidence of renovation on the central tower, with its new roof, and the multiple belts of low-lying defenses around the whole complex. But it was not details that counted. It was the sense of an apparition.

In moments we had rounded the ravine and were on the route du Château, with the castle gate straight ahead. On our right we passed M. Meunier's house, though no one seemed to be home. Then we were at the *bourg*, the town proper. There, anchoring the harmonious ensemble of golden buildings, was the *Mairie*, bedecked this year with red and white petunias. The shutters on the front door were closed, but sitting on a low wall next to the door was a gnarled old man in a blue béret holding a walking stick. With a look of suspicion, he watched us pull the car into a small space. We got out and gave the wiry old man a friendly greeting, which he returned with a wary *bonjour, monsieur, madame.* That was something. He could have remained silent. We smiled and nodded, then with mounting excitement, scurried past the tourist shop and the *Mairie*, under the stone arch, and up the path, to be struck by a view of our house, with the afternoon sun full on it.

It looked larger and more impressive than I remembered. The full sun brought out the outline of nearly white blocks of stone framing the door and window and anchoring the walls at each corner. Between those smooth, creamy-white blocks, the rough stones of Périgord created a variegated face, ranging in color from tan to orange. There was one major change from last year. The wall that held up the hill for our side terrace had become overgrown with ivy and weeds, and there were even some brambles on the porch steps. But the house itself was intact. Side-stepping the brambles on the stairs, we stood in front of a huge oak-plank rustic door with massive hinges and hardware.

"Now for the key," Michael said, pulling out the French men's purse he had bought especially for the trip. (He had nearly lost it twice, not having the woman's habit of checking constantly that the purse is touching her.) He unzipped the center pocket and then an inner one, and pulled out the long iron key that M. Meunier had sent over the waters. It took a minute to jostle the heavy key into its right position in the notch and to turn it once (the door didn't budge) and then twice. The heavy door swung in, dragging a bit on the floor tiles of the kitchen. It was still pitch dark inside, with the shutters closed. Michael fumbled to find the closet and to locate the electricity main within it. He flipped up the switch, and then there was light—a naked bulb hanging from the ceiling. The bulb spotlighted a bottle of walnut brandy, left on the sink by M. Meunier as a house present. *"A la jouissance de la maison!"* read a note penned on a torn piece of newspaper.

Walking across from the sink to the window, I struggled with unfamiliar locks and threw open the shutters. Sharp sunlight streamed in, and the musty odor of a house shut up for a year assaulted our noses. I saw mouse droppings all over and grimaced at bare, peeling walls. Michael went out around the side to open the water main, hidden under a stone lid. He groped for the valve, which was lost under a pile of straw—used for insulation over the winter, of course. (We had to remember that on departure.) Finding the valve, he twisted it sharply, and the satisfying sound of water rushed into the taps. Nothing seemed to be leaking. The tank filled in the toilet, and it flushed! *Très bien!* With water and electricity, any other unanticipated problems would be minor. Next he opened the gas valve of the knee-high butane tank hidden underneath the sink and tried to light the hot water heater. It missed a few times, then caught. We mounted the winding stairs to the *séjour*, threw open the shutters and felt fresh air. Then up the winding stairs again to the bedroom: Pah! Stifling hot and littered with mouse droppings. We both banged our heads on the low ceiling beams trying to open the windows, and then the air was much better. We sat on the floor a moment, catching our breath. From the little window, which was at floor height, we could see the castle barbican, the tiled roofs of neighboring houses, and a glimpse of wooded hillside in the distance. The yard below looked like a Mayan ruin overrun with brambles, but we would clear it tomorrow. We were really here.

The hours remaining until sunset passed in a flurry. Hauling, scrubbing, cleaning, unloading, with scarcely a moment to glance outside. By dusk the bathroom and kitchen were in proper shape, essentials had been unpacked, and the bedroom was assembled. (Standing on a borrowed ladder outside on the terrace, Michael had passed the disassembled bed and bedding to me through the window. There were treacherous moments, as Michael leaned back to give the bulky but pliant mattress a push, and I cried out, "Careful, careful, don't lose your balance—I can pull it in just fine.") When it was clear that we were set to spend this first night under our own roof, we broke off our labors, returned the ladder gratefully to the jocular young man who had come over from next door to offer its use, and washed up minimally for dinner.

"First," said Michael, "we've got a date to keep."

He fumbled in one of the IKEA boxes and pulled out two glasses. Then he reached for the bottle of walnut brandy that was our housewarming present and declared that dinner would be delayed. We were having an apéritif at the castle.

With bottle and glasses in hand, we mounted the path to the castle guardhouse. At every step there were magnificent vistas. As we neared the barbican, there was a glimpse of the church, and below it the river, at its confluence with the little river Céou, a thin shining thread weaving in and out between stands of poplars to meet the grander Dordogne. The massive castle remained silent, closed. (Later we learned that it was being renovated inside in preparation for its opening as a museum of medieval warfare.) But we were free to roam the grounds. We were drawn to the overlook where, a year ago, we had made our decision. The view from this eagle's nest was just as compelling as we recalled. Far beneath us, the river curved like a blue road through cultivated fields. Only a handful of houses dotted the green valley, for this was a land for castles—Marqueyssac directly across the way on its own peak, our own Castelnaud, and the rugged fortress of Beynac to the west. The river led the eye toward Beynac, then looped farther westward. From there, armies had marched out across the plain to harass our citadel, held by the English for most of the Hundred Years War. Five times the English were driven from this ground, and five times they recaptured it, until the French finally forced the English back across the Channel. It was easy to picture French troops in armor picking their way on horseback along the riverbank and English archers standing where our feet were planted menacing the horsemen from above. What was difficult to picture was the brutality of that dreadful age against the backdrop of all this beauty. Michael positioned himself to sit on the wall and swung his legs out over the valley.

"To Castelnaud!" he raised a toast, clinking glasses with me.

We sipped our sweet walnut drinks and looked out over the valley, lit by the sunset. In the distance to the east we could just make out the houses of the village of la Roque-Gageac, where we were headed for dinner. When hunger overcame the moment's contentment, we scrambled back down to the house, secured the doors, and were on our way.

It was only a ten minute drive to la Roque-Gageac. Earlier we had spotted a roadside *crêperie* at the entrance to the town and thought we might feel comfortable going there in our working clothes. The little restaurant was unpretentious and did not disappoint. Ham and cheese *crêpes* accompanied by a green salad and washed down by a bottle of tart hard cider made a delicious meal. Afterwards we strolled the main street of the village, which follows the river's edge. The stone houses of la Roque-Gageac are strung out beneath a burnt orange cliff that overlooks a generous bend of the Dordogne. The town's houses form a lovely ensemble at night, with their golden exteriors illuminated by floodlights and their reflections undulating in the water. That evening we discovered that powerful outdoor lighting enhances the major monuments of the valley. Returning to Castelnaud on a dark country road, we were delighted to see our castle from a distance, perched high above the river and lit from below, a beacon in the night atop its steep cliff. Beynac, too, was illuminated in a pool of yellow light on the far side of the river.

The village itself was inky dark by the time we reached the little square in front of the *Mairie*, where we parked as quietly as we could. Stars were clearly visible overhead, despite a street lamp that cast a cone of buggy light on our house. Not a soul was about, not a sound to be heard other than a cat's complaint. Despite the warm evening, all the windows of the village were shuttered. We pushed open our door, taking care not to let it scrape too loudly across the floor, climbed the winding staircase to our snug bedroom in the attic, and tumbled into bed, exhausted. But not too exhausted. After all, it *was* the first night in our new house. Later, studying the worm-eaten beams supporting the ceiling over our heads and wondering if they would hold, we drifted off to a very sound sleep.

It's fun to fling open your shutters in the morning. We don't have shutters in Wisconsin; nobody does—or if a house has them, nobody uses them. It's not quite the same to twirl open the blinds, draw back the curtains, or just raise the shades. Shutters swing open with a squeak and a clatter as they clap against the walls. The commotion announces to the village that you're ready to go public. Your house, that intimate space that up to a minute ago was strictly off limits, is part of the common sphere again, open for socializing. You belong to the town, and you had better be dressed. And sure enough, just as soon as our shutters flew open that morning, we were hailed by an elderly woman standing in her garden below our window and gesticulating in the direction of our door.

"Cuckoo! Cuckoo!" she shrilled in a sharp-pitched voice, insisting by her arm movements that we come down immediately. Obviously, she had been keeping watch and waiting for the right moment. Pulling on jeans and sweatshirts, we spiraled down the staircase and opened the door. There on the threshold were several plastic bags containing walnuts, a fresh lettuce, potatoes, and bunches of string beans straight from the garden. Mme. Boucher (we soon learned her name) beamed up at us, clearly proud of her housewarming gift.

She was a tiny, white-haired woman in her eighties, with surprising strength in her limbs from a lifetime of farm work. Now a widow, she lived alone in the house behind the garden, which the window of our main room overlooked. It wasn't long before we were chatting away—she in the clear country accent of southwest France, Michael in the gliding French he had learned in Paris, and I in the twangy accent I had copied from my Quebecois high-school teacher. Our interest in each other soon overcame the differences in our versions of French. It became clear that Mme. Boucher had spent all afternoon yesterday watching in fascination as we lugged bags and furniture up the steep incline to our house. Were we newlyweds, she wanted to know? No, but why did she think so? Why, because of the bed. She explained to us that the custom of the country was to pull pranks with the bedding of newlyweds, so naturally she thought something like that was afoot when someone tried to push a mattress through the upstairs window of our house. Michael explained that he was the one pushing the mattress, and then we described the various pitfalls and triumphs of the previous day's labors. A half hour went by in good-natured conversation before we begged off to attend to our chores (actually, to our breakfast). But a lasting friendship was established that morning and was to grow closer over the years.

We had breakfast at a small roadside restaurant looking out over the river at the foot of Castelnaud. The waiter brought a blue tray to the table bearing plates of croissants and walnut bread, a small bowl of strawberry jam, a tall metal coffee pot, a glass full of hot milk, a pot of tea (for me), two cups, and a pile of sugar cubes. Michael, one of the great coffee lovers and a connoisseur of morning luxuries, was delighted. We took our time, gazing out at the river and alternately craning our necks to look up at the castle, which soared overhead.

After breakfast, I resumed housecleaning while Michael attacked the terrace. At some point in time, our dirt terrace had been a garden, but now it was overgrown with thick, chest-high grass (not the lawn kind but the thatch kind), prickly thorns, and nettles. There was no alternative but to take a scythe to it. The surface wasn't large enough to justify a lawn mower, and the task was too daunting, anyhow. So, at a hardware store on the road leading out of Sarlat we purchased an old-fashioned scythe and a small electric trimmer that came with a long extension cord and spun a spool of plastic wire at its cutting end. Once the tall grass had been cut below knee level, the trimmer could do the rest. But first, it needed the scythe. This ancient implement looks easy to manage, but it isn't at all until you acquire the knack. The tool is cumbersome, and it takes practice to find the best angle of approach and rhythm: sway, swing, cut, and again—sway, swing, cut, and again. It's heavy toil, and a straw hat is advisable to keep the sun off your head.

Aptly attired, Michael was just finding his rhythm and beginning to move through the thicket at a decent clip when I glanced out the window and noticed a stirring on the pathway below. A tourist passing alongside Mme. Boucher's garden wall was tugging at her husband's camera strap, urging him to catch this authentic rural scene of *la France profonde* before the straw-hatted peasant with his ancient implement moved out of camera range. They were speaking French: Parisians, no doubt. I watched as the couple surreptitiously snapped Michael's photo as he angled the blade and adjusted his grip. Sway, swing, cut went the scythe. Whiz-click went the camera, long focus, short focus, a series of frames. Congratulating themselves on their artistic coup, the couple moved on to the castle, snapping shots all along the way. Perhaps in the fall, somewhere in Paris, dinner guests would be looking at an album of the Dordogne, and there would be a picturesque series of a local laborer swinging his scythe through the mist of time—in reality an American professor on his first day in town who had never used a scythe in his life.

Once the terrace was cleared, we set up our white metal picnic table and its swaying umbrella and enjoyed our first lunch outdoors, which consisted of Madame Boucher's lettuce and several items from the tourist shop near the *Mairie:* a thick-crusted bread, a pleasantly aromatic cheese, and a half bottle of Bergerac red. I recounted the story of the Parisians' photographs, much to Michael's amusement. Our spirits were high. From our table, we could survey most of the village below us: a maze of narrow streets and clusters of houses with red-tiled roofs wherever there was a purchase to build on. Directly below us was Mme. Boucher's garden and a ridge of forested hills in the distance. Behind us was the formidable castle. The back wall of our terrace, about six feet high, marked the edge of the castle grounds, which rose steeply up toward the huge base of the battlements in a series of stepped and walled embankments. Directly behind us was the castle keep with a massive *lauze* roof and crenellations. We watched workmen dangling from ropes cleaning ivy from chinks and patching stonework. Shrubbery shielded us from the house to our left, while the roof of the house to our right, whose wall served as a retaining wall for our terrace, made the enclosure complete.

After lunch, on our way to do errands, we took an exploratory turn around the neighborhood. Our little *bourg* was quite compact. The *Mairie* was the principal structure on the square (it had, we discovered, a little fossil museum on its second floor). Next to it was the tourist shop, a public telephone box, a café with outdoor tables arranged in a small courtyard, a long stone building that appeared to be a barn, an old wooden shed for drying tobacco, and several houses, the largest of which belonged to our new neighbor, Mme. Boucher. The barn and tobacco shed, we later learned, were hers but no longer in use. Leading down from the square in one direction was a cobblestone path that passed under a mortared archway and led to the village church. Going uphill in the opposite direction was a road that branched off to the small parking lot where we found our car. The lot was flanked by a long school building, with two entrances, one marked Girls and one Boys. Beyond that were empty fields. The other houses of the village clung to the descending slope of the hill leading down toward the river, where, on the flat, another little square connected a few larger homes and housed the post office.

We got in the car and stopped in at the post office to announce our presence. The perky postmistress was delighted to learn of our arrival. Three cartons of books that we had shipped ahead were waiting for us, and she was pleased to have us take them off her hands. We continued on our way to buy appliances, which was our objective for the afternoon. At an Electro-Ménager store on the road to Sarlat we selected our stove and refrigerator. Delivery was promised before the end of the day. The refrigerator we chose was an awkward size, larger than the drink-and-candy model you might find in a hotel room, but smaller than the standard size found in American homes. It was the French custom to shop for the day, not for the week, so we hoped the size would be right for our daily needs. The stove was a lightweight, flimsy contraption designed to operate on the bottled gas that also fueled the water heater. Warning labels cautioned that one must not use the oven and run hot water at the same time—no showers while the chicken was roasting. Likewise, one must remember to lift the white enamel cover for the gas burners before lighting the oven. (Who had seen a stove-top cover since grandma's time?) For their quality, both the fridge and the oven were expensive compared to their U.S. counterparts, but we accepted the salesman's assurance that they were the best available and would see us through a lifetime.

We stopped at a market on the way home to pick up the makings of our first dinner, trusting that our stove and refrigerator would arrive as promised. Naturally, the stove would require a new tank of butane gas. I recalled M. Meunier saying that the concession was handled by the Daniel family, father and son, who owned the village café. We unloaded our boxes and packages at the house and wandered back to the café to introduce ourselves, feeling the heat of the afternoon. M. Daniel *fils* (the son) was a short, middle-aged man with close-cropped hair, thick glasses, and a brusque, though friendly, manner. Michael put in our request for a gas tank and followed M. Daniel around the side of the café, as he jangled a huge ring of keys. There was a wait while he fumbled to find the right one to open the iron gate to the *cave*. With a grunt, he hauled one of the heavy gas canisters out on a dolly, which Michael would need to lug up the steep path to our house.

M. Daniel *père* (his father) was sitting in the shade of a sprawling linden tree that covered the little courtyard of the café. We recognized him as the old gentleman who had greeted us warily yesterday as we drove into town. He was again in his blue béret, with his thin frame hunched over his cane. We exchanged greetings, this time more familiarly, based on our mutual recognition. His aged wife, wearing a blue print apron, sat next to monsieur with a basket of walnuts at her feet and a thin slab of *lauze* (the same stone used for roofing tiles) on her lap. She was cracking walnuts with an antique wooden mallet. With impressive dexterity, she picked the dark nuts from her basket and cracked them on the stone, shattering each shell in a single stroke that left each kernel whole. M. Daniel the elder was sorting them into baskets on the table, the first for the best quality, whole hemispheres that were perfectly intact; a second for those that were patchy in color or chipped; and a third for those that were in pieces.

Soon we were engaged in conversation. The best kernels, he told us, would be glazed in honey and marketed as confections; the broken ones would be used to make a local specialty, *gâteaux aux noix*, dry walnut cakes baked without flour and sold in small tins. His daughter-in-law baked them by the dozen and did a brisk business selling them at the café. Another specialty was her *confiture de noix*, a breakfast spread made of sugar and walnut paste, to which we soon became addicted. (There is nothing better on a warm croissant.) We had an education on walnuts that afternoon. We learned that they can be used in a variety of dishes from salads to dessert; that during the war, when people here had little to eat, whole families depended on the walnut for their principal source of protein; that ownership of a walnut grove was a source of pride in Périgord; and that in the village walnuts were associated with longevity. For reasons of health, monsieur told us, he and his wife ate walnuts every day. She was ninety-two years old, and guess how old he was? Ninety-three? No. Ninety-four? No. One hundred! Indeed, he looked that old but nevertheless was animated, had his wits, and seemed in remarkable condition. We congratulated him on his longevity and bought a supply of everything walnut on the premises: walnut cakes, walnut candies, walnut mustard, walnut liqueur, and walnuts. I carried the stash up to the house while Michael hauled the tank of bottled gas on the dolly.

For the remainder of the afternoon, we busied ourselves with household tasks while awaiting delivery of our stove and refrigerator. At five-thirty, two burly delivery-men, their van parked in front of the Daniels' café, manhandled the appliances up the footpath to our house, bullied them into place in the kitchen, and disappeared as quickly as they had arrived, leaving the set-up to us. Michael went about attaching the stove with a length of rubber hose to the gas tank, which now sat under the sink, and tested the pilot light—it worked! Then he plugged in the refrigerator. Nothing. Dead, no hum, no light. What could be the problem? The electricity was on in the house. Was there a starter button or something to push? Nothing of the kind was apparent. Suddenly the good cheer of the day was diluted. Something must be wrong with the unit—did the refrigerator come with a guarantee? What was the French equivalent for getting stuck with a lemon? We had food that would spoil if left unrefrigerated.

The appliance store would be open until seven, so we dashed to the car with our purchase papers and sped back to the showroom. The manager, getting ready to close, did not appear happy to see us.

"Monsieur has a problem?" he asked, with an incredulous expression. The accent was southwest, but the manner was off-puttingly Parisian.

"*Eh, bien*, the refrigerator doesn't work," Michael replied.

"*Impossible!*" asserted the manager. They had tested *le frigo* themselves before delivery. Had we plugged it in?

*Plugged it in?* Of course we had plugged it in. One was familiar with electrical appliances. Feeling slighted, Michael made the mistake of attempting irony. We were *au courant*, he jibed, but the *frigo* wasn't.

Irony is a tricky tack even if you happen to be a native speaker, and it's hardly ever advisable if you're not. Unfortunately, this mangled attempt at a pun failed to register and noticeably soured things, since the manager knew an irate customer when he saw one. He held firm, the honor of his establishment, not to mention that of French-made appliances, having been challenged by a foreigner who didn't quite speak the language.

The refrigerator, insisted the manager, was in perfect working order. Perhaps our outlet was defective; that happens all the time in these old houses.

"Have you tested the outlet?" We hadn't.

"*Non? Voilà!* One tests an outlet before plugging in the appliance."

"But . . . " He would hear no further complaint.

"You must test the outlet, then report if there is a problem. Tomorrow, since now it is closing time."

Disgruntled, we had no choice but to follow instructions. Back we went to Castelnaud and discovered to our embarrassment that indeed our outlet was at fault. The refrigerator hummed into buzzing life once we maneuvered it against another wall and tried another socket. So the haughty manager was right! But now we needed to repair the problem, since there was only one convenient placement for the refrigerator. I recalled Mme. Gulessarian's advice to talk to the owner of the souvenir shop if we ever needed work done in the house. Mme. Laval was her name, and her husband was the town electrician. Her shop was only a few steps from the Daniels' café. I had dropped in there earlier for lunch fixings but had not introduced myself. This time I brought Michael and we made a production of giving our names and passing on the Gulessarians' compliments.

Mme. Laval, or Anne-Marie, as she insisted on a first-name basis—which is typical of the younger generation in the village—was a full-figured, merry woman with a free-flowing laugh and down-to-earth manner. She was then only in her late twenties and had two small daughters clinging to her apron. When she came closer, you could see that the laughter in her eyes lit a soft pink complexion, giving her the glow of one of Mary Cassatt's contented mothers. She was sitting on a stool behind the till of her shop, surrounded by shelves of local products including pâtés, wines and fruit liqueurs, jams and walnut specialties, and displays of souvenir crockery ranging from ash trays to tea pots bearing images of the castle and the town name. We explained our mission and were assured that there was nothing to worry about; she would send Antoine, her husband, up to the house when he returned from his rounds and before they had dinner. Antoine, she explained proudly, had his own van and spent his days driving from one village to another on emergency calls. He would fix things in no time.

Sure enough, at about eight Antoine appeared at the door, toolbox in hand, trailed by his inquisitive daughters, Nicole, eight, and Babette, not quite three. Anne-Marie had sent them to meet *les américains*, and to them we have remained *les américains* ever since. I showed the girls the house and engaged them in a little chat while their father and Michael attended to business.

Nicole asked where we were from, and I said near Chicago. Her eyes lit up. "Bang, bang!" she said in English. Then, back to French: *"Grande ville, Chicago! Beaucoup de mauvais types! Très dangereux, n'est ce pas?"*

I explained that actually we had never seen anyone with a gun in America—no, not even in Chicago—and that Americans did not shoot each other that often, really. Looking a bit disappointed, Nicole leaned over to listen to something Babette was trying to whisper in her ear.

"My sister wants to know where your dog is," Nicole relayed. I explained that we did not have a dog. Both girls expressed disbelief and asked several times more, certain that the problem was in my understanding of their question.

"No, no—your dog in America, where is he while you are here?" Nicole demanded. "Did you leave him with your mother? Why didn't you bring him on the plane? You can do that, you know."

In later days we would learn that no French family is complete without its little dog, and unless there are relatives at home to keep him company, he goes with the family on any outing, whether to restaurants, shops, hotels, or foreign countries. Our lack of a dog had planted a doubt in the girls' minds about our suitability as friends. Thankfully, soft drinks and homemade cookies would eventually win them over, but for now they retreated into wary silence and watched their father do his work.

Antoine, a few years older than his wife, had a good-natured, well-fed air about him and eyes that crinkled up amiably when he smiled or was perplexed. Unlike Anne-Marie, he was not much given to small talk. Rather, he seemed preoccupied with the mysteries of his profession, poking around and furrowing his brow with concentration. After chipping away a bit of plaster, he soon found the source of our problem, a faulty wire running from the wall to the outlet. Out came snippers, a screwdriver, some odd plastic doohickeys, and within minutes he had worked his magic. For only a second, he paused to feel pride in his expertise—and relief to be done so quickly with an unexpected job. Under firm instructions from Anne-Marie, he resolutely refused payment. He gathered up his girls and went home to dinner.

We were pleased to find that we were able to return this neighborly favor later by entertaining Nicole and Babette, who soon started to drop by on a regular basis. Nicole at that age was serious and plain spoken, but Babette was a playful imp. The girls' routine was to ask about life in the United States, correct our French like tiny schoolmarms, sip Coca Cola, and take home a treat. For their amusement, Michael became Michel, but the girls had trouble pronouncing the "ts" in Betsy (a sound combination with no equivalent in French), so I became Bet-ty (with an accent on the last syllable). Now they are older, of course, and with practice, they are able to pronounce Bet-sy (but the accent is still on the last syllable).

Looking back on our first days in Castelnaud, I am amazed that within forty-eight hours of our arrival we had made friends with the oldest and youngest members of the village, and we were on business terms with the generation in between.

5

D O R D O G N E   D A Y S

When people hear we have a house in France, they usually ask the same set of questions. Where? (We tell them "the Dordogne," but that draws a blank.) Who takes care of it when you're gone? (No one, really. We close it down when we leave.) Do you rent it out? (No, that would involve more trouble than it would be worth). And: What do you do there? How do you spend your days?

At seven in the morning, when the church bells chime, Michael usually turns over and burrows under his pillow, but I slip out for an early walk. At that hour the air is cool; fog wells up from the valley and mists the castle in a veil of white spume. Though Mme. Boucher is out in her garden, most of the village is still dozing. During the two hours that I'm gone walking, the sun warms the valley behind the castle's east wall, edges over the top of the round artillery tower, and begins to heat the tile roofs of the town. I'm back by nine with fresh bread and croissants, which I pop into the oven for a few minutes to make the buttery crusts even more flaky. Michael, wakened by my entry through the noisy front door, winds down the stairs. He sets about preparing his filter-drip coffee and its pot of steaming milk, while I fix a pot of Fauchon vanilla tea for myself. To go with the croissants there is locally made raspberry and strawberry jam and Mme. Daniel's sweet walnut paste, *confiture de noix*, which we consume in shameful amounts. Our kitchen window looks out on a cheerful stone wall with a patch of flowers in front, taking the morning sun. During breakfast we like to listen to the news in English on the BBC, using our shortwave radio, which sits next to the coffee grinder on a small oak night table with a black marble top that must have been part of someone's bedroom set a hundred years ago.

The time to get things done is after breakfast, before the heat of the day builds up. Afternoons in the Dordogne can be hot. We usually bring work with us from Madison—writing projects, books to read for the preparation of new courses, correspondence, and the like—whatever can be accomplished without benefit of a library. In the mornings we work at our tiny desks, a pair of small walnut tables that we spied at an outdoor antique fair. Michael's is in the corner of the *séjour* next to the fireplace; mine sits beside the doorway to the terrace, which offers me a view of the dry stone wall that separates our property from the terraced grounds of the castle. There is something soothing about a hand-built wall where the placement of each stone has involved a human choice, and I never tire looking at it.

In the Dordogne, you own the wall that separates your land from the property below you; you do not own the wall that separates you from the property above. That means that the castle owns the wall I look at from my desk. One year when the wall collapsed, it was the castle's responsibility to reconstruct it, even though all the stone fell onto our terrace. We in turn are responsible for the steep retaining wall that keeps our terrace from tumbling down onto the footpath below us. Over the years it developed an alarming bulge, but we had a mason point the stones with *chaux* (lime mortar), since nothing but earth was holding them, and so far the wall has held, bulge and all. Its solidity encouraged us to plant a large hibiscus bush in front of it. This "Rose of Sharon" (the French don't use that nickname, preferring "ee-bees-koos") has grown to an impressive height and produces masses of white blossoms each July.

Except for the couch, the room we work in is furnished with nineteenth-century rustic antiques. We spent the better part of our second summer scouting furniture at antique shops and outdoor fairs before settling on the pieces for our small rooms. Those antiquing jaunts gave us both a purpose and an excuse to visit towns and villages that weren't on the tourist circuit. In a way I was sorry to fill up our last remaining space, but it took us several years to find the final item we were looking for, a small cherry armoire that fits just so in the four-foot space between the fireplace and the terrace door. (As there are no closets in old Périgord homes, a wardrobe is a necessity.) We saw larger armoires for sale at fairs, some of them huge pieces that must have come from great country homes or manors, but the smaller ones seemed impossible to come by. When we asked one dealer why, he explained that Parisians snapped them up for their apartments and that the small ones sold for as much as similar pieces twice their size. In fact, ours *was* expensive by our lights, but it is the centerpiece of the *séjour*. Made by an artisan in the eighteenth century, it waxes to a lustrous russet shine and is quite an improvement over the white plastic wardrobe that served until we found it.

When we're not working at our desks, house maintenance can take up a morning. The first summer, we worked steadily and throughout most days. We stripped the wallpaper from the pitched ceiling in the bedroom and painted it white, carefully covering the ancient beams with masking tape to prevent spotting. We spread multiple coats of walnut stain on the new untreated beams in the living room, then followed the masking tape routine and gave two coats of white paint to the particle-board panels between the darkened beams. We sanded and stained the oak floor of the living room, which the previous owners had left unfinished. We washed, scraped, and whitewashed the plaster walls of the kitchen, put new stain on all the shutters and doors, scraped the wallpaper from the bathroom walls and painted them white, as well, to offset the blue-and-white flowered tiles. Everything wooden needed wax and received it.

The first week of renovation tested the mutual tolerance we had worked out over the years to accommodate our different schedules. I'm an early riser and would, if left on my own, go to bed each night by ten and pop up cheerily at six. Michael is a creature of fluctuating bio-rhythms. Left on his own—and he is left alone, since I'm always asleep and awake before him—he tends to drift off twenty minutes later each night and awaken grumpily seven hours later. His ten-day cycle of falling asleep has a perigee just before midnight and an apogee well after three. At home, we work around the gap in our schedule by breakfasting separately and planning no shared events before noon. But, settling into our summer home, we came up against a major time crunch. We needed to get our work under way before the house heated up; one sweltering afternoon of stripping wallpaper from the bed-room ceiling at fainting temperatures convinced us of that. The problem was that Michael's habits were in major conflict with the French timetable.

In the Dordogne, every storekeeper worthy of his blue work smock keeps the tradition of closing shop be-tween noon and three. Only the foreign born are out and about during those hours when any civilized person is at home eating lunch with the family. Now, if Michael's sleep cycle happened to be at apogee, he would just be getting going when the shopkeepers were closing their doors. Meanwhile, I would be stomping around the house, reminding him that we could not get started on the day's work without buying more paint, a roll of masking tape, a bottle of white spirits, or a higher lad-der—we always needed something. Michael, who sticks to his morning routine with the tenacity of a clam, would proceed at his own pace, with the result that we often had to delay our work until late afternoon, since we would not find a store open until three.

As a result, we had some cranky moments, but the outcome was good for our subsequent summers.

Michael decided that days in Castelnaud need to start by nine o'clock, so he encourages me to bang that front door and generally make a ruckus when I come back from my morning walk. That puts us on schedule for doing chores before lunch.

Thankfully, our maintenance now is minimal. Even so, a house that is a century and a half old and abandoned for ten months of the year constantly needs work. Michael's is a familiar face at Brico Plaisance, our hardware store on the road to Sarlat. Over the years he has picked up some unusual skills. Now he can track *les petites bêtes* in old ceiling beams by following their powder trails, and he has learned to administer a pitiless *coup de grâce* to the bugs through a needle-nosed spray can. He can bat-proof crannies in an attic ceiling and fashion wasp traps for the terrace by using the local method. (You fill a plastic food container with sweet vermouth, cut a hole in the lid, then cut a plastic water bottle in half and place the neck of it in the hole. The wasps land in the vermouth by flying through the open end of the cut-off bottle, can't figure out how to fly back up out the neck, and die happily in an alcoholic stupor.) He's learned when it's time to decalcify the water heater, de-moss the interior stone walls, and clean out the distribution box of the septic tank, which sits under the front stoop. (It took several summers of experimentation with vents and pipes and special treatments to tame the tank's malodorous fumes whenever the wind blew in from the wrong direction.) Another skill he has mastered is waxing the floor of the *séjour* wearing strap-on foot brushes, like a skater on a pond.

Michael's proudest accomplishment, though, is our window screens, the only ones in the village. He puzzled over their construction a long time. French windows open out, not up and down, and they work with shutters, so fixed screens aren't practical. But what does work are roll-up screens made of flexible plastic netting, which can be attached to the top of the window frame by Velcro strips. A section of broom handle anchors the bottom, which is secured when the casement windows are open by pushing wedges between the frames and the wall recess. For a screen door, Michael used the cord mechanism of a rolling roman shade, replacing the shade with plastic screening. He suspended the mechanism from the top of the door frame, again using a section of broom handle for an anchor at the bottom. With these contraptions, we fend off flies, bees, and night-flying bats, for we have a colony living under our attic eaves. It was bat droppings, not mouse droppings, as we first thought, that had littered the floors on our first arrival. But with the screens in place, we are protected from unwanted creatures.

I'm the gardener and housekeeper, knocking down cobwebs, scrubbing the tile floors, and washing clothes in the kitchen sink between trips to the *laverie self-service*. It's my *boulot* to plant and water the flowers, which I do by carrying watering cans around and up the back stairs to the terrace, since there's no exterior water outlet and cans must be filled at the kitchen sink. Each summer I tug at weeds and try to suppress dogged nettles to plant geraniums, petunias, impatiens, flowering clover, basil, thyme, and mint—which just have time to blossom before we have to leave them behind. Also, I do the marketing and cooking, the pleasures of which I hide from Michael so he won't ask to trade assignments.

After lunch, we go on vacation. By July, that means the beach or pool. We shut the house up tight to seal out the heat not only by pulling the shutters and darkening the room, but by locking the windows too. The practice seems counterintuitive, but the local wisdom is to make sure that not a crack of air can penetrate, so that the cool air that has been stored overnight in the thick stone walls can maintain a shield against the afternoon sun. We put our beach paraphernalia in a basket, don straw hats, and make our way to the village parking lot, where our car has been sizzling since about eleven.

We have learned to leave an extra twenty minutes for departures, since it is customary to stop for a brief conversation with anyone we recognize who may be about. At home, a cheerful wave and greeting is usually sufficient for neighborly encounters, which don't always necessitate breaking stride. But in the village it is considered rude to recognize someone and just keep ambling along. The expected courtesy is to break your trajectory, change course, and greet your neighbor by physical contact, whether a peck on two cheeks if the relationship has so progressed, or a laborer's handshake, that odd custom of brushing limp wrists to which M. Meunier had introduced us. There has to be a little conversation, especially if it's the first encounter of the summer. But people don't linger. In fact, the elders of the village have a habit of ending each such encounter with a playful wave of the hand and an order of *"Allez, allez!"*—that is, "Go on, go on!"

Eventually we do make it to the car and head down the winding hill to the valley below, stopping midway at the dumpsters, where we drop off the day's garbage. (In a village this small, there is garbage deposit rather than garbage collection. Then again, taxes are low.) At the foot of the hill, flanking the arching bridge that spans the Dordogne, is the tree-lined Castelnaud beach. Some years ago, the commune dredged out a shallow swimming area and brought in sand and pebbles to make the wooded shoreline comfortable. By midsummer, the sun-dappled beach is abuzz with kids and parents. Reposing, you look up at the bridge and the castle (or if you're Michael, you surreptitiously look for the occasional topless sunbather) while the Dordogne bubbles by. The water is cold, the current swift. Really, the river is for wading rather than swimming, for if you move too far from shore and the current doesn't carry you off, you are likely to be run down by a kayak or canoe paddled by some inexperienced tourist. For wading, you must have plastic slippers to keep from cutting your feet on the sharp river stones. Nevertheless, the beach of Castelnaud is a delightful spot, where there is always a cooling breeze off the water. On hot afternoons we bring camp chairs down with us and read under the trees.

For real swimming, there is the Olympic-sized pool in the shape of a J, built for Josephine Baker in the 1950s at the nearby Castle of les Milandes. Today this opulent pool is open to the public for a nominal fee. By midafternoon it is packed with kids, but the pool is deserted at noon, when everyone is at lunch. Ideally, that's when we arrive, so Michael, an enthusiastic swimmer, can do his laps. We often bring a picnic lunch and spend the afternoon relaxing on the grounds in our favorite shaded spot, under an enormous weeping willow, where we lounge until five or six o'clock. Baker's graceful Renaissance castle sits on a high hill above the pool and is the elegant backdrop for splashing kids shrieking in delight under the watchful eyes of their sunbathing moms.

"*La Bay-caire*" is still a legend in this part of France, where she is truly revered, but Josephine's renovation of les Milandes had a poignant end. Constructed in 1489 by one of the lords of Castelnaud as a gift to his wife, les Milandes was designed as a *château de plaisance* and built on a bank of the river just a few miles from Castelnaud. The castle survived the French Revolution and even was expanded in the nineteenth century, but then fell into decay. Baker bought it in the 1930s, after her rise to fame as one of France's most celebrated cabaret singers.

Josephine's story is as dramatic as any work of fiction. She was born in a St. Louis slum and came to Paris in the 1920s as a dancer in the chorus of *la Revue nègre*. Almost overnight she became its star, causing a sensation with her scantily clad "banana dance." By the age of twenty, Baker was the queen of the *Folies Bergères* and the most famous Black entertainer of the era, admired as much for her sweet, high-pitched singing as for her dancing. Her theme song, "*J'ai Deux Amours*" ("I have two loves, my country and Paris"), captures the generosity of spirit that so endeared her to the French. During the Second World War, "*J'ai Deux Amours*" was played constantly on both sides of the Atlantic as an emblem of the Resistance and of the partnership between the Free French and the United States. Baker's role during the war years extended beyond boosting morale through her music. After the fall of France, she remained at les Milandes and worked with the French Resistance, sheltering downed Royal Air Force (RAF) pilots and refugees trying to flee the Nazis.

She also served as a military courier, using her concert tours as cover to convey messages for the Allies. For these efforts, she was decorated by General de Gaulle.

After the war, she and her husband, Jo Bouillon, the French band leader, embarked on an idealistic plan to create a "World Village" for orphaned children of various races and nationalities at les Milandes. One by one, they adopted twelve children—from Europe, Africa, Asia, the Middle East—and set about transforming les Milandes and its park into a combination orphanage, concert center, working farm, restaurant, amusement park, and casino to raise money for their project. At one point Josephine employed almost the entire adult population of the village. She had ambitious plans to expand the castle, which had fifty rooms, but sadly, Josephine overextended herself, and before long her debts began to outrun her income.

When she and Jo Bouillon divorced, Josephine was left to raise her "rainbow tribe" alone. By 1964 she was bankrupt, and her creditors forced the sale of les Milandes to recoup their debts. There is a heart-rending photograph of Josephine that made all the French newspapers, showing her sitting on the steps of les Milandes in a robe and nightcap, shielding a kitten from the rain. She had been evicted that morning and would suffer a heart attack later that day. During her convalescence, Princess Grace of Monaco took Josephine in, with some of the children. Others were sent to live with friends or former employees. When her health again permitted, Josephine went back on the concert circuit in order to raise money for her family and spent the last decade of her life on tour. In 1975, after a triumphant comeback in Paris, she suffered a stroke and died.

A few summers ago, to launch the opening of a Josephine Baker Museum on the castle's grounds, the commune sponsored a reunion for Baker's adopted children, now grown and scattered around France and several countries. A platform with a microphone was set up in front of the castle. There were speeches by the Mayor of Castelnaud and other regional dignitaries. Then the returning members of the "rainbow tribe" rose to share their *souvenirs* of living with their famous parent in the Castle of les Milandes. These middle-aged men and women of different races seemed to have little in common on the surface, but they recalled the shared memories of childhood and the burden of press attention while they were growing up. Several writers have criticized Baker's child-rearing experiment as exploitative; some journalists have implied that her motive in adopting the children was to seek publicity. If so, there was no sign of bitterness among the speakers. Several became teary-eyed and sentimental, recalling the remarkable woman who brought them to live in a fairy-tale castle in the Dordogne.

Afterwards, there was champagne served under a tent for the attending guests and the public. While we were standing and sipping, an old-timer in work clothes and a béret, with a cigarette dangling from his lips, sought us out. He was bursting to tell someone about his personal recollections of *la Baker* and was buttonholing anyone who would listen. We were happy to hear his stories. Monsieur had been one of the original workers hired by Josephine to help run the village farm. "She was *extraordinaire*," he kept repeating, and famous as she was, made no distinctions between the rich and the poor. His fondest memory was of the star going off to pee behind the bushes one afternoon, rather than returning to the château, after drinking wine at an outdoor lunch for her workers. Wasn't that *extraordinaire!*

Recently I came across a black-and-white photograph in one of the Baker biographies that shows a smiling Josephine and her happy brood sitting by the pool at les Milandes. Today the pool shaped as her initial still echoes with the squeals of children, who splash at the bottom loop of the J at the shallow end. Adults swim the stem of the J, some doing the sidestroke while looking up at the castle that Josephine loved.

On afternoons when we're not at Josephine's pool, we go exploring or revisit favorite haunts. It has taken us years to check off the most highly recommended visits listed in *le Guide Michelin* for *Dordogne/Périgord-Quercy.* In the guide, sites and attractions are described as "Worth a Journey" (drum roll: three stars), "Worth a Detour" (still compelling: two stars), or merely "Interesting" (one star). We have worked our way through all of them, and sometimes it takes the fresh eyes of our guests to make a return visit still "worth a journey." For instance, one visit to the *Gouffre de Padirac* (Padirac Chasm, with its boat ride on an underground river) is sufficient, and not even the Pope himself could drag us back to Rocamadour, a famous pilgrimage site in the Middle Ages spectacularly built against the rugged face of a perpendicular cliff (three stars in *le Guide Michelin*). True, the approach to the fortified town is awe inspiring, but the climb to the top of the precipice (223 steps) leads through a vertical mall of trinket shops. In the thirteenth century, penitents climbed the Grand Staircase on their knees and believed they would be rewarded with merit in heaven when they reached the top. Today's climbers are harangued at each level by hawkers of dashboard saints. There is an elevator for those impatient to arrive at the principal souvenir shop at the summit.

On the other hand, there are quiet, out of the way places that we never tire of. Cadouin is one of these. The abbey there was founded in 1115, and like Rocamadour, the town became a popular pilgrimage destination in the thirteenth century. Its attraction was its holy shroud, reputed to be the linen cloth that had been wound around Christ's head on the day of the Crucifixion. Richard Coeur de Lion (the Lion Heart) came to genuflect before it, as did many of the era's royalty. For centuries Cadouin was a major site of worship. Then, in 1934, the shroud was proved to be a forgery, and the pilgrimages ended. From our point of view, the town was saved. Today, few tour buses pull up to the abbey, but the church and its cloisters, dating from the Renaissance, are peaceful havens on a summer's afternoon.

When we are restless and ready for a day trip, we sometimes head for Carennac, about an hour and a half's drive east from Castelnaud into the Quercy. The town is noted for its Romanesque cloisters and the elaborately carved doorway at the entrance to the Church of Saint Pierre. But the town as a whole is the real attraction, with its peaceful ensemble of sixteenth-century houses, most finely restored. There's also a quiet park along the riverbank, where we lay out our picnic, usually a simple affair of bread, cheese and fruit, and something cold to drink. The French picnickers nearby—whether a single man out fishing or a family on a day's outing—are engaged in a much more elaborate event. With the respect the French give to every meal, the picnickers have brought along folding chairs and a folding table. They drink wine, not soda, and use glasses, plates, and silverware. The first time we observed such a repast *en plein air*, we thought it was the aberration of a rigidly formal family—aristocrats perhaps. Now we know that we are the ones who are out of step. To the French, we must seem culinary slackers. Headed back to the car, we still have a treat to anticipate, for the route home takes us along the most dramatic stretch of the Dordogne, with craggy cliffs shading the far side of the river and marshy wetlands edging the road.

It is not necessary, however, to go far afield for an afternoon's pleasure. There are art galleries and *ateliers* tucked away in the otherwise sleepy village of Meyrals. If what we want is solitude, we seek out one of the forgotten hamlets situated on roads that the map renders with a light thin line. When we see houses ahead, we pull the car off the road and go for a little exploratory amble. We may discover a communal oven from centuries past, a medieval chapel lined with fading murals, a ruined manor, or a new (to us) configuration of the classic Périgordian stone house. Often the hamlet has been abandoned for years.

Some outings are occasioned by a town's weekly market day. Others are prompted by posters advertising upcoming festivals, which are major events for both locals and visitors. The summer calendar is crowded with street fairs, contests, outdoor communal dinners, and of course *la fête nationale* on July 14, Bastille Day. To observe the celebration, we go to Domme to see the fireworks, followed by dancing in the street supplied by an accordion band. Even more colorful is *la félibrée,* held the first weekend in July and hosted by a different town each year, with towns and villages vying for the honor. The festival honors the folk customs of old Périgord and celebrates *la langue occitane,* which is still spoken by some of the older residents. The host village is decked in swags of handmade paper flowers strung between buildings and over the streets. Men and women dress in the traditional costumes of the region, the men with black broad-brimmed hats and vests, white shirts, and black pants; the women with bright patterned blouses and colorfully trimmed white skirts. Wandering street bands, carrying old instruments, provide music. There are poetry and declamation contests in the ancient tongue, folk songs and dances, demonstrations of by-gone crafts and farming practices, and plentiful wine and food available from street stands. *Les périgourdins* take this holiday seriously and look upon the displays with pride.

Even the smallest hamlet has its annual *fête;* Castel-naud's is held on the third weekend of July. Posters go up around the village announcing events, and Antoine Laval knocks on the door collecting donations to cover the fireworks and the stringing of colored electric lights from telephone poles. It is more or less a civic duty to attend. During our first summer, the *fête* of Castelnaud was an arcadian delight, but though we didn't know it then, we were witnessing the last of its kind. A large field had been cleared next to the river at the bottom of the cliff. The posters announced a *fête champêtre,* an old-fashioned country fair. Lights had been strung and a stand set up for food, mainly grilled *merguez,* a cross be-tween a spicy sausage and a hot dog, and cheap red wine pumped out of plastic barrels. People began to gather at dusk, carrying blankets to spread on the ground. The whole town, it seemed, was there, though not Mme. Boucher, who even then retired early and no longer went to the *fête*.

The crowd seated themselves in a wide circle, leaving an open ring in the center for a grassy stage. Into it sprang a man in his thirties wearing jeans and a bright-colored shirt, carrying a hand mike that was plugged into a portable amplifier: he was the *animateur*, the master of ceremonies. He roamed the circle, bouncing with kinetic energy and telling jokes that we couldn't follow but that pleased the crowd. Introducing the evening's entertainment, he moved things along at a lively pace. There was a juggling act, some slight of hand, a milk bucket race for girls, a hay-pitching contest for boys, and an accordion player, who came on just as a silver full moon rose over the trees on the opposite shore of the river. Everyone waited for the main event, a bare-backed donkey race for the men, with a big country ham as a prize for the winner.

The race was actually a bucking bronco contest, with obstreperous donkeys instead of horses. As the donkeys circled the ring kicking up their heels, their riders were flung this way and that, to the crowd's amusement. One cocksure teenager was tossed from his mount but grabbed onto the donkey's tail and was dragged full circle in a cloud of dust and straw and encouragement. Miraculously, he seemed to walk away unharmed. The eventual winner was carried off on the shoulders of his pals, swinging his ham and wearing a crown of laurel leaves.

The race was followed by a *kermess* on the flattened grass, with music provided by the accordion player and a fiddler, who materialized for the purpose. Young and old whirled around in a two-step, men with women, women with women, girls with girls, and a few old men with their contemporaries (but not boys with boys). We danced, too, jostling into M. and Mme. Meunier, who were twirling at a clip that defied their age.

At midnight some of the revelers crowded along the bank while others walked out to the middle of the bridge spanning the Dordogne to watch the traditional ending to the *fête de Castelnaud,* the descent of the Dordogne by boats carrying illuminated torches, or *flambeaux.* Slowly snaking down the darkened river came a flotilla of canoes, moving in graceful synchrony, at first seen only by the torches in their bows, which cast pools of dancing light in the water. Then, as the boats drew closer, their outlines became faintly visible, along with the shapes of human figures silently turning their paddles in the current. As each boat passed under the bridge, the paddler in the bow extinguished his torch while the other in the stern guided the canoe to a gentle landing. At the moment that the last boat touched shore, a spectacular fireworks display erupted from an island in the middle of the river, illuminating the castle with flickering colors. The crowd ooh-ed with pleasure.

Our village *fête* was delightful, and we looked forward to its repetition the next summer. But the following year, the town fathers of Castelnaud, in their anxiety to keep up-to-date, felt the need to modernize their *fête* to attract more local youth. That meant no more donkey races. No more accordion players. No more sitting on the grass. Huge flat-bedded trucks now hauled in motorized attractions that filled the parking lot in front of the post office at the bottom of the hill. There was a shooting gallery, an electric bumper-car rink, a disco truck with blaring loud speakers that could be heard up at the castle, and a variety of gut-shaking rides that squealed and belched oily fumes into the air. The *boom! boom! boom!* of a pounding rock-and-roll beat echoed across the valley, and the teenagers did show up. The new highlight of the *fête* was the crowning of "Miss Castelnaud," the English term chosen to mimic the "Miss America" and "Miss Universe" contests familiarized by television. We tried to explain to Mme. Boucher why we regretted the change, but she was at a loss to understand our preferences. Everyone else said that the new *fête* was a success; the crowds were much larger now. Since a poster for the *fête* was always tacked up on the door to her cellar, which was visible from the square, she had acquired a proprietary interest in the event and would have been insulted had we not attended. Michael subsidized the shooting gallery until he finally won a stuffed chartreuse frog, which he bestowed upon Mme. Boucher, who giggled.

One tradition that persists is the annual planting of the *mai*. Since pagan times, Europeans have celebrated the coming of spring by dances and fertility rites around a maypole. The custom continues in Périgord, but the origins and meaning of the ceremony have been forgotten. Nowadays Périgordians raise the *mai* to honor their employers or the winners of elections, a concept that strikes Americans as strange. Driving through the countryside in late spring or early summer, you may come across tall pines stripped of their branches with a little tuft left on top, bedecked with ribbons and the French tricolor. They are erected in town squares and bear plaques with such inscriptions as "Honor to our Elected

Officials" (*Honneur à Nos Élus*) or "Honor to the Boss" (*Honneur au Patron*). This reverence for authority seems out of character for the people who launched the French Revolution, but since maypoles are thought to be symbols of power (if not male potency), maybe the political connection makes some kind of sense.

One summer we were invited to witness the raising of a *mai* to honor the reelection of the mayor and the new members of the town council. The ceremony was held before the entrance to les Milandes. For administrative purposes, les Milandes is considered part of the commune of Castelnaud, and on this occasion the present owner of the castle was sponsoring the event. Next to the pit that had been dug for the *mai*, a huge, gaily colored tent flapped in the breeze, waiting to house a reception for the team once the pole stood upright in its place. A complicated tangle of ropes attached to the stripped tree lay loosely on the ground. The maypole itself looked enormous as it leaned at a steep angle in its hole—a tractor had moved it into position. But how would it be possible to drag the pole upright, we wondered, even with a team of a dozen men? Antoine Laval, who served on the council in addition to his work as an electrician, was in charge of the operation and invited Michael to join the rope line. Everyone took his place, laid hold of a piece of rope, and waited for the signal.

"*Allez, tirez!*" came the cry. With a shudder and creak, the monumental pole swayed in a cloud of dust, then suddenly and easily rose into place in one haul, as the men pulled in unison, with the spectators cheering them on. The *mai* was vertical within moments and held there while the receiving hole was quickly filled in. There were back-patting and hand-shaking all around. Michael was elated. Afterwards, the pulling team posed with the mayor for a group photograph, then repaired to the reception tent for champagne and cake. Fluttering at the top of the pole was a small French flag and a placard proclaiming: "Honor to our political victors!" The slogan struck me as comical; yet there was something timeless about the moment, too, a vestige of some far-off day when fertility rites in sacred glens welcomed the spring.

Which reminds me, we also have attended one marriage. A few years ago, the young baker at Beynac was dating an American stewardess, and they decided to wed. Whether they had met in the air or in the bakery, we never learned. Because Castelnaud was the groom's home, the couple chose the *Mairie* of Castelnaud for the ceremony, with the mayor, a family friend, officiating. But since the bride spoke hardly a word of French, they needed translators. At the last minute, we were invited, or rather, pressed into service. There was a small procession from the parking lot to the *Mairie*, where the mayor, draped in his ornate sash of office, performed the rites. We wrote out a little speech in English for him to deliver, which he pronounced in a language incomprehensible to everyone, including us. The stewardess, a quiet girl who came from a small town in Texas, seemed dazed and looked a little puffy around the waist; the family looked resigned. That November we received a baby announcement in Madison. We heard that the couple settled in Houston, which now must have a very authentic French bakery.

In the evenings, there's lots to do: concerts in the surrounding towns and churches (ranging from Gregorian chants to jazz), a lively theater festival in Sarlat starting in late July, various spectacles at some of the castles: historical plays, *café* entertainment, street dances, lawn-bowling tournaments, and even *discothèques*. But most evenings, for us, the main event is dinner, either at home or at one of our favorite restaurants.

I still like to cook on vacation but prefer to keep meals simple. Veal scallops sautéed with *cèpes* (a delicious local mushroom), potatoes fried in a tiny bit of goose fat (left over from the last can of pâté), and newly picked string beans, along with a fresh *pain du pays* and a bottle of *Bergerac sec*, is typical fare when we're at home. Eight o'clock is the right time to be out on our terrace. It will still be light for another two hours, but the sun has dropped behind the west side of our house, casting the yard into shade. Michael cleans the previous night's bat droppings from the picnic table, cuts the bread, and carries the bottles, dishes, glasses, and utensils up on a tray. It's tricky carrying trays up a narrow, winding staircase—a lighthouse keeper must have a similar challenge—but we're used to it by now. Two more trips bring up the meal. Though the sun has sunk behind the top story of our house, the castle still remains in sunshine. As we eat, flocks of long-tailed swallows circle the towers, squealing eerily as they search for insects. The setting sun soon turns the castle gold, then orange. When the light is gone, wheeling bats emerge from under the eaves of our house and join the birds in the hunt for food. We collect our dishes and descend to the kitchen, spiraling down our wrought-iron staircase, mimicking the movements of the bats and swallows.

We do the dishes, read for a while in the *séjour*, then wind up the spiral staircase to our *chambre*. The small bedroom with its low, pointed ceiling still retains the heat of the day, but a fan placed in front of the window, flush with the floor, brings in the night air. A spotlight on the hill opposite us mounted to illuminate the castle floods through a low side window, but we block it by moving a wicker basket into place. We check for *moustiques*, fly swatter at the bedside. A sheet is all the blanket we need. Overhead the old beams, brittle with age, form an arc, like the inverted frame of a boat hull, almost close enough to touch.

# 6

## NEIGHBORS

We hadn't realized at first that so many of the permanent residents of the village were elderly. Like the young of Najac, Castelnaud's sons and daughters had moved away to the cities to find employment, as over the years the town's economy had dwindled to a narrow base of artisan wares, small-scale agriculture, and tourism, which clearly was the engine of the future. When we first arrived, there were hardly any shops in Castelnaud, but we patronized the few that beat out a living, and we were acknowledged gratefully by the proprietors. Most services were provided by merchants who drove up at fixed hours of the day in little minivans. There was a butcher, a baker, a fishmonger, and a general grocer. Once you knew the schedules, it was a great way to shop. Each day as we waited or stood around with purchases, we got to know the neighbors and what they ate.

It wasn't long before we were on nodding terms with most of the village. Foremost in stature was the smart and energetic young socialist mayor, whose office we could see from our living room window. He had been the teacher in the one-room schoolhouse, had risen to mayor, and then, to the pride of the village, had been elected to represent the Department of the Dordogne in the National Assembly. Yet he found time to run a walnut farm and compete in the Olympics on France's kayak team. To him, we were part-time constituents, and we received the same brisk handshake and efficient attention that he parceled out to the other townsfolk who met him in passing as he dashed in and out of the mayor's office.

To some of the other residents of the village we were at first curiosities, then, tentatively, accepted as time went on. We had chats and occasional drinks with M. Fauré, a day laborer who did odd jobs for the commune. He was the kind of man who could tease a woman without seeming to flirt and who made friends with every man he shared a drink with. We looked forward to having him over for apéritifs. Each evening, we waved to Sophie, a dark-haired beauty in her fifties who flashed gold teeth when she laughed and rode astride her husband's tractor as it puffed up the hill at the end of the day. We visited the makeshift atelier of octogenarian Mme. Calais, whose passion for wood sculpting had flourished in her widowhood. We even helped chase after her neighbor, Mme. Moreau, who raised rabbits and chickens for sale, had bouts of dementia, and would wander away from home.

One evening shortly after our arrival, while we were doing the dinner dishes, we heard a loud rap on the door.

M. Meunier was standing on the threshold, smiling, carrying an armful of wine bottles. He and madame had been away in the north visiting their daughter and son-in-law, but now they were back, and he wanted to welcome us. How did we like our house? We liked it fine. Had we found everything in order when we arrived? *Mais oui.* No leaks, no unexpected repairs to make? We assured him we were pleased. Then, so was he. He grinned broadly. We noticed that he no longer was wearing his arm in a sling. Yes, the arm was much better now, he said. And he had brought us a gift, some bottles of homemade wine. The grapes, he told us, came from his own little vineyard and were completely natural, untreated by chemicals. He had picked and squeezed them and bottled the wine himself. We insisted that he join us to sample his gift. After a polite hesitation, he eagerly pulled up a chair.

The dark green bottles looked as homemade as the wine. Of uneven shape, they bore no labels. On inspection the wine had a suspicious cloudy color and an aroma resembling mildewed rope. The taste, frankly, was alarming. M. Meunier swirled his glass, held it against the light, squinted, and tossed back a swig. He smacked his lips several times in quick succession.

"Not as good as last year's," he pronounced, judiciously. Evidently not.

To be polite, we tried to keep up with our well-meaning guest, matching him glass for glass. But first one, then the other of us flagged. M. Meunier, however, seemed perfectly pleased with his product and accounted for most of the bottle, then opened a second one for the sake of comparison. It tasted just like the first.

The wine may have been sour but not M. Meunier's company. As the evening wore on, our guest grew more talkative and began spinning tales. He was proud of the fact that he had been born and raised in Castelnaud and had remained here all his life—except for a period during the war before France capitulated, when he fought against the Germans and was taken prisoner. After enduring months of hardship, he had managed somehow to escape from the prison camp with a friend, and together they made their way back to Périgord, where they hid out on a farm until the armistice. M. Meunier recounted his joy on that day in 1945 when he finally was able to return to Castelnaud and cross the stone bridge over the Dordogne. At the time, the bridge was still riddled with bullet holes from German machine guns.

We were surprised to learn that there had been fighting around Castelnaud during the war and that there had been a period when resistance in the region against the Nazis had been spirited. Indeed, a band of partisans had made the castle their stronghold for a few days but had to abandon it when the Germans brought cannon up. M. Meunier called the Germans *les Boches;* they had brought nothing but misery to France, he said grimly. He recounted how his father, too, had fought the Germans in World War I, had served as a prisoner of war himself, and had come back gravely wounded, a broken man.

"It was pitiful to see him like that. And there were many others like him."

Two generations of men in the village had been scarred by war. Our friend had no use for the Germans, and it irked him to see German tourists in Périgord.

Most of all, he hated to see them buy houses—there was a German writer who owned a big house on the hill opposite the town. No, he didn't like it at all.

It was compelling listening to these stories, which kept alive the presence of two world wars. Every village in this part of France has its monument to the dead of the Great War inscribed with the names of sons who died *pour la Patrie*. And the same family names appear on monuments to the dead of World War II. Here in the southwest, the Resistance had pockets of strength, and the Nazis exacted brutal reprisals. At Rouffignac only the church was left standing when the Germans burned the town in March 1944, killing a large number of civilians. Rouffignac was rebuilt, but the town of Oradour-sur-Glan, which the Nazis burned that same year (killing five hundred women and children who were locked in a church that was then set on fire), remains a charred ruin, a museum village offering mute testimony to the massacre. Bitterness toward Germany is a living reality in the Dordogne. Everywhere you come across plaques on buildings or along the road asking you to remember the name of someone who was captured and shot by the Nazis at this crossroads or against this wall or in front of this building on such and such a date. "Shot by the Nazi Barbarians." "Hero of the Resistance." "Died for France, Age 21." "Remember them." We made an effort to, pronouncing their names aloud. M. Meunier had survived the war, but the names on some of the signs were those of his schoolmates.

As the evening wore on, our conversation turned to life in the village in the days before the war. The farther back M. Meunier reached in time, the more animated he became. There were jokes and stories of infidelities involving people long dead, the parents, grandparents, and even the great-grandparents of some of the current residents whose names we recognized. There were tales of ill feeling between the nobility and peasant families dating from the Revolution but continuing to this day and still coloring village politics. There were childhood memories of working in the fields and pulling pranks on companions, tales of customs vanished, and anecdotes that we couldn't quite follow. One of them had to do with how M. Meunier got into real estate after the war instead of continuing as a farmer, but we lost the thread.

For as the hours went by and we consumed more wine, M. Meunier's stories became more difficult to understand. It didn't help matters that our senses were dulled when our guest began slipping in and out of the local dialect and slurring his words. When we compared notes the next morning, we admitted to each other that neither one of us had understood much of what had passed for conversation toward the end. Whether it was the lateness of the hour, the growing incomprehensibility of our visitor, or the potent effect of his homemade wine, I couldn't say, but by eleven o'clock our heads and stomachs were spinning, and we had all we could do to remain upright on our straw-bottomed chairs. Seeing that we were nodding, M. Meunier took his leave, and we pulled ourselves with difficulty up the staircase to our bed.

The next morning we both were wretchedly sick and remained so all day. I stayed in bed, Michael on the couch. Only Mme. Boucher's soup passed our lips; there was nothing else we could keep down. Imagine our consternation when M. Meunier, looking fresh, reappeared at our door that very evening bearing additional bottles

and an invitation from Mme. Meunier to Sunday dinner. He was delighted that we liked his wine. There
would be plenty more of it to drink on Sunday.

We couldn't refuse the invitation—not that we
wanted to—but how could we face any more of the
wine? We couldn't just put our hands over our glasses,
and yet another exposure to the pungent wine would lay
us low for days. There had to be some preventive measure we could take. Pepto Bismol! It had worked for
Michael in Mexico. On a trip to Oaxaca, he had followed his doctor's advice and had taken two pink Pepto
tablets before every meal. The idea was to coat your
stomach before eating, rather than after, when the bugs
had already entered your system. At the time I pooh-
poohed the idea and refused to follow the regime, which
created the conditions of a controlled experiment. We
ate the same food and drank the same liquids. I got
sick—very sick—and Michael didn't.

We started on the Pepto twenty-four hours in advance, after lunch on Saturday. By the time we arrived
at the Meuniers, our innards were surely coated, as our
tongues certainly were, having turned completely black.
Sure enough, the first sight that greeted us on arrival
were eight bottles of "Château Meunier" arranged on
the sideboard in two military rows. For some reason, I
thought of Goya's painting *The Executions of the Third
of May*, the bottles reminding me of Napoleon's firing
squad lined up in their tall hats and facing their victims
at point blank range. In addition, there were bottles of
gin and scotch and apéritifs of every description. It was
going to be a long afternoon.

We were six at table, or rather five, since Mme. Meunier would spend most of the day in the kitchen. M.

Meunier had invited another English-speaking couple (though we spoke only French at the dinner), clients to whom he had sold a house in the region a few years earlier. They were the Lairds, a retired couple from Scotland who had purchased a second home in the Dordogne, a much grander house than ours, with considerable land to garden. We would always be grateful to the Meuniers for this invitation, for we became friends not only with the Lairds but also with their grown daughter and her English husband, who lived in a town nearby. By an odd coincidence, they in turn introduced us to another English professor—from Wisconsin of all places. David had retired from the English department not at Madison but at the University of Wisconsin–Milwaukee. He and his partner, Sean, an artist, had summered in France for years and now lived here permanently in a converted farmhouse only a half hour from us. By their considerate gesture the Meuniers had connected us with a small network of English and American expatriates with whom we became close friends.

But that was later: first we had to get through the meal. With the before-dinner drinks we had olives and light salty crackers. M. Meunier and John Laird drank scotch, while we sipped sweet vermouth. When we were seated, Mme. Meunier brought out several trays of homemade pâtés and *terrines* made of duck and rabbit she had raised herself. These smooth-meats were served with half-dollar-sized pieces of toast, their crusts neatly cut off. Delicious. With everyone seated, Mme. Meunier gave the signal for the wine to be opened. Her husband filled each glass to the brim and kept them that way. We tried to sip sparingly.

Michael was holding his own through the soup, a clear chicken *consommé*. When we had emptied our bowls, M. Meunier got up with mischief in his eye and announced that it was time to acquaint us with a local custom known as *faire chabrol*. With mock ceremony, he ladled another serving of soup into his bowl, poured in half a bottle of the home-brewed wine, swirled it, lifted the mixture to his lips, and chugged it down. I blanched; fortunately, the women were excused. Not Michael. With great merriment M. Meunier ladled a spoonful of *consommé* into Michael's bowl and filled it to the brim with homemade plonk. Fumes actually rose from the mixture. From the hot broth? From the witch's brew of wine? At any rate, there was no escape. With fortitude Michael rose at his place and performed as required, to applause and laughter, but he appeared somewhat unsteady as he sat back down. Under the table, he tore the cellophane from a packet of Peptos, palmed a couple, and raised them to his lips, using his napkin for cover.

Next Mme. Meunier brought out a hearty platter of succulent roast chicken accompanied by shoelace-thin string beans and heaping mounds of *pommes de terre sarladaises*, which are potatoes fried Sarlat-style in goose fat with onions and truffle shavings. Everything was fresh, Mme. Meunier assured us, the potatoes and beans from her garden and the chickens from her own coop. The chicken was cooked to perfection, with crisp skin, moist meat, and a marvelous tang, which Mme. Meunier attributed to basting with *verjus*, the tart juice of wine grapes picked in summer. When she offered us second helpings, Michael accepted, though I demurred, to save room for dessert.

But instead of dessert, the next course was an even larger platter of *confit de canard*, local duck fried to a golden brown. *Confit* is a specialty of Périgord, and M. Meunier had requested it for his guests. To make *confit de canard*, you begin by partially cooking the duck, then preserving it in its own melted fat and sealing it in a tin or jar, which will keep for months. When it is time to prepare the meal, you unseal the jar and fry the duck in its preserved fat. In the days before refrigeration, preserving fowl and game using the method of *confit* ensured ready meat the year round. This specialty dish is found on menus in all the local restaurants and is a favorite of tourists.

Mme. Meunier's *confit* was the best we had tasted—or ever would—but we weren't prepared for it. There were two main courses to the meal, and even though Michael had taken second helpings of the chicken, he had no choice but to find room for the duck too.

There followed next a *salade périgourdine*, composed of tender lettuce, fried duck gizzards, and toasted walnuts, dressed with walnut oil, a meal in itself. Then came the cheese course, an assortment including the small, dry, round goat cheeses known as *cabécou*. With each change of plates came a new basket of breads—country tourte, walnut bread, white rolls, and now baguette slices—and of course another glass of wine. Dessert was the traditional *gâteau aux noix*, a one-layer, unfrosted cake made with plenty of ground walnuts, just a touch of flour, a few eggs, some butter, and a splash of walnut liqueur. In the walnut cake we savored the deep flavors of the Meuniers' own walnuts, from the grove we passed each day on our way down to the river. No sooner had we set down our cake forks than madame ducked out to fetch the dessert for which she was known for towns around—perfect, crisp *gauffres*, feathery light twirls of cookie dough, magically stamped with a beehive pattern and lightly powdered with sugar. Then coffee was poured, and then *eau de noix*, a walnut-based digestive liqueur. Followed by chocolates.

When it was over, we dragged ourselves back up the hill. Never before had we coped with such a gargantuan meal, or so much wine, especially if you counted the soup. In the morning, we marveled at the Meuniers, their hospitality, and their culinary feats. By the way, the Peptos worked.

By the end of that first summer we were familiar with our immediate neighbors—on the one side Jean-Louis, a good-humored young woodcarver who lived alone, and on the other side a Portuguese couple, Fernando and Maria, the caretakers of the *château*. A few steps down lived Paulette, who drove the grocery wagon that came to town late in the afternoon. She was a nervous, stubby woman with disheveled brown hair and the chiseled bones and flashing eyes of a gypsy. Divorced, she had a high-spirited tomboy of a daughter who was ten and given to naughty pranks. From Paulette we learned our first tidbit of gossip: the mayor's secretary was having an affair with the roofer, who was a nephew of M. Meunier. Everyone knew about it, she claimed, except perhaps the secretary's husband and the roofer's wife. We were wide eyed, remembering the sweetness of the pretty, intelligent secretary as she explained our taxes to us, and recalling the charm of the handsome roofer, with whom we had felt fast friends after one consultation on missing roof tiles. Ironically, the village would bless this unlawful union, while Paulette, the scandal-bearer, would herself become the subject of village gossip in another year and would not find forgiveness.

By then tourism was on the rise, and Castelnaud needed new shops, but there was scarcely any space in the hilltop village for expansion. The town council mulled over the situation and decided to embark on a development plan. Next to the little beach on the river was a stretch of town property that had been leased as a corn field. The commune cleared the land and erected several small commercial buildings in the local style connected in the shape of an L. A graveled parking lot was added, and Castelnaud soon had its own little shopping mall to compete with the traveling food trucks that until then had enjoyed a monopoly. Within a year, the little shopping area, which the townsfolk called *"en bas"* ("down there") boasted a row of shops including an all-purpose grocery store. Its proprietor was Paulette. She had quit her truck route, borrowed heavily from the bank, and opened her own business.

The result was disastrous. Paulette had a generous heart but lacked the experience to run a store. She overstocked inventory, and produce spoiled on the shelves. She sold on credit or gave away food to friends in spontaneous gestures of magnanimity. She made a complete botch of the books. She stocked goods that nobody wanted except us, like orange juice, Ritz crackers, and peanut butter. She kept a freezer full of ice cream but not enough staples. And all along, while she was losing money, Paulette thought that she was making it. She confused cash flow with profit and went on buying sprees, showering her daughter with presents and sprucing up the house.

Tourists kept her afloat the first summer, but when the season was over and they were gone, her losses grew. Villagers who had patronized her truck and then switched to the store became uneasy with Paulette's folly and took their business elsewhere. Paulette closed the store for a month during the winter. When summer came around, cash started flowing again, and she cheered up. With money temporarily in the till, Paulette went out and bought a car and a computer, leaving unpaid her debts to the town, her suppliers, and the bank.

That computer, as Anne-Marie later told it, was Paulette's downfall. Years before Americans were surfing the Net, the French had the *minitel*, which offered services and business links by phone and then computer. On the *minitel* Paulette joined an electronic lonely hearts club, and from time to time, she would disappear for weekends or longer on distant jaunts. Her daughter would be sent to stay with her grandmother in Toulouse for weeks at a time, and someone else would be minding the store, usually a young relative from one of the nearby towns. Sometimes the relative would live in Paulette's house, which she rented from Anne-Marie, who owned the building. This July, it was a nephew who was supposed to care for the house, water the plants, walk the dog, and feed the daughter's menagerie of pets, which included birds, cats, and a brood of rabbits. One night at about three in the morning we were awakened by the unhappy howling of the dog, which had not been let out all day. When we encountered the nephew, he was evasive. He would no longer be sleeping over, he said (meaning, we surmised, that he had moved in with a girlfriend), but he promised to return once a day and feed the animals and do chores.

Sometimes he came, sometimes he didn't. Neighbors complained to Anne-Marie about the howling dog, but what could she do? Paulette was off somewhere "on a vacation" and had left no forwarding address. The nephew didn't come for days, and then he stopped in only to take the dog away and set out food and water for the other pets. That was the last we saw of him. The place started to smell, and soon there were sounds of animal feet scurrying over the wooden floors inside. When Anne-Marie finally brought the mayor up and got his authority to break down the door, no one had been inside for a week. The apartment was in ruins, the new furniture scratched and soiled beyond cleaning, the drapes reeking, and the floors covered by pools of urine and piles of excrement from the cats and the rabbits, which had broken out of their pens. Those rabbits had been cute bunnies at the beginning of the summer. Now they had grown to splattering adults who had the run of the house. In the end, the place had to be fumigated and the floors refinished.

Paulette never returned. It was said that she was living somewhere with *un type* whom she met through the *minitel*. We never knew what became of her smart little daughter. Eventually the grocery store *en bas* was bought by a sober couple from Saint Cybranet, who turned it into a going concern. The husband wore an official-looking white grocer's smock behind the counter, whereas Paulette had always worn jeans.

After the apartment had been fumigated, the mayor's secretary moved into it with the roofer, M. Meunier's nephew Serge. By now both were going through divorces and were living openly together. We liked our new neighbors. Like his uncle, Serge, who was sinewy and dark and had a quick grin, would occasionally drop by after dinner carrying a bottle of wine and looking for a chat. Once we watched him at work, replacing old tiles on the roof of Mme. Boucher's house below us. He tossed the old tiles to the ground, using the exposed wooden roof slats to bear his weight like a ladder as he moved up and down the steeply pitched roof. An assistant threw the replacement tiles up to him, which he caught skillfully. Serge then lodged each in place, fitting them perfectly, without any adhesive. For someone in his line of work, he had a hazardous liability: Serge was deathly allergic to bee stings, and the angry insects are attracted to tile roofs in the summer heat. He carried a syringe and vial of anti-bee-sting serum with him whenever he was working.

One evening he arrived at our door after dinner. We offered wine, and he accepted happily, even though he already had done justice to a bottle over his meal. He wanted to talk about American houses. Was it true, as he had heard somewhere, that American houses were made of wood? Yes, quite commonly, we assured him; in fact our house in Wisconsin was made of wood. That fascinated him. And what kind of roof did we have? We couldn't find the words to describe asphalt shingles, and eventually we gave up.

"One day," said Serge, "I will build myself a wooden house. That's my dream."

We protested that houses made of the local stone were more charming.

"Maybe to you Americans," he said. "For me, a wood house is more romantic. One day I will build my own."

At this point, a startled expression crossed Serge's features, as if something had taken him by surprise. He quickly got up to excuse himself.

*"Un petit besoin,"* he said by way of explanation, and hurriedly exited the front door to attend to his "little need."

A few seconds later we heard a happy sigh and a distinct gushing sound outside the door. There was no doubt about it; Serge was relieving himself against the front wall of our house. Why hadn't he asked to use our bathroom? We were told once by Parisian friends that the French think it impolite to use their hosts' toilet while visiting. And it is true that none of our French guests have ever asked to do so, despite imbibing large quantities of drink. The cheerful splashing continued. Michael cupped his ear in an exaggerated listening pose and wisecracked: "That's why the houses here are made of stone."

Our relations with one couple in the village who since have moved away led to an embarrassment during our first summer. Maurice Crotté was a semiretired mason who sometimes assisted in projects at the castle and seemed always on the lookout for some extra work. He was a compact, surly fellow who nursed a perpetual hangover and usually sported a bandage somewhere on his person, if not a cast. Maurice was accident-prone— a condition no doubt related to his habit of imbibing. Often at night he would be the lone remaining patron in M. Daniel's café, sitting at the bar and recounting his latest mishap, while M. Daniel feigned interest, with a towel draped over his shoulder and one eye on the clock.

Camille, Maurice's wife, was a thin, nervous woman with a facial tic. She was somewhat younger than her husband and busied herself with advice to anyone who would listen concerning home improvement schemes that Maurice would be happy to undertake. One evening she arrived on our terrace buoyed by an opportunity to advance a proposal. At the edge of our terrace was a shaky wooden fence that served as a flimsy barrier above a drop to the sidewalk of about twelve feet, and it needed repair.

"It must be hard for you to take care of so many things at once," Camille said to me, nodding, affecting a tone of sisterly commiseration. "Just look at this fence. What you need is a stone wall. Don't worry, I'll get Maurice to build it."

It was true we needed the job done, and it would be helpful to the couple to provide some extra income, yet somehow I had misgivings. Michael appeared at that moment, and Camille repeated her suggestion. He had been thinking about the fence and agreed before I could signal my unease. Nothing was said about cost, but it was understood that Maurice would arrive after he finished work the next day to build a barrier wall for our terrace.

At six o'clock the next evening Maurice and Camille appeared on the terrace carrying a bucket, a trowel, and a plastic tub in which to mix cement and sand. But where were the main materials, the stones? The volunteers were evasive. Finally it occurred to me that Maurice intended to filch them from the construction site for work on the castle and that he expected Michael to help him carry away the stones. I was aghast, but Camille assured me that there were many more blocks at the castle's construction site than were needed for restoration, and Maurice had permission to use them.

What's more, the wall would be for the good of the village. No one would complain. She beamed in her mode of connubial loyalty, but then her cheek twitched involuntarily.

What, I wondered, was the penalty for removing building supplies from a classified historic site? And what would the other neighbors think of us? Yet we had no real proof that mischief was afoot, so how could we back out now without insulting the Crottés?

We tried to temporize, but the ambiguity of our situation defeated us. Was it clear that Maurice was working for us and therefore subject to our direction, or— since no payment had been discussed—was he at this point just a fellow helping out a neighbor with a backyard building project, in which case we were expected to pitch in? While Michael and I talked strategy, Maurice and Camille scampered up the hill to the construction site and soon returned carrying their first load of bulky stones. Out of gallantry, Michael relieved Camille of her burden, and before he realized it, he was laden with contraband. Relieving her of a second load seemed less of a transgression than the first, and by then it was too late to regain any pretense of innocence. By now I was mortified and kept imagining the eyes of the entire village on us, signaling banishment from the circle of respectable company. I began to feel nauseated and felt the first signs of migraine.

I became so upset that I took to my bed and refused to have anything more to do with the enterprise, while Michael soldiered on. I stayed in bed a good part of the next day, too, but by then our new wall, about three feet high, twelve feet long, and enclosing the open end of our terrace, was drying, and the heavens hadn't fallen. When

Mme. Boucher called from her window that the wall improved her view and was *quelque chose de beau*, I ventured out to inspect it and felt relieved. If Mme. Boucher wasn't scandalized, then perhaps it was all right. In fact, no one called the *gendarmes* or ever mentioned the incident. Within a couple of years the mortar and stones of the wall had acquired the patina of the surrounding buildings and blended harmoniously with the castle. And why not, considering the origin of the stones? The wall looked as if it had been there forever.

We consulted M. Meunier on the subject of fair payment for Maurice.

"How many hours did he work?" Michael told him, and our advisor calculated a sum.

"What about materials?"

"Materials," Michael said, coughing behind his hand, "were included."

M. Meunier came up with a figure that seemed reasonable, to which we added 20 percent just to be on the safe side. We wadded up the large bank notes in an envelope along with a thank-you card, and took it down the path to the Crottés' cottage. Camille beamed and immediately suggested a landscaping project and several other improvements to our property, which led us to believe that the payment had been generous.

The Crottés tilled a small plot of land on the hillside behind our terrace. The first summer we were installed in our house, they grew beans and other vegetables there. The next summer, though, they put up a chicken coop and installed hens and a full-throated cock of the walk. Every morning at dawn the rooster crowed his bloodcurdling shriek, until one day Michael could stand it no longer. We considered various options, then hit upon a ruse. I went to see Camille and asked if she would consider selling us the rooster to make *coq au vin*, one of Michael's favorite dishes. Camille grasped the situation and made a counteroffer. She would deliver the rooster to her mother in the next village if we could provide the transport. It happened that their car was out of commission (a result of a road mishap), and she was stranded in Castelnaud, unable to do much marketing, or visit her mother, or get to the doctor. We understood this negotiation as follows: Chanticleer gets the axe if you agree to provide me with wheels. First we visit my mother, then we go to market, then to the doctor in Saint Cybranet. Honorable terms. We accepted.

Without sentiment, Camille wrestled the flapping rooster into a big cardboard box, which Michael locked in the trunk, and off we drove. Inside the trunk, the belligerent bird struggled to escape, shrieking and scratching all the way to Beynac. After climbing the winding road toward Beynac Castle, then branching off, we eventually arrived at a small, unprepossessing house in the hills behind the town. The stucco house was close to the road and had a small yard on the side with chickens stepping gingerly and pecking the dirt. An old woman dressed in black was waiting outside and greeted us with a mournful expression. Camille had apparently explained the situation over the phone. It didn't seem as if she had given her mother much choice.

When we opened the trunk, there was an uproar of noise and feathers. The box was in shreds and the stench revolting, as the rooster had fouled the carpet. Our passenger seemed no happier to have arrived at his new home than to have departed his former, and he attacked with a well-honed beak as Michael tried to help

Camille lift him from the trunk. Pure malevolence gleamed in the bird's yellow eye. With a hop and a yelp, Michael let go, and the prisoner was free, but only for a moment. Camille and her mother both grappled with the creature, who suddenly went limp as an audience of chickens scurried about, beating their wings and adding to the commotion. The lull was temporary. With an outcry, the rooster made one final attempt to escape and left a terrible mess on the old lady's shoes. By then the women had him—Camille grasping him by the neck, her mother holding his feet—and he gave in, solaced perhaps by his act of defiance and the clamor of interested hens, who circled the car. The last we saw of Camille's mother, she was dragging the rooster off to a shed, where we imagined a chopping block.

True to our word, we spent the rest of the day ferrying Camille on her rounds, adding a stop at a car wash, where we cleaned the car as best we could, including vacuuming and spraying scent in the trunk. It was useless. For the rest of the summer, the car smelled like a chicken coop. One day M. Meunier got in and sniffed the air with a puzzled grimace until we explained our plight. He nodded in understanding, as if the conveyance of roosters in car trunks were an everyday practice in Périgord. "*Eh, bien,*" he said with a nod, expressing solidarity as he rolled down his window.

I sometimes wonder what became of that car. The leasing agency always provides us with a new vehicle, which then is sold on the used-car market after the rental period. Were they ever able to remove the stench? Luckily, because our return flight left Bordeaux early on a Sunday morning, we were able to drop off the car at the airport when there were no agents at the return counter to ask awkward questions. I imagined Michael having such a conversation:

"A rooster?"

"Yes, Monsieur, a rooster. We are desolate."

"Do you mean to tell me, Monsieur, that you put a live rooster in the trunk?"

"Truly desolate. We have paid for comprehensive insurance."

"It is strictly prohibited to transport animals in our vehicles, with the exception of small dogs."

"It was just for a short trip."

"Come this way, Monsieur. I hope that you are not pressed for time."

Fortunately, there was no need for this exchange. At six in the morning on a Sunday there is hardly a soul at the Bordeaux airport. Following instructions, we left the car in the designated parking lot, dropped the keys into the slot at the unmanned car-rental booth, and skulked aboard our flight.

## MADAME BOUCHER

Our closest companion in the village was Mme. Boucher, whose memories extended back to a time before automobiles were seen in Castelnaud. From her kitchen window, Mme. Boucher could see the house where she had been born and where, from age twelve, she had kept house for her father and brother, who were farmers. In the heat of a July afternoon, she liked nothing better than to sit in the shade, looking up at her birthplace, telling tales of the past. Her fair cheeks would redden and lift into laughter as she told of running like a rabbit on the ramparts of the castle with the boys—her brother and the young Paul Meunier—when she was too small to know the difference between the sexes. Then her face would tighten and her voice crack as she told of the change in her life when her mother died. Suddenly she had to take the mantle of the matriarch, wear a dark apron, and stay indoors keeping house for the men. Her eyes would fill with tears as she mourned her last days at school in the year before her mother became ill. The teacher had always said she had a prodigious memory. She could to this day recite the names of the old regions of France. And though outside of school she spoke *patois*, her formal French was impeccable, as was her handwriting. *Mademoiselle l'institutrice* had said she should be sent to Sarlat, to the sisters, for instruction in arts and letters, but at twelve those dreams were nullified by her mother's death. For the eighty years thereafter, through housework, marriage, farm labor, childbirth, and the tragic deaths of child and husband, she kept up her reading, wrote letters regularly to practice her hand and her art of composition, and leaped at every chance to demonstrate her agility with numbers. She was proud of these skills and as delighted to exercise them as she must have been to learn them, in the girls' schoolroom just up the hill.

On her melancholy days, there would be no sign of Mme. Boucher all morning. In the afternoon, we would find her seated by her fireplace, with a navy blue coverall over her black-and-white nylon paisley dress. This was her grieving attire. No matter how we would start the conversation, it would lead to her life's great sorrow—the loss of her son, Charles. We heard the story scores of times, it's true. Yet through the gravity of her telling, the tale cut the heart each time. Her handsome son, the one real friend she had ever had in the world, had been taken from her at the height of his success. She had fought for his chances, protected him from family expectations that he would become a farmer like his father, insisted that he be well educated, and then had swelled with joy as he succeeded in the tobacco business and was elected mayor of Castelnaud not once but four times in succession. Through the first two terms, he was unmarried, and she was his social partner. She accompanied him to mayoral receptions in the stately city hall of Sarlat and, on one memorable evening, she and her son received the great Josephine Baker in their very own salon. When, in his third term, her son married, her happiness was complete. Even if she no longer had first place at his side, she reveled in his continued success as mayor and his contentment as husband and father. But then one day, *"la catastrophe."* He collapsed. There was nothing to be done. He suffered unspeakably. (At this point, Mme. Boucher would go silent. It was many years before we pieced together an understanding that it was a brain tumor that caused her son's collapse and killed him after a lingering illness.) She still occupied the house that he had expanded to include a reception room for official occasions; it was filled with photographs, yellowing election placards, and even strips of old bunting.

Listening to Mme. Boucher's tale, we were at first at a loss, wanting to comfort her and reaching for consolations—how fortunate, for example, that her son had left a baby daughter, who was the grandmother's chief joy in her old age. We soon came to see, however, that what our old friend wanted most was a witness to her heartbreak. We learned that when the day dawned as a day of grief, there was no avoiding it, and the most helpful thing we could do was to echo her litany:

*"Mon pauvre fils."*
*"Oui, Madame. Le pauvre."*

*"Comme tout le monde l'a bien estimé."*
*"Eh, oui. On l'a bien estimé."*
*"Élu comme maire quatre fois—imaginez-vous!"*
*"Eh, oui, Madame!"*

"My poor son, esteemed by everyone, elected mayor four times—imagine that!" After a half hour of such incantations, Mme. Boucher would rise from her chair, fetch her son's formal photograph from the living room, set it on the kitchen table, and propose that we drink some prune brandy with her. Suddenly she would be full of scurrying energy, lifting from the shelf the huge jar of prunes preserved in *eau de vie,* reaching for glasses made for the purpose, plopping a moist prune into each glass, and filling each glass with brown liquor. We would drink to each other's health, salute the portrait of M. Boucher the mayor, eat the prune with a spoon, and shift the conversation to village gossip. We would slip away just in time for Mme. Boucher to turn on the radio for the four o'clock weather report—her only traffic with electronic media.

These visits took place in her large kitchen, which now was the principal room in her house, since the *salon* remained as it was on the day of her son's funeral and was a museum to be shown to visitors rather than occupied. Not much had changed in the kitchen, either, over time. The floor was tattered green linoleum. The walls once had been whitewashed but now were brown with cooking grease and smoke from the old wood-burning stove in a corner. (A butane stove stood next to it with its hose attached to a tank of gas, but Mme. Boucher preferred cooking the old way and kept a basket of wood stacked underneath the sink.) The large fireplace had been blocked off and replaced by an oil burning heater to warm the house in winter; the tank stood in the fireplace but was hidden behind discreet wooden doors set into the wall. Above the former hearth hung a pair of old hunting rifles, which once had belonged to her husband, who had passed away within a year of her son's death. The loss, Mme. Boucher said, had been too much for him. That was all we ever learned about her husband; his memory had been all but eclipsed by the death of her son.

As for furniture in the kitchen, there were two tall standing cabinets and an ancient wooden table with four sturdy straw-seated chairs. Mme. Boucher had one proud possession in the room, a magnificent grandfather's clock from the eighteenth century, which stood in one corner in a floor-to-ceiling walnut case. The face of the clock was adorned with a golden sun and a silver moon, with the hours etched delicately in roman numerals. Behind a glass door, a three-foot brass pendulum swayed inexorably. Mme. Boucher wound the clock with a huge key once a week, and it still kept meticulous time. About time and dates she was obsessive. Around the kitchen hung four daily calendars—one from the telephone company, one from the electric company, one from the post office, and another from an insurance firm. Every evening Mme. Boucher made her rounds about the kitchen, pulling a page from each of the four calendars, marking the passage of hours, days, and years since *la catastrophe.*

On a good day, I would waken to the sound of Mme. Boucher's hoe meeting hard earth in the garden. I would peek out through a crack in the shutters and see our friend dressed in her sky blue house dress, a wine red sweater-vest, and a straw hat with a ribbon to match the dress. Her hoe would rise and fall with the force of a miner's sledge hammer—and we would blink, hardly able to believe that the tiny old lady in her finery could swing a hoe with such strength. But the evidence was all around her. Well into her eighties, and with legs swollen from diabetes, she worked a garden free of weeds and flourishing with tomatoes, fava beans, string beans, lettuces, potatoes, and budding squash. We contributed indirectly to this cornucopia, as the runoff from our septic tank, which sat encased in cement beneath our front stoop, trickled downhill and must have issued right under the ground she was tilling.

Our neighbor's gardening routine was invariable. As the church bells rang seven times, she began her day's hoeing. Starting with the fava beans—the staple of her diet—she wound her way down row after row, hacking at weeds, inadvertently hitting stones, tossing weeds (roots and plant) into her basket, and periodically carrying the full basket to her compost heap. By the time the bells rang eight times, she had checked the rain barrel that sat against the garden wall. If the water was high enough, she rolled up her sleeves, bent over the barrel, and plunged her watering can down for a deep drink. If the barrel was dry, she brought the watering can to the spigot at the back of the house. In either case, she then began a tedious circuit, back and forth from the source to the thirsty plants, which she frugally gave just enough, and not too much, to drink. Once she had watered the last row, Michael might be ready to stir. When he looked out the little spy window in the attic, there she would be, bent over from the waist, legs straight as poles, straw hat a foot from the soil, as she leaned over to drip the precious water carefully around the root of each plant. Then, just as suddenly, she would be up-right, glancing up at our house to see if the lay-a-bed Americans were showing signs of life (a light behind the shutters, a creak on the iron staircase).

When the last row was watered, she was ready to savor the best moment of the day—picking the produce for her dinner and for giving. For this purpose, she kept a clean basket, to which she had pinned a white cloth. As she moved down the rows, gathering her beans and tomatoes, she would carefully lift the cloth, and slip the treasure under it, where no morning sun could strike it—and no neighbor's eye could pry.

We never witnessed the ritual of preparing the pro-duce for gifting, but it would have been a pleasure to watch, for Mme. Boucher did not simply hand over a fistful of vegetables; she presented a bouquet. One day it would be a brown glass jar, brimming with stems of flat parsley surrounding one giant red dahlia. Another day, a head of lettuce would arrive enveloped in gift wrap saved from her last birthday. Or a pound of beans would arrive on a white plate—with the beans washed, trimmed, and bundled into four neat packets, each tied with a white silk ribbon.

With her offering prepared, Mme. Boucher found her-self at a loss as to when to present it. The gift ought to pass over the wall by nine or ten if the Americans were to use it in the day's main meal. But the Americans didn't seem to keep any hours. Eight is the proper dead-line for shutters to open and doors to unlock, but most days the house up there was shut tight until nearly ten. If Madame Bet-sy could be counted on being there when the shutters opened, that would be one thing. But some days—one could not predict when—she would have slipped out of the village early, to go walking in the hills or shopping in nearby towns. She usually returned by nine, but she might return as late as one, and Mme. Boucher wanted to be at her own table at noon sharp. How could she get the produce to them in time for the midday meal? She hated to summon Monsieur Michel, for a man should not be bothered with meals and groceries, but sometimes in desperation she did cuckoo to him at half past eleven, handing the packet over the wall and asking him to make sure that madame saw it the instant she returned from her wanderings.

From her kitchen table, the worried Mme. Boucher would watch our doorway until the prodigal's return, wondering why such a nice young woman would so neglect her husband and the requirements of "equilibrium." She only hoped that the proffered beans or zucchini would prompt the cooking of a warm meal, however late it might be served. For, to her confusion, she had seen us set up for lunch on the terrace at one, two, or even later—and the neighborhood children, who popped in at any hour, reported that the Americans ate only fruit and cheese at their afternoon meal. But this she would not believe.

If smoke rose from her chimney in the late morning, that meant that Mme. Boucher had lit her wood-burning stove, and soup was on the way. The smoke signal gave notice for one of us to appear at the wall at precisely noon and to adjust whatever other plans we might have made for lunch. Michael or I would loiter at the wall at the appointed time to receive the steaming blue saucepan covered with a strip of crinkled tinfoil to disguise the gift from curious neighbors. Sometimes, when we just couldn't face another bowl of fava bean or noodle soup, we would freeze the contents, and soon our minuscule freezer would be overloaded with plastic bowls of rock-solid soup. In return, we supplied our neighbor with a steady stream of store-bought edibles, such as fruit, cheese, yogurt, or *pâtisserie*—Mme. Boucher had a sweet tooth (in a manner of speaking, since she no longer had teeth).

On the occasion of one of these over-the-wall gifts, Mme. Boucher mentioned that there was a service we could render her if we possibly had the time. On the coming Sunday, there was to be a memorial Mass for her son at the church of Castelnaud, and she wondered if we could come along and help her navigate the steep cobblestone path that leads down to the church from the *Mairie*. We ourselves aren't churchgoers—I'm a lapsed Catholic and Michael, though Jewish, is nonobservant. But we told our friend that it would be an honor to accompany her, and when we did so, she came forth with more details.

Castelnaud is too sparsely populated to support a priest, but once a month a curé from the diocese makes a rotational visit, and the old church, which perches halfway up the hill and looks out over the river, is opened for Mass. Until this past winter, when her legs weakened dramatically, she had always walked down the hill to the monthly Mass, after which she would visit the graves of her son and husband in the little cemetery behind the church. But this year she had not been to the graves since November. Now there was a special reason to make the journey. The third day of July was the anniversary of her son's death, and the curé always held a memorial Mass for him on the Sunday nearest that date. She had not had the heart to tell the curé she would not be able to attend this year—and with our help she could keep the tradition.

That Sunday we awakened to the long pealing of bells at eight o'clock, the special call to church. We opened the shutters forthwith, to reassure Mme. Boucher that we were up and would be on time. By half past eight we were at her door, with a bouquet of daylilies from our terrace. When we saw Mme. Boucher's glossy black straw hat and her white gloves with seed pearls at the wrist, we were glad we had decided on our best outfits. She, too, had a bouquet, tucked in a bowl-sized basket, which also held her lace handkerchief. We commended each other's bouquets and started down the hill.

With one of us on either arm, Mme. Boucher took the familiar walk to church. Though we scrambled down the path daily on the way to the post office or river, we could never get over its beauty. You start in front of the porch of the *Mairie*, pass the awnings of the tourist shops, skirt the iron crucifix on a stone pedestal, which used to mark the official center of town, and cross through the terrace of the café and under a stone archway to a cobblestone path that winds through a little neighborhood of tiny golden houses, each with its architectural flourish—a Juliet balcony, a Renaissance window, an alcove with a medieval-looking statue of the Virgin. As you're looking up at these features, the path suddenly zigzags right and left. You look down, to get your footing on the turn, and you see you are on the side of the hill, overlooking terrace after terrace of grapevines and household gardens.

Here the slope is steep, and an older walker like Mme. Boucher needs a friend's support. Her eyes were on her feet, while ours took in the vista—the cultivated hillside, the road at its foot, the town growing up around the river and, on the right, unmolested by building or farming, the darkly wooded hills that gave Périgord Noir its name.

Soon, though, the path veered to the left, between rows of three-storied houses, which blocked the view. Suddenly, a turning opened onto a view of the church, which looked massive and dark (its stones uncleaned, in contrast to those of the houses). But as we descended the path and approached the front door, we felt the church's homely proportions. A simple stone lintel topped the doorway at a height of no more than six feet, and there was just room on either side of the door for a dried-up four-foot Christmas tree to be propped up, oddly bestrewn by balls of white tissue paper. (We learned that the bedraggled evergreens were left over from a wedding celebrated months before. It is the custom for the wedding party to cut down two small evergreens, decorate them with white crepe-paper flowers and streamers, and prop the trees at the sides of the church door. These "wedding bushes," which look fresh and joyful on the wedding day, are left to decay and eventually blow away—the superstition being that honeymoon bliss will last as long as the bushes themselves.) There was just room for Michael to assist Mme. Boucher past the wedding bushes, through the doorway, and into the stone cavern.

Though we had arrived early, the church was nearly full. On each side of the central aisle were ten simple pews, each designed to seat no more than four adults. Into the two back rows were squeezed two dozen wiggly boys in blue shorts and shirts, with red scarves—a group of Catholic boy scouts, accompanied by their two adolescent troop leaders, who each rated a pew to himself. Mme. Boucher looked annoyed at the presence of these children and marched firmly to the middle rows, from which, suddenly, the hands of friends grabbed out to touch her sleeve or to pull her toward them for a quick kiss on the cheek. The whole "upper village" seemed to be there—but, no, only those over seventy, on second look. Mme. Calais (the wood-sculpting widow) stood to usher Mme. Boucher into the first row next to a hunched-over old man, who leaned over to accept her kiss and then looked straight ahead without speaking. With a brusque flick of the hand, Mme. Calais indicated we should join her in the pew behind Mme. Boucher and her elderly companion.

"Her brother," Mme. Calais indicated. "Ninety-four. He walked up the hill—with his cane. The right thing to do."

Empathizing with her friend, Mme. Calais gave a nod of satisfaction. "Now, this is going to be something special. You're very lucky," she said with narrowed eyes, as if she were not so sure we deserved our good fortune. I nodded and said something to the effect that to be here for the memorial service was very special.

"*Non, non!*" she corrected. "It's the hermit. The curé is ill, and in his place he asked Father Anselm, the holy man."

She went on to explain that Father Anselm was pastor in Castelnaud when Charles Boucher was an altar boy. Many years ago, Father Anselm had renounced the world and had gone into the hills.

"Now he comes out to say Mass no more than once a year. Hush up! Here he comes!"

At that, the low mumbling that had made the stone walls echo halted, and the only sound was the swish of skirts brushing on the altar floor. In a few brisk steps, a strong, upright old man stood before us, draped in a brown monk's habit, tied with a rope. For a long moment, he stood looking out at the little congregation with a look of tender affection. A patient smile spread across his face as he turned to touch the shoulder of the plump girl beside him, who was also draped in a monk's robe. With a turn of his eyes, he reminded her to open his missal to the page for the start of the Mass. Here was a modern touch—a girl as altar boy.

"Retarded!" whispered Mme. Calais. "This could be a long Mass."

Then, thinking better of her remark, she added, "*C'est gentil.* She's the curé's niece, slow since birth. She's awfully proud of herself for learning the responses."

There was something especially moving about this Mass, which lasted no longer than any other. Using the French of the modern missal (Latin having been foregone decades ago), Father Anselm made each phrase fresh for his small congregation. Looking with compassion at Mme. Boucher and her brother, he spoke endearingly of the Charles Boucher he knew as an altar boy, going on to a sermon on the child within each of us. He even made the boy scouts laugh with some phrases about worms and dirt that we did not quite understand. Moments later, he had the adults moist eyed as he spoke about valuing what one most had loved in childhood. Though we didn't get the local references or the quips in *patois*, we shared the feeling of accessing some old well of happiness, there since childhood and too little visited.

"You may go. The Mass is ended."

And with that said, Father Anselm was out the sacristy door and on his way back to the hills. There would be no chatting with the priest at the church door. The group observed decorum, letting Mme. Boucher and her brother exit first, though they were slow and in the front row. It was they, not the priest, who greeted the members of the congregation as we passed out the door and by the wedding bushes. Those who had known Mayor Boucher shared their memories and gave their condolences. Those who did not—the two dozen boy scouts included—did not fail to shake the hand of the bereaved mother and uncle. We were among the first out, with Mme. Calais, who tugged at one of her old friends to arrange a ride in their car for Mme. Boucher's brother. With that settled, she waited, along with us, for the crowd to disperse. She intended to go with her friend to the cemetery.

We held the bouquets, ours and Mme. Boucher's, as the two women joined arms and supported each other the short way from the church to the graveyard. The church was perched midway up the hill from the river to the castle. The small cemetery, enclosed by a gate, hung off the cliff side of that hill, looking out at the river and the valley below. Through the wrought-iron gate, we could see descending rows of tombstones, and beyond them a blurred panorama of gold and green landscape. As we passed through the gate, we noticed on our left the one showy tomb, a miniature temple in black marble, dedicated to the baronial family occupying the Château de Lacoste for the last couple of centuries. Otherwise, the rows were tightly crammed with coffin-sized family vaults raised a few feet above the ground.

In this graveyard, as in most French ones, the accent was on gestures of remembrance, actualized in little objects left on the top of the tomb. On many, the tablelike surface of the tomb was stuffed—with pots of flowers, with framed photographs of the dead, and with paperweight-sized mementos made of stone and bearing touching legends: "*Maman*—We will never forget you"; "With respect, to a brave veteran of war, from his fellow combatants"; "Friend without equal."

Five such ranks of decorated graves descended below us like rows of chairs in a well-banked theater. Detaching herself from her friend, Mme. Calais marched briskly to the end of the top row and then four steps down the far aisle to her husband's grave. That left us in charge of Mme. Boucher, who indicated our destination: a stolid gray tomb right in the middle of the cemetery. With full attention on the narrow pathway, we maneuvered our charge to the Boucher grave.

It was modest enough—a slate-colored box with no fancy carving—but it was bedecked with decades of remembrances. Amid a clutter of stone testimonies to grief, the chief memento stood up proudly—a photograph of Mayor Charles Boucher framed in marble and laminated under plexiglass. He looked to be in his forties, a vigorous man of accomplishment, with strong features and a frank gaze. All around him, set on little slabs of stone, were statements of devotion—from his loving wife, his bereft daughter, his grieving mother, and—to Mme. Boucher's pride—from the mayors of Sarlat and Domme. A vase of cloth flowers had weathered the winter, but Mme. Boucher snatched them up and replaced them with her fresh bouquet. She sent Michael down the aisle for a watering can, which some kind soul kept filled for mourners. He carefully filled the vase with water and helped Mme. Boucher brush away debris and generally neaten up the memorial display.

"Now, *mes enfants*," she said, standing straight as a soldier and looking out at the splendid view of river and valley, "here is where I will take my rest. *C'est beau, n'est-ce-pas?*"

We could truthfully say, *"Oui."* Nothing surpasses the view from the Boucher plot—a length of the Dordogne flanked thickly by poplars and willows, groves of walnut trees and fields of sunflowers; on the other side of the valley, the gardens of Marqueyssac on their cliff top; just opposite, and in the distance, Beynac Castle on its heights.

On the way back up the hill to home, Mme. Boucher and Mme. Calais renewed a long-running debate as to whether the cemetery view was truly the best in town. Mme. Calais allowed that she preferred it to the view from the castle, which, taken from a greater height, has more majesty but less warmth. Mme. Boucher agreed but admitted that her true favorite was the view from her own pasture. She still owned the hillside opposite her house. The former pasture faces the castle and rises almost to its height. All through her childhood and marriage, it was her job to milk the cows and walk them from the barn up onto that hill. She had loved her cows dearly, and she didn't mind the steep climb to pasture them, because from the hill she had the most magnificent view of the town and the castle. In the mornings, the sun would be coming up from behind the castle. Through fall and winter, a white mist would sometimes rise up thickly from the river and encircle the broken towers—nothing was more beautiful. And when she went up before sundown, the face of the castle was ablaze with light from the west.

"Do you mean you have never been up there?" she asked. "Photographers ask me all the time if they can climb up there to take pictures. I see no harm in it, so I let them. If my legs could stand it, I would go with you. But there's no more of that kind of climbing for me now."

Mme. Boucher asked to be left at her gate. We knew she liked to lunch alone, leaving the indignities of old age unobserved: eating without a full set of teeth, favoring soups and puddings over meat and vegetables, and dining on child-sized portions. For socializing, she preferred afternoon, when time began to hang heavy, since she took no siesta and was forbidden by the doctor to go out in the afternoon sun. So after settling the two ladies back in their houses, we mounted to our terrace, put up the powder blue parasol over our white round table, and lunched, American-style, on tuna-fish sandwiches, while the whole rest of the village (Mme. Boucher excepted) filled the village air with the aromas of the roasted chickens and garlic-fried potatoes of five-course Sunday family meals.

We lounged the afternoon away, writing letters, reading, and gardening a little in the few shady nooks. By five, we were restless and ready for an adventure. Why not mount that pasture and go on a photo-taking expedition? So while Michael got his photography gear together, I ran down to ask Mme. Boucher for that permission she seemed to like to give to trespassers on her land. She was seated outside in one of two chairs that her granddaughter had installed under the roof of the woodshed. The space was airy enough to catch the summer breezes, and it was well protected from sun. It was Mme. Boucher's favorite spot for a rest or a chat. She motioned me to sit down, but when I told her my errand, she clapped her hands in delight and then shooed me away, saying, "Go, make the most of it. *Il faut en profiter.*"

So we headed up the hill, past the entrance to the old schoolhouse where Mme. Boucher once had practiced her penmanship, with its two doors marked *"Filles"* and *"Garçons,"* by the school playground with its fountain and outhouse, and around a corner where the hillside banked steeply, next to an outcropping of granite and a tiny waterfall. Just beyond the waterfall we found the footpath, which zigzagged up the hill through knee-high grass. Though it was already July, the grass was still mingled with purple and red wildflowers. Once upon a time, Mme. Boucher's cows would have forestalled such beauty, eating up the greenery before it had time to flower. Now the pasture was cut just a few times a year by a neighbor for his cows. Poppies and purple foxglove had plenty of time to root and blossom.

After the path stopped, we brushed onward through the grasses to the crest of the hill. Then I swung round and saw our town and its castle as if for the first time, an ensemble of staggeringly large buildings scattered over more than an acre of hilltop and belted together by a line of enclosing walls. In the slanting light of early evening, the turrets glowed orange, setting off the green of inner courtyards and hillside garden plots. The castle and its grounds seemed to come alive, looking ready to serve the scores of nobles and vassals who must have constituted its community in days gone by. Below lay the village houses, made of the same stone, with the only modern touch being the red tile of the slanting roofs. And, to the right, where the hill of the town dropped down a notch, lay a grand royal blue stretch of the Dordogne River. Mme. Boucher was right: this was the only vantage point where the full expanse of the castle, the town, the church, and the river could be seen at once. Our house was part of the picture too. Set, as it is, just at the base of the castle's lowest enclosing wall, it faced us directly, with its centered doorway, single window, and pretty little terrace on the side. Michael's shutter clicked away, as I walked from side to side of the field, watching the river come in and out of view.

Now when we think of Castelnaud, it is this picture that we visualize. To the left of the frame, the tall, peaked tower of the castle; in the center, our house, directly below the castle keep; to the right, the round artillery tower, half in ruin; and the slope of the hill leading down to the church with the village cemetery hidden behind it, perched above the ribbon of river. And we think of our friend, who rests there.

8

LA GRANDE RANDONNÉE

France may have the best walking trails in Europe. *La Grande Randonnée*, or "the GR," a network of rustic paths, extends unbroken over the entire country and is open by right and at all times to the public. In addition, every local area has its traditional communal footpaths, which dedicated walkers fight to keep open when the occasional property owner posts a No Trespassing sign. Nowhere are the walking paths more appealing than in Périgord.

Michael gets his exercise by swimming, and I get mine by walking. While house hunting, I always asked realtors about hiking possibilities in the vicinity, but finding them thoroughly blank on the subject, I did my own research. At a stationery shop, I found a walker's map covering Sarlat and Beynac. From that, I discovered that the area was crisscrossed by three of the major

*Grande Randonnée* routes—the 6, 64, and 36. Then one rainy afternoon, when we were sipping hot chocolate at a Sarlat café, I spotted, next to the postcard rack, a set of booklets detailing local GR walks. A few early mornings, I set out with map, booklet, and a compass, to follow the GR for an hour and a half and then double back by a different route, creating what the French call a *circuit*.

The challenge of the GR for a small-time walker is that its routes are designed for hiking straight across country in four- or five-hour stints, with no doubling back. But with a good map and a little courage, you can create your own circuit. Fumbling along this way, I learned the GR system—how it marks the correct route on a building or tree, with short strokes of red or white paint (sometimes both, looking like an equal sign); how turns are indicated with elbowed arrows and wrong turns warned off with an X; and how the trail leaves you in suspense until about one hundred yards into the new path, when the sight of a red mark blazing ahead relieves your mounting anxiety. There is also an ancillary system resembling the GR signage but marked instead in yellow or orange. The yellow signs mean an attractive local pathway, which might or might not eventually join the GR but which is worth a detour in its own right. It was years before one of my hiking friends revealed that the orange signs were for bridle paths—no wonder they seemed squishy under foot!

When I set out on the marked trail, I am seeking what every walker walks for—the physical pleasure of moving through fields like a fish through water and the fascination of discovering what people have done with the land, which is often as curious and as graceful as nature itself. My walks in Périgord have never failed to deliver these satisfactions. Wanting to share these riches with Michael, who is more of a stroller than a hiker, I took to adding a challenge to the morning's walk. While wandering to my heart's content, I would occupy my mind by designing a half-hour's walk for him that would capture the best features of the day's jaunt in the fewest possible steps. At some prime hour—four on a cool June afternoon or eight on a warm July evening—we would stroll out together to review my finds. Our first such walk took place during our house hunting near Sarlat, when we climbed all over the ruins of the bishopric of Temniac. On another day when we had spent a tedious afternoon examining badly restored town houses, I led Michael to a fallen-down château I had discovered just off the GR 6 near Sirey. Its exquisite fifteenth-century Renaissance grace renewed our determination to find a house that had kept something of the spirit of old Périgord.

It was Michael who pointed out, after we had our offer in for the purchase of the house at Castelnaud, that there were GR markings all over the village. What could this mean? We stopped in at the *Mairie* and asked the mayor's secretary, who laughed, saying "*Mais, oui*—we are practically standing on the GR 64. It passes the *Mairie* on its way down the hill to the river. In the other direction, it goes up to the *croix de la mission*. Have you seen it?"

We had not, and there was no time like the present. Suddenly the GR markings shone at us like beacons. There they were, one next to the village letterbox and one on the door of Mme. Boucher's cellar. That marking sent us up the hill past another house, where the cornerstone sported an elbowed red arrow. We turned into a flowered alleyway between two houses, which led toward the cliff on which the castle was built. As we approached another house, hidden back away from streets and neighbors, the path veered left, climbing slowly and following an ancient wall set against the cliff. We followed the counseled trail, which grew steeper and ever more forested. Finally, a V brought a moment of decision. The path to the left was marked by the GR and led off to the west. The path to the right looked steep, and it was marked, unofficially, with a small cardboard placard hand printed with the word *"Croix."* We veered to the right and forged ahead, bowing under drooping branches and securing a foothold carefully.

Another few minutes brought us into the open. We were on the cliffside, within feet of the precipice, and there before us was a disappointing modern iron crucifix, mounted on concrete. Doubtless there had once been a carved stone cross here, but it was long gone. Like many a hiker before us, we steadied ourselves with a hand on the cross and peered over the cliff. What we saw was a sheer drop of tawny stone, ending finally in a jade green terrace, giving onto the wide, inviting river. An image of falling bodies flashed through my mind. I stepped back as Michael caught my arm, looking a bit rattled himself. As we climbed carefully back down the path, we speculated that maybe this particular mission cross had been mounted more to frighten sinners than to praise creation.

The next year, when we were settling into the house, I established my regular morning walk: down the steep hill out of town, by a few houses to fields and a sheep farm, past the principal manor-farm of the region, *la Maison Blanche,* by the *lauze*-roofed cottage whose new owner had installed a swimming pool in the foundations of the erstwhile cowshed, up to the grounds of the stately Château de Lacoste, and through the dying hamlet of Generilles into the woods, to emerge at our mayor's farm, whose driveway is marked with the one remaining stone cross in the village. From there it is steps to home.

With the help of neighbors, I also discovered the bridle path between the châteaus of Castelnaud and Fayrac—which locals still call by its grand old name, *les allées de Fayrac*, though it is overgrown and rarely sees a horse these days. Other days I followed orange markers and found myself retracing the path of nobles between Castelnaud and the pleasure palace of les Milandes. Before long my wandering ways were the subject of *badinage*. M. Fauré, often out in his garden when I passed by at half past seven in the morning, would call out, *"Bon foot-ing!"* (This was the latest Franglais for "jogging.") As I passed his turf again on the return route, he would ask, "Any adventures?" and I would tell him about the bull I found in the middle of the road or the lynx that crossed my path in the woods.

One noontime early in August, I heard the bang of the knocker on the front door. I dashed down the spiral staircase and flung the door open, expecting to see one of the neighbor children. Instead, poised with her ankles touching in a kind of gymnast's pose of readiness, was a lithe and tiny woman of my own age, looking up at me expectantly. After the obligatory apology for possibly disturbing us, she announced, "My name is Annie Delechaux, your neighbor." She pointed vaguely up the hill beyond the schoolhouse. "M. Fauré has told me that you are a walker, and so am I. I wonder if you would care to accompany me on a *promenade à pied* one day this week."

Here was an opportunity not to be missed—a local walker to show me the hidden pathways and a potential French friend of my own generation. This I sorely needed, since my practice in French, aside from shopping, was mainly with elderly Mme. Boucher and children under eight. Summoning up my most cordial phrases, I invited my visitor into the house, using the formal "vous" to address her. (I did not dare call her "Annie" but thought "Madame" or "Mme. Delechaux" too formal.)

To my surprise, she looked startled. "Oh, no," she insisted, backing away. "I didn't mean to disturb you at lunchtime. I thought we could make a rendezvous for a walk during the week—but perhaps this is not a good time."

Life in a foreign country is full of awkward moments like this. You try your best to be friendly and communicate, but either you break some social rule, or worse, you corner your interlocutor into breaking one. Here, I had offended a potential friend by implying, with my invitation to step in, that she was rude enough to knock on a stranger's door and expect to enter and visit. Far from it. She thought she was crossing the line by presenting herself with only the reference to M. Fauré as an introduction. Concluding this quickly, I stood in the doorway, accepted her invitation with pleasure, and fixed the next morning at ten for a rendezvous in front of the *Mairie*. She stepped away pleased, saying smartly, *"Très bien, à bientôt, demain matin à dix heures!"* I smiled, waved, and called, *"D'accord, à tout à l'heure,"* as she departed.

By ten the next morning, the sun was already hot, and I regretted that I had been too shy to propose an earlier departure. In all my morning walks, I had never seen another early walker—not even a boy scout, so it felt more normal to suggest an after-breakfast hour. Dressed as coolly as possible, and slathered with sunblock, I made my way to the *Mairie*, which was just opening, and sat on its porch to await the arrival of Annie. Five minutes went by, ten, and I began to think my French had created a misunderstanding. But I decided to wait a little longer, just in case.

At quarter past ten, an old blue Peugeot pulled up in front of the *Mairie*. Annie emerged from the passenger side and came round to the driver's window to introduce me to her husband. Pierre Delechaux was his wife's contrary: large, warm, and droll, where she was small, cool, and earnest. With an amused smile, he asked what we planned for a route. We hadn't planned a route at all, so this led to a quick exchange of possibilities and a sudden decision on Annie's part to lead me to Lacoste by a cliffside path. Skepticism warred with indulgence on Pierre's expressive face.

"A little difficult for a *randonnée*, don't you think? Well, I'll think of you while I drink my coffee and read the paper at the café by the river. *Bonne promenade, Mesdames!*"

As he departed, Annie explained that her husband, like many French men of his generation, was not much given to exercise. (Indeed, joggers, who are usually tourists, are subjected to ridicule.) That's why she was interested to hear from M. Fauré that I went out for walks by myself.

"In this area," she said, "it is not a good idea to walk alone. Haven't you had trouble with farm dogs?"

It was a relief to confess that in fact two local dogs terrorized me every time I took my staple walk. One— the big one—was fenced in and only barked and leapt wildly at the chain-link as I passed by, while the other, a little dog at the sheep farm, quieted down if I stayed on the far side of the road and spoke to him nicely in French. (English didn't work.)

"If you walk alone, you must carry a stick," warned Annie.

I could not picture myself defending myself from canine attack with a stick, however hefty, but I nodded politely.

"We shall be all right together," she continued. "A dog is smart enough to know when he is outnumbered."

As I got to know Annie, I realized that her take-charge, advice-giving manner went with her occupation. She taught four-year-olds at a state nursery school in a Parisian suburb. This set us up for a working relationship. I must have seemed like a grown-up version of her favorite kind of pupil—alert and curious but untrained in the proper French ways, a bit inarticulate but able to make myself understood. For all her perfectionism (from the first hour she corrected my French as we walked along chatting), she had the patience of a nun. She never minded giving the same correction over again, and she calmly supplied vocabulary when a silence showed I had drawn a blank. She seemed as pleased as I was when I managed to get out a complex thought. And, though she was the teacher, she was also eager to learn. We exchanged information about our countries' systems of education, medicine, and social security. We traded political scandals and compared the French left and right to their American equivalents (not near equivalents, as it turned out). Eventually we got round to describing our families and our daily lives.

On this first day, however, the talk focused on hiking—which routes I had taken, which ones she would take me on before she had to return to her job, and which I should explore on my own. To start on this walk along the cliff, Annie had led me to a wooden stairway along the roadside, which I had wondered about many times. It seemed to lead up to a house perched high above, but the stairway was marked *"Propriété Privée."* That brought me to a halt.

*"Ridicule!"* scoffed Annie. "This path has been public since Pierre was a little boy, and long before that, I'm sure. The people who bought the house up there installed this fancy stairway, which is fine. But they can't make the pathway private just by 'improving' it. This is a communal footpath, stairway or no. *Allons-y!"*

With the *sangfroid* for which the French are famous, Annie mounted the stairs, chin held high. I trailed hesitantly, with eyes darting round to see if we were being observed. When we reached the top of the two flights of stairs, we entered a wooded path and were mercifully hidden from view.

Just as I was beginning to relax, Annie said, "Now here's where we may meet difficulty. We are approaching the house, and I believe they do have a *chien méchant*. Let's get a stick." And she ferreted around on the side of the path until she found a sturdy branch almost a yard long. She snapped off the side twigs and brandished her weapon.

*Chien méchant* is a term that commonly appears on signs posted around French properties. Literally it means "bad dog," but that depends on which side of the fence you are on. Would-be intruders are warned that the resident canine is anathema, a ferocious, foaming-at-the-mouth beast; but for the home owner, he is a devoted guardian and therefore, logically, a good dog. As a walker, you want nothing to do with such an animal. I looked around nervously but saw no posted sign. Annie led the way.

The woods continued to shelter us, but the green in front lightened with every step, as a yard and a house perched high up ahead came into view. Soon we were on the edge of the lawn, looking up at a rather grand version of the Périgordian manse—one long story of golden stone, with enough windows to suggest four rooms in front, and to my discomfort every one of the windows wide open, making it likely that we would be observed. At least, there was no one on the long flagstone terrace that swept the whole front of the house. But bounding around the corner of the house came the feared *"chien méchant."* My heart stopped, as the German shepherd lunged straight at us. In a flash, Annie drew herself up and pointed her stick like a toreador's foil straight ahead at the dog.

*"Arrête!"* she barked, in a deep, commanding voice. *"Arrête! Tais-toi!"*

Astounded by the assertive masculine sound coming from this little woman creature, the dog stopped short, with his wolflike head cocked in puzzlement. Annie had him mesmerized. She stared at a point over his head, not into his eyes, then called out, *"Vas-y!"* as she threw the stick clear to the other side of the lawn. Off he went after it! With an eye still on him, we continued walking the path, which skirted the edge of the lawn. When the brow-beaten beast returned with the stick, we were just at the edge of the terrace and ready to take the path deep into the woods. Annie pulled the stick from his mouth, gave it another far fling, and counseled me to hurry up and get out of sight. We hustled into the woods, leaving the bewildered dog to find another playmate.

The next half hour was an invigorating hike in the open, on the top of the cliff, sometimes through the field at the very top, sometimes on a perilous pathway set on a rock ledge a few yards below the top. I would have been terrified, except that the dog had taken all my adrenaline for the day, and Annie was a confident guide. Finally, the cliffside trail was over, and we were approaching a satellite dish, attached to a summer house hanging off the cliff. We squeezed ourselves between the dish and a retaining wall, and I recognized the hamlet of Generilles.

Now we were on my daily walk, just doing it backwards, and I knew what path we would follow to the Château of Lacoste. Just as I expected, we passed by deserted stone hovels, several *bories* (beehive-shaped stone huts of indeterminate age and purpose), and field after field of unmown hay. Glimpses of Lacoste revealed a cool, white expanse with classic eighteenth-century lines, nicely broken up by the Gothic form of a tiny attached chapel, which must have predated the château by centuries. Approaching it with Annie, I saw it with new eyes, as she recounted tales of the Revolution of 1789, which downed whole courts of aristocracy around Périgord but left the Baron of Lacoste with his good name and newly built castle intact, because he had been a mild and generous landlord.

After a long climb, we finally stood underneath the last sycamore in the lane, gazing at the beautifully arched stone gate and perfect proportions of the house. With a nod of appreciation, I was ready to move on, but Annie was moving toward the gate. With authority, she reached for the latch and lifted it. A pull and a shove got it open, and Annie was inside the grounds, calling "Cuckoo!" in her flutiest voice—to whom I could not imagine. I followed her through and watched her tap on the guard's booth, which was empty, then march straight for the front door.

Seesawing between awe at Annie's gumption and fear that the Baron's retainers would appear to shame us for our intrusion, I held back in the shadow of the guard's booth. Just as Annie rang the bell (a real bell, with a resounding clapper), a retainer did emerge from a sort of garage I had not noticed on the side of the lane opposite the guard's booth. Truth be told, she wasn't much of a threat—a meek-looking woman in housedress, apron, and the kind of hairnet that waitresses used to wear in the fifties. To my discomfort, she approached me questioningly. It hadn't been my idea to trespass on castle grounds, but now I would have to do the explaining.

*"Excusez-moi de vous déranger, Madame, mais . . . "* I began, using the formulaic phrase Annie had told me should begin all difficult encounters. That is, "I'm so sorry to trouble you, Madame, but . . . " (here, insert your dilemma of the moment). I racked my brain for a plausible excuse that could necessitate knocking at the castle door. I couldn't think of one. My real dilemma was that my friend was knocking at the castle door, and

I had no idea what was in her head. I was stammering lamely. In another moment, the housekeeper was as surprised as I to see the Baron himself (for who else could it be?), portly but elegant in a flowing white silk shirt, murmuring something inaudible as he took Annie's hand and bent over to kiss her wrist. The puzzled housekeeper froze in place. She looked at me for explanation, but I stood mute. The Baron, without missing a beat, whisked down the lane, holding Annie's hand high in air, as if he were crossing a ballroom to start a dance. When he reached us, he released Annie's hand, took mine, and bestowed the baronial buss.

"My dear ladies," he said with an amused twinkle and an accent that had tones of the French Baroque theater, "you are most welcome to tour the grounds this afternoon." And with a turn of the head to his employee and to me: "Madame has just been reminding me of the friendship between her mother-in-law and my late mother. I am so pleased that memories of garden parties at Lacoste have not entirely passed away in the neighborhood."

Turning back with a gracious smile toward Annie, he added: "It would give me great pleasure, Madame, if you would show your American friend not only the rose gardens but also the grotto at the end of the cliff walk. It was a favorite spot of Mother's—and of your mother-in-law as well. Just take care to avoid the lawn behind the château—I have friends visiting from Paris, and I believe one or two of them may be sunbathing. And now if you'll excuse me, I wish you a most enjoyable visit to the gardens."

With that, the Baron bowed deeply. I think I bowed back, not having had much practice in curtseying. I do recall calling out thanks as our host gracefully strode back toward his castle. The housekeeper watched skeptically as Annie and I began our turn around the gardens. Today I remember nothing about them, but the cliff walk and its grotto were unforgettable. To the east of the great house was a long *allée,* wide enough for a horse and coach but so grassy and smooth that it clearly had been used solely by walkers, at least in recent years. The inside of the *allée* was marked by a high straight boxwood hedge, which shielded the castle grounds from the walker's view. (On the other side, no doubt, lolled the sunbathing house guests.) The far side of the path was adorned with topiary—first in the form of animals: squirrels, rabbits, roosters, geese; then in the form of card suits: hearts, spades, diamonds, clubs; and so on, through many a playful permutation. Craftily, the topiary designs lured one's eye out to views that the manicured forms only partly obscured. For the topiary edged a promontory of limestone, and the fanciful green masses framed magnificent tableaus of the Dordogne valley.

We walked on in delight until we reached the entrance of a small cave. On the walls near the entrance, engraved plaques gave thanks to Our Lady of the Grotto for cures, for "a great wish," for answered prayers of all sorts. There were too many of these messages for this chamber to be the private chapel of the castle. The grotto must have been visited by the faithful of the whole neighborhood. Most of the plaques were undated, but the dated messages started in the 1860s, just a few years after the apparition of Our Lady at Lourdes, not so very far away. So, Lacoste had its own little Lourdes. Where, then, was the statue of Our Lady? A strike of a match deeper in the cave revealed Annie, who stood before a bank of candles, which in turn stood before a statue of the Virgin no more than a foot high. Once we had one of the candles lit, we could see that the Virgin was old and faded and only painted plaster, but her presence was potent enough that someone kept her niche supplied with dry matches and fresh candles. In spiritual matters Annie is a typical Frenchwoman—Catholic by upbringing but agnostic by rational conclusion. She smiled, feeling the tug of her youthful devotion to Mary, but pushing it back into the cave with a gesture of combined irony and respect. At one and the same time, it looked like a wave of goodbye and repudiation.

The grotto marked the last navigable point on the promontory, so we wound our way back the way we came, this time grateful that the tall hedge was beginning to cast some shade. On the way back, Annie explained that her mother-in-law had been on visiting terms with the Baron's late mother. The two ladies had shared a love of tea roses and consulted on each other's gardens (though it was always Mme. Delechaux who came to Lacoste and not the other way around). In early June each year, the Baroness held a garden party to which she invited all the women of Castelnaud. Mme. Delechaux acted as the social bridge, introducing her shyer neighbors to the Baroness and helping everyone feel welcome at Lacoste. So it was that Annie had thought it quite proper to stop by and ask "a family friend" if we could see the garden.

Annie is never without courage, but on occasion courage isn't enough. This we learned on our first attempt to follow a GR guide to the letter. Each summer we pooled our two stashes of walking guides, and we had found most helpful a loose-leaf notebook of *"Chemins de petites et moyennes randonnées en Périgord Noir."* You can pull out a single sheet and follow instructions for a rural walk of short (three to ten kilometers), middling (fifteen to twenty-two kilometers) or long (thirty to forty-two kilometers) distance. Within two summers we had covered the short routes and had wiped ourselves out once or twice getting through a so-called middling circuit by giving it the better part of a day and taking strategic breaks for snacks and water. There was one destination, though, that was not covered by the notebook and that we were sure would be pretty. The hillside village of Montferrand de Périgord had an attractive twelfth-century castle and covered market, and it was smack on the GR 36, so if we just used our ingenuity to invent a circuit, we could go out on the GR to see it and return by some charming back roads.

The GR 36 booklet for the area of Belvès, an unspoiled medieval town shortly to the west of Castelnaud, showed a walking path that could be picked up out of town, just behind the cemetery of the sleepy village of Bouliac. Annie and I drove there late one sunny morning, pulling up at the frankly ugly little graveyard, laid out in a flat field on a side road, far from both church and houses. In its location it was not so different from other local cemeteries, which often were set off from the village, perhaps to avoid contagion. But this one seemed awkwardly placed—nude of trees and lacking a vista. It did have a parking lot, though, and seemed a safe place to leave the car. We pulled out our light gear (fanny packs filled with water, maps, and guidebook) and set off, per instruction, on the dirt lane to the south of the cemetery. We were led by potato fields, corn rows, and hay stacks; told to ford this stream and cross that road; and offered the lovely respite of a path through a leafy wood. According to the map and the guide, we were now supposed to trespass straight into a farmyard in front of us, hug the side of the barn, and follow the farmer's tractor path through the cornfields ahead. As we stood looking at the gate to the farmyard, we doubted our directions, but there was the red GR slash right on the gatepost of the driveway. If we were going to be *Grandes Randonneuses*, keeping the communal footpaths open for posterity, we would have to violate a little personal property here and there, *n'est ce pas?* Well, yes, unless challenged. So we pulled our rib cages up straight and marched resolutely into the yard, past the farmhouse, past the stone barn attached behind it, and finally past animal pens that fortunately were empty, so our presence didn't even cause a goose to cackle or a cow to moo. Since it was shortly after noon, there were no people in sight, either, but we could hear little clinks of silver against dishware and could smell poultry fried in garlic. We began to regret setting out without a picnic.

All at once two farm dogs came racing around the back of the house to block our path. A huge black hound stood us off, barking, growling, and bounding from side to side. At his heels yapped a little terrier, imitating his leader, looking ridiculous hopping back and forth on his chicken-sized legs. Annie was caught off guard. Since our approach had raised no sign of dogs, she had not armed herself with a stick. But an arm can be a stick— so Annie stuck her arm out stiffly at a forty-five degree angle, pointing down at the hound.

"*Tais-toi! Arrête!*" she repeated, as we edged our way backward. It seemed a lifetime until we were out the gate and back onto the road—neutral territory, we hoped. Annie kept herself turned toward the dogs, still with her arm pointing like a gun at the hound's head. I moved ahead, eager to get out of there.

Suddenly I felt a surge of pain up my leg. Shocked, I looked down to see the scruffy little terrier attached to my ankle. His razor-edged teeth bore down hard. I yelled and tried to jerk away, but the savage little beast held on, until Annie whacked him across the back with the side of her hand. He yelped and ran back to the hound, which seemed cowed by Annie's prowess. I limped ahead, and Annie tried to tend to me while keeping an eye on the dogs. I couldn't have been badly hurt, because I was wearing jeans, and the dog had caught me just above the ankle, over the fabric. When we got far enough ahead to feel safe, we checked and found no great harm, but a reddening welt, and four puncture wounds from the little beast's longest teeth gave proof of the attack. Annie pulled out tissues and her nearly empty water bottle, and we gave the wounds a wiping down. We decided to return home and expressed our disgust with ill-brought-up dogs, while we wondered if we would be in our rights if we complained to the farmer. His dogs shouldn't be attacking passersby. But then again, we were more than passing *by*. We were passing *through* his property. The GR said his lane was a communal right of way, but the dogs hadn't read the GR guidebook. As far as they were concerned, they were doing what dogs were supposed to do—protect their territory.

The ache subsided until we got in the car. Then the muscles made their complaint. The hurt could be managed with aspirin, we agreed, but Annie raised a more distressing prospect—rabies. Oh, no, I did not want to get into that. I had heard the stories of the long needles and painful injections used to ward off rabies. Nobody got rabies these days, anyhow. And there was no reason to suppose that little dog had rabies—he was just your typical *chien méchant*. I promised Annie I would wash the puncture wounds and apply alcohol, but that was all the treatment I intended to get.

I was forgetting that we lived in a village. It was not enough to fight off Michael's insistence that I see the doctor. No sooner had I washed, lunched, and napped than the barrage of advice began. First our neighbor Maria and her daughter came by, telling tales of the cousin in Portugal who failed to go to the doctor after being bitten and died in an agony of pain and dementia. Then Anne-Marie telephoned and repeated Maria's message. She had heard about the dog bite from M. Fauré, who had heard from Pierre Delechaux, for whom he was repairing a wall. She insisted I must go to the doctor and had the telephone number ready. A trip to the doctor was *de rigueur.*

Michael made the call and reported that the doctor said there was no time to lose—we should get in the car that minute. But our first stop must be the pharmacy in Cénac. This was the country. A doctor who kept his *cabinet* at home didn't have refrigerator space for every serum he might need. It was the pharmacist's job to keep the stock for all the doctors in the area, and it was the patient's job to purchase and pick up whatever would go into the shot the doctor ordered. We were told to get gamma globulin and tetanus vaccine. I prayed this meant no rabies shot.

Doctor Maleville's office—and home—is centrally located, just outside the quiet town of Saint Cybranet on the road between Castelnaud and Cénac. From there he serves the surrounding towns and hamlets. By the time we pulled up in his driveway, it was well into the apéritif hour, but he seemed unfazed by our late arrival. He was just patting the back of his last patient, an ashen-faced boy with a heavily bandaged knee and an arm in a sling. "No more rock climbing for a few months, eh, Robert? Maybe your balance will have improved by then."

*"Les américains?"* he asked. "This way, please." No smiles. No introductions.

We were ushered into a brightly lit room just big enough for a desk, two chairs, and an operating table. Anticipating the worst, I sat on the table and let the two men take the chairs. The doctor swiveled my way and took a look at the offered leg (I had changed into a skirt, so the wound would be accessible).

Then the questions began. What did the dog look like? Was he dirty or clean? Did he behave erratically? Did he foam at the mouth? Had I provoked him in any way? Ah, if he was a farm dog, and I was on his property, then, we knew he belonged to someone and we knew the address, did we not? We were going to have to call this someone.

This seemed overkill to me, and I assured the doctor that the dog did not seem crazed. He was just copying his larger companion—making a fuss to make the intruders go away. Was rabies really a problem in France, the land of petted and cosseted dogs? No, he had to admit. But tetanus was a problem in recent years. If I could not remember my last tetanus injection (I did remember; it was when I stepped on a nail at age nine), then the least we must do is start a tetanus series, which I must finish upon my return to America. Then, in case the wound held other infections, he would give me gamma globulin to boost the immune system and antibiotics to fight bacteria. If I had the least fever or sweating, I should call him, whatever the time of day or night. I behaved stoically through the shots, took the prescription for tetracycline, said thank you, and paid cash on the line.

I wish I could say I exited with my dignity intact. However, the good doctor gave me the same treatment he had given the teenage rock climber. With a stern fatherly look, he warned, "No more entering private property, Madame. *C'est la campagne. Ce n'est pas Chi-ca-go!*"

Chastened, I let Michael take me to Beynac and buy me a serious walking stick. We had seen them in the antique shop there, but I had sworn I was not old enough for a cane and would let Michael know when I needed one. The time had come. We picked a sturdy one, with a gnarled walnut handle and a sharp brass tip. Whether alone or with Annie, I now set out for my walks with the stick as my companion. It reminds me to hold my ground firmly, like Annie—and to stay out of people's farmyards, whatever the GR says.

## 9

PÉRIGORD TERROIR

If you ask any Frenchman where the best food is in France, you're likely to hear, "In the Dordogne—there they eat well."

It took us a long time to appreciate that saying. After our first hotel dinner in Périgord, we assumed the adage referred to a peasant's ability to pack away a hearty meal, with the main course fried in goose fat. Eager to try the local cuisine, we ordered the *menu du terroir,* or so-called meal of the region. Noting our interest in local food, the *patronne* offered us an apéritif of walnut wine. It was a good choice for that cold, rainy night and our first dinner in the Dordogne. The mellow brown liquid with its nutty aroma warmed our tongues. As an accompaniment, the young waitress brought out a pot of the house *rillettes,* with an accompanying basket of toasted sourdough bread. What we knew about *rillettes* didn't sound appetizing. They consist of chopped up pork from the least desirable parts of the pig, lavishly larded with fat. To be polite, we each spread a little on a toast and took a bite. A bite led to a munch and was followed by seconds. The savory taste of the homemade *rillettes* nearly made us forget that a whole meal was coming.

When the waitress succeeded in separating us from our appetizer, the real menu began—a first course of *terrine de campagne* (a coarse pork and liver pâté, as it turned out, and therefore redundant on top of the *rillettes*); a main course of *confit de canard* with *pommes de terre sarladaises*; a green salad dressed with walnut-oil vinaigrette and sprinkled with chopped walnuts; and to finish, the classic walnut cake. With the help of a carafe of Bergerac red, we cleaned our plates. Everything had been delicious. But we had overeaten.

If this was a typical meal, why weren't the locals fat and grumpy, which is how we began to feel by bedtime? The answer is not simple. First, the restaurant's *menu du terroir* is not, strictly speaking, a typical dinner, if by that you mean an everyday meal. Yes, the dishes are made from local ingredients and are prepared from recipes inspired by those of the local grandmothers. But much else about the *menu du terroir* is a tourist's construction. For one thing, the timing is wrong. When Périgordians eat such a meal, it is not in the evening but at noon. Nowadays, such a meal is reserved for Sunday company and is served at a time that provides a good half day for digestion.

Second, in trying to showcase the most distinctive dishes of the region, all but the best restaurants allow combinations that a sage Périgordian cook would avoid. Typically, walnuts, which are fundamental to the local cuisine, will appear sparingly, not with every other course. Nor would *rillettes* be posed before a pork-based *terrine*—that's too much pork. In fact, neither *rillettes* nor a *terrine* would be the most likely offering before a main dish of *confit* and *pommes de terre sarladaises*, since that delicious duo gets its oomph from duck and goose fat, just as the *rillettes* and *terrine* get theirs from lard. It would be better to start such a meal with a soup of wild greens or a vegetable *terrine.*

We have an American friend who jokingly refers to the *menu du terroir* as "the menu of terror." But if there is blame to be placed for the heavy combinations, it's more likely the customer than the chef who is at fault. In effect, the *menu du terroir* is a sampler. It is the customer who must be aware that if she chooses the *terrine de campagne* for a starter, she would be advised to take the trout, not the *confit de canard*, as her main course. When people talk about "learning to order" in a French restaurant, they don't mean working on your French accent or even being able to translate the names of all the dishes. Rather, the challenge is to select a meal that is balanced and "correct" in terms of ingredients, preparation, and spirit. It takes time to develop a sense of what is *convenable*, a sense of what goes with what. It has taken us years to get to know the foods of Périgord, the typical ways of preparing them, and the combinations in which they are most suitable.

The best way to learn the local cuisine is to attend an open-air market. Sarlat, the *foie gras* capital of France, has world-renowned gourmet shops that sell every conceivable brand of canned duck or goose liver. However, the town is at its culinary best on Wednesday and Saturday mornings, when the local farmers set up their stands of vegetables, cheeses, breads, jams, poultry, meat, and of course, *foie gras*—but bottled on the farm, not tinned in a factory. Whether you're doing the week's shopping or just sightseeing, the Sarlat market is not to be missed. A carnival of color and sound animates one of the most beautiful ensembles of medieval and Renaissance buildings in all of Europe. While you focus on the choice between homemade sausages (of duck, boar, donkey, bull, or pork, and mixed with chestnuts, walnuts, Roquefort, or Cahors), your peripheral vision may catch the glare from light bouncing off mullioned windows. The narrow lanes are crowded with rows of stalls wafting heady aromas. Makeshift shelves and carts hold mounds of pink peaches, bright yellow lemons, and several shades of green parsley, lettuce, and beans. Boxes of spices, in seeds or ground fine, scent the air. A little square where two alleys meet forms a flower market, overflowing with scarlet geraniums and mauve gladioli. In the main square, small vans pull down their sides to reveal itinerant storefronts for butchers and cheese makers. As you read the proud sign over the sausage table—"*Je suis producteur*"—you sense the pride that lies behind the integrity of Périgordian cuisine.

To host a traditional farmers market, a town must verify that the vast majority of its vendors are small producers on local plots of land. Although Sarlat draws visitors from around the world, it has not let its market become cosmopolitan. The cheese truck that pulls into town weekly may have a little Brie or Bleu de Bresse, but the market's tables offer only local cheeses. Here that means goat cheese. Young *chèvre* comes smooth as cream cheese, shaped into serving-sized disks called *cabécous* (pronounced "kah-bay-koo"). After a spell of drying, a *cabécou* graduates to gourmet status, ready to be savored for its intriguing combination of milky mellowness and goaty tang. A longer rest on the shelf leaves a dry *cabécou*, which will take well to marination in walnut oil and fresh herbs. Producers sell their *cabécous* plain and wrap them for the customer in a simple fold of white butcher's paper, but some artisans sell shallow boxes the size of a slipper filled with bite-sized rounds of goat cheese, each rolled in a different condiment: red pepper, black pepper, walnuts, fennel, tarragon, or dill. Beyond goat cheese, there is only the rare sheep cheese (*chèvre de brebis*), and to round out the tray, two cow's-milk cheeses from the neighboring region of the Auvergne: the sharp, firm Cantal and soft and creamy Saint Nectaire.

When we were new to the region, we would end our restaurant meal with old favorites such as Camembert or Pont l'Évêque. We noticed that although waiters politely offered these exotic items (all the way from Normandy), they did not warm to customers who chose them. It was the selection of a *cabécou* or *brebis* that got the nod of approval. Such a choice would prompt the suggestion of a mild Roquefort—which, the waiter would relate lovingly, was also made from pure *brebis* but with a totally different taste and texture. So, slowly, we learned about cheeses local, neighboring, and foreign—and came to prefer the local as a fitting close to a meal made from other products of the surrounding land.

"*Terroir*" means of the earth, *this* soil, this particular place. Each parcel of land has its qualities of minerals, moisture, light, and past cultivation that give any food produced there a special flavor. The farmers market at Sarlat is a showcase for the integrity of "*Périgord ter-*

*roir.*" While you may find oranges and lemons that were trucked up from Spain or Portugal (and are so labeled), nine-tenths of the vegetable tables in the market abound with purely local produce. For every bin or pile on the table, each farmer has filled out an "etiquette," a little sign with spaces for the name of the product, its variety, and its exact place of origin. Onions grow rampantly all over Périgord, and there are many types to choose among: the apple-fat fresh onion (sweet as a Vidalia and young as a scallion, but ten times bigger), the teardrop-shaped red onion called Simione, the standard round yellow onion, the queenly leek, and, braided into ropes to be hung from the kitchen ceiling, the pungent shallots and garlic that make all the difference in sautés and sauces. Red and yellow new potatoes also thrive all over the region, as do simple leaf lettuces—there are only one or two varieties for sale, and these are the same ones you see in your neighbor's garden. The best turnips and beets, though, seem to profit from the thinner soil south of Domme, close to Salviac, just over the departmental line dividing the Dordogne from the Lot. Strawberries, raspberries, and currants appear in patches (or plastic-covered greenhouses) all over; it is the care of the individual producer that matters here, ensuring that berries are picked before they are too plumped up with moisture and that they are kept cool and unbruised until sale. As for the precious wild mushrooms—*cèpes, girolles*, and truffles—you won't be told where they come from, for that's the picker's great secret. You'll simply be grateful that there are any, since, at least at the farmers market, wild mushrooms are really wild. They appear only at certain seasons and in the right conditions of rain and temperature. In addition, they must be found by a *chercheur* who knows the hidden spots where they are prone to flourish.

*La truffe* is the queen of the fungi, and her season of glory is winter. Being summer folk, we have not yet attended the December truffle market in Sarlat. In old books you can find photographs of men and women wrapped tightly in black cloth coats, huddling over baskets of the "black diamonds" and worrying over what price to pay. In summer the truffles come bottled or canned, unless you fall for the summer truffle, which connoisseurs scorn as a pale ghost of the real thing. If you cut through the black skin of these fair-weather cousins, they are white inside, not black through and through—and the flavor, we are told, is insipid. As amateurs, we are content to let the local chefs decide which source of preserved truffles is the best. They know how to use a cutting of truffle judiciously, whether to accent a mellow pâté or to permeate an omelette with smoky warmth.

When buying walnuts, I'm on firmer ground. The walnut markets occur in October and November, just weeks after harvest, when the nuts are still moist. Admittedly, the best time for cooking with walnuts is winter, when the body wants a dish with substance. The great walnut recipes of Périgord (superb dishes like Roquefort-walnut quiche, duck with walnut sauce, walnut-prune cake) are designed for the cold season, just after the harvest. In summer there is still room for walnuts on the menu, but in lighter form: lemon-sole rolls with a walnut crust; fresh fig salad with candied walnut halves; celeriac, apple and walnut salad. Whereas in the old days the nuts tended to be too dry or even rotten by summer (the source of a law requiring walnuts to be labeled "old harvest" after June 1), today's packaging allows for sale of walnuts all summer long. In the summer Sarlat market, you can buy them whole in string bags, shelled and vacuum-packed, bottled in honey, ground with sugar to make *confiture de noix*, and glazed with caramel or powdered with cocoa. Bottles and tins of many shapes hold walnut oil, which preserves the essence of the walnut. The good cook samples the pressings of all the producers but makes at least one summer pilgrimage to the Moulin de la Tour in the tiny village of Sainte-Nathalène, where the same family has crushed walnuts with a stone wheel since the sixteenth century. Here is a local product worth taking home in the suitcase. For depth of flavor, no walnut oil we have bought in the United States has held a candle to even the least costly bottles we have bought at the Sarlat market. And a tablespoon of walnut oil will make a salad a triumph.

While we are thinking of what to take home for ourselves and friends, we are susceptible to the allure of gold tins of *foie gras*. We have found that succumbing is a mistake. *En place*, in France, and handled by a knowing cook, *le foie gras* is marvelous—in any form, even spread straight from the can onto toast. Back home in the States, unsupported by the ingredients and the meals that normally surround them, these imported goose- or duck-liver products tend to disappoint. The best chefs do make *foie gras* work in restaurants and banquets outside France, but most of us don't have the knack. So much the better for the *cachet* of Périgord's most important product.

Today the visual symbol associated most certainly with Périgord is an old black-and-white postcard photo of *la Gaveuse*, a grandmotherly farm woman in the process of force-feeding her goose with corn mash. Ducks too are thus over-indulged, with the same desired result: a plump, blonde liver. The raising of geese and ducks and their loving care through the process of *gavage* (ever so gentle force-feeding) was traditionally the farm wife's special province. She was the cook and preserver, just as with the farm's vegetables. But today's artisanal production of *foie gras* tends to be a family affair. The market tables from which you'll be offered samples of pâté on bread cubes may be staffed by Mama, Papa, Grandma, Grandpa, or teenage son or daughter, all of whom had a hand in developing the product from chick to can.

There's a type of preserved liver for every taste and pocketbook. At the summit is the *foie gras entier*—a whole liver, and if it is on the small side, lobes of other livers to fill out the space. Cans labeled as *foie gras* of duck or goose will be filled with good liver pieces, with up to 15 percent lard as filling. Moving down the luxury line, the *bloc de foie gras* is a cube made from liver chunks pressed together, with a paste of ground liver as mortar. *Parfait de foie gras* is ground *foie gras*, though not the best quality, and then you move to the various pâtés, *purées, galantines,* and *terrines* made of *foie gras* mixed with unfattened livers, meat from duck, goose, or even pork, and lard from any of the three. If you want purity, you need to read the labels carefully and be prepared to pay the price. But if you're looking to make a satisfying supper out of a baguette and pâté from an inexpensive can, you can hardly go wrong in Périgord. By just plunging ahead and reading the label afterward, you may learn you have a taste for duck liver mixed with turkey meat, to name just one available concoction.

The combination most prized over the centuries is *foie gras* with truffles. Once a year, we have the good fortune to encounter this delicacy in its perfect ambiance. Our friend Antoine Laval, the town electrician, is a truffle hunter, coached by his aging father and aided by the hound they have trained together. Anne-Marie Laval raises her own geese, ducks, and quail; but being busy with her own job and the raising of two daughters, she leaves the *gavage* to her mother-in-law, who lives just next door, a short walk from the poultry pen. The family store of *foie gras d'oie aux truffes* is put up in winter, in association with preparations for the Christmas and New Year feasts. Luckily for us, some is left conserved and re-frigerated for safe consumption in summer. When we arrive in early June, Anne-Marie or one of her girls invariably spots us before the suitcases are all mounted up to the house. We embrace and stand in front of the luggage, agreeing that once we are unpacked and have made the house livable we'll come up to the Laval's homestead on the hill called Soucaillou, or "under the pebbles"—that is, beneath the cliff, which washes down pebbles in the rainy season. Sometimes Anne-Marie is so insistent and we so compliant that we make the visit on the first night. In other years, the press of visitors on our part or work on hers puts the reunion off until our last evening.

At Anne-Marie's house, life offers its best pleasures. When we arrive, she crushes us in a hug and smacks kisses on both cheeks. While she's settling us at the out-door table, she asks her younger girl to fetch the glasses and get us started with drinks. She apologizes that Antoine has not yet arrived (often he's been out handling an electrical emergency; this past summer he was more happily employed, hunting for *girolles* with his father and his dog). Anne-Marie lets us know that champagne will be opened on his arrival; we get the hint and choose Badoit as our first drink. Over crackers and bubbly water, we catch up on each other's news. The girls bring their photo albums to the table and review the high points of the year—communions, confirmations, birthdays, marriages (not yet theirs), and visits from friends from Basque country. The photos record the meals that celebrated those occasions, with the same set of friends and family caught smiling at table. A prime topic of discussion is the menu at each of these feasts. We discuss the logistics of serving roast duck to fifty people (the butcher *en bas* roasted the ducks, but everything else came from Anne-Marie's kitchen) or of creating an impressive dessert that children will like as much as adults. Each of the girls has her opinion. Nicole must have chocolate, while Babette prefers meringues and fruit. As we talk, skinny green beans from Anne-Marie's own *potager* are trimmed at the table.

Eventually Antoine arrives jubilantly, with a sack full of saffron yellow *girolles*, to be divided between his house and his father's. The elder M. Laval rounds the corner of the house, limping a bit, and lights up with pleasure at the sight of company. He vies with Antoine in relating how they knew when and where to find the *girolles*—they pop up after a good soaking summer rain. He chuckles and casts his eyes down when we tease him about revealing the site (that's a family secret). Though he's asked to stay for a drink, he declines and instead takes his bowlful of mushrooms from Anne-Marie, who has done the division discreetly in the kitchen. She too looks pleased and knowing. We expect that *girolles* will feature in the night's menu.

Indeed they do, but that is not the *pièce de résis-tance.* The crowning jewel of the meal is the first course, a pâté of duck liver and truffles, made by Anne-Marie and her mother-in-law from the ducks they've raised and the truffles their husbands foraged the previous autumn. It is for that triumph that the champagne, left over from Babette's confirmation, was put on ice. (In the Bergerac region and in fancy restaurants, a Monbazillac Sauterne is the recommended accompaniment to *foie gras,* but our friends in the Sarlat region prefer to serve it with champagne.) Anne-Marie revels in our appreciation. She watches Michael's reaction to the first bite and bursts out in delight: *"Qu'il aime la truffe! Regarde—il est au ciel!"* And it's true—we are both in heaven, from the pungent truffles, the succulent *foie gras,* the sparkling champagne, and the pleasure of enjoying them with people who have put their souls into the creation and serving of the specialty of the region.

The rest of the dinner rolls from the kitchen to the terrace table with casual ease. While we were chatting with the men about truffles, Anne-Marie must have cleaned a handful of *girolles* and set them to sizzle in hot oil. While we savored our *foie gras* and champagne, she added a little tomato and garlic to the pan and set it on low heat. Now that we are ready for the second course, it is ready for us: slices of roast lamb, sauced with *girolles* and accompanied by green beans sprinkled with walnut oil. I am allowed to decline seconds; Michael is not—males have a duty to eat heartily. The girls clear the table and bring on the simple lettuce salad, which they dress at the table. The family routine respects the work of the cook and lets her take her ease for the rest of the evening. When the girls bring in dessert, it's a raspberry and white-chocolate charlotte still in its box—to show the label of the best *pâtissier* in the region. As night falls and the girls excuse themselves to go off to bed, the adults sip their coffee and count their blessings, among them good friends, good children, and good food.

Ten years into our family friendship, Nicole, then eighteen and curious about the United States, came for a fortnight's visit to us in the Midwest. She was thrilled to see Chicago's architecture, Madison's capitol building and university, the Mississippi River, and how we lived. But she was appalled by the food, or perhaps more by the attitude she found toward food in the United States. She returned home with a firm set of opinions: Americans regard food as fuel, to be injected like gas into a car whenever the tank is empty. There is no regard for meal hours; there are in fact no meal hours. Worse, there is no respect for the ingredients themselves, no attention to proper ripening, proper preparation, or the construction of a balanced meal. Until the last night of her visit, when she discovered fudge brownies with vanilla ice cream, Nicole could not find a good thing to say about American food. She declared that the visit had settled one thing in her mind. She intended to make her life in Périgord, where there is always something delicious to eat!

This sentiment may have been seeded a decade before, when we served the Lavals what we billed as an American dinner. They had been over for drinks several evenings, but it was time to repay their hospitality with a full meal. What to serve? Feeling a bit insecure, I chose each course not for its typicality, but rather on the basis of how many times I had served it with success at home. We started with olive-stuffed cheese puffs served with gin and tonic (the evening was very hot), followed by cold potato-leek soup (I hoped they would recognize this under the name of *vichyssoise*), a meatball dish that I thought would be interesting served with a lemon-based sauce over egg noodles, a green salad dressed noncalorically with citrus juices, and for dessert, the best approximation of gingerbread cake that I could make without molasses.

Apéritifs began nervously. Antoine and Anne-Marie sipped their gin and tonics, joking about not having experience with hard liquor. They politely ate one cheese puff each and then watched while the children consumed one after another (after delicately splitting them open and removing the olives). As the pile of discarded olives mounted, the parents hid their embarrassment by accepting a second round of drinks, which left them slightly stupefied. At the table, little Babette confided, *"Maman—il y a une faute. La soupe est froide."* I was sure French cookbooks contained cold soups, but apparently they were not the custom locally. This time the adults did their duty, and it was the children's plates that were full when removed. The main course daunted everyone, even Michael. The meatballs were just fine— tender and mild after hours of painstaking mixing and poaching. But the sauce had gone wrong. The recipe called for an addition of Worcestershire sauce and sour cream at the end. Neither was available, so I substituted lemon juice and *crème fraîche.* Though I whipped mightily, the sauce separated into grayish clumps irrigated by streaks of yellow liquid. In desperation, I poured the sauce over the meatballs, stirred, and decided against presentation at the table. I served each plate from the kitchen, trying to position noodles and parsley garnish so that the worst sins of the sauce were concealed. The effort was in vain, because the worst sin of the sauce was its taste—sharp and sour. Each plate came back to the kitchen minus its meatballs but still containing noodles and a pool of coagulated sauce. If only the salad and dessert could have saved the day. Instead I learned that a salad without oil is not a French salad and that gingerbread without molasses is not gingerbread, anywhere. Not a word was said about the food that night—or ever after. Now when I cook in Périgord, I stick to local tastes.

Fortunately we don't rely exclusively on my cooking. Wonderful restaurants have drawn us back season after season, and they are half the reason why we love the Dordogne. Our photo albums are full of pictures of us with our parents, our sisters and brothers, our near-neighbors from the Lot, our friends from the Loire and Paris—all at table on the second-floor balcony of la Belle Étoile, an unpretentious family-run hotel that overlooks the river at la Roque-Gageac. Its restaurant is the one where we most feel at home and to which we return on a weekly basis. As a twosome, we have watched many a twilight dim here, as we sipped and ate with pleasure. But the meals we remember most clearly are those we've shared with family.

In the premature heat of our first June in the house, my father came to visit us from Boston. Mom had broken her ankle and couldn't make the trip. Worried about Dad's response to the heat (he had just recovered from heart failure the previous winter), we sought out cool spots for dinner, and the riverside balcony of the Belle Étoile promised an evening breeze. Dad was enchanted by the way the owners had grown an arbor on the second floor by arching grape vines over a flagstoned terrace set between the roof lines of two parts of the hotel. The *patronne* escorted us to the best table on the terrace, on the edge of the balcony. Years later, Dad still talks about his dinner. It started with a bed of tender lettuce topped with three small mounds of diced savories—smoked duck, *foie gras*, and marinated beets. With the taste buds thus piqued, he proceeded to see what the French would do with his favorite dish, grilled salmon: it came on a stone plank, fresh from a roasting oven, with flecks of red and black pepper clinging to its pink flesh; in a bowl at the side was a *purée* of celeriac and potatoes, a new taste that delighted him. After doing justice to his main course and his share of a platter of goat cheeses in various stages of ripeness, Dad chose for dessert the *crème brûlée aux noix*, a heavenly bowl of baked vanilla custard with a caramel-walnut glaze flamed to amber crispness. What I remember of that evening is the pleasure on my father's face as he savored his food, gazed on the river and the pastures beyond it, and told us for the first time about his adventures and trials as a naval officer in the Pacific during World War II. Over dinner each night during that visit we heard a chapter in the story of his war, a story that somehow, in the atmosphere of home and family, had never been told.

I remember another family evening one summer at la Belle Étoile when the temperature had risen above ninety degrees. This time my mom was with us as well as my dad. The terrace was full, and we were relegated to an elegantly furnished dining room inside. Mom took pleasure in each detail of the table setting, menus, and service, but she nearly suffocated from the heat. We ordered as cooling a menu as possible, but the hot, still air took away our appetites. Hardly having the energy to lift a spoon, we watched our specially ordered frozen walnut soufflé melt into a puddle. Today the restaurant boasts an air-conditioned salon, which is quite a rare thing in Périgord. The staff still doesn't have the hang of it, though. The waiters keep leaving the doors to the dining room open as they enter and exit the kitchen, which of course lets out all the cool air. The French are befuddled by air-conditioning—that's all there is to it. So now if it's hot and we can't be seated outside, we simply reserve for another day when the terrace is available.

Whereas la Belle Étoile is family run, le Centenaire in les Eyzies is professionally staffed and as formal as resort dining gets. We find that our visitors need a push to get over their sense that either the pomp of the place or the sophistication of its food will be too much for them. But once there, they melt with pleasure under the meticulous care of the Centenaire staff. As they enter the ground-floor restaurant, they find its modern stone construction reminiscent of a design by Frank Lloyd Wright. Put at ease by the airy space and simple furnishings, they are ready to study the elegant menu with its oversized cream cover, in the middle of which is embossed in gold and brown a drawing of a bull and its hunter in the Lascaux style.

If you're willing to brave duck gizzards in the appetizer, the lowest-priced menu offers the intrigue of lasagna stuffed with tuna lox and slivers of that suspicious summer truffle, followed by roast rabbit moistened by sauce thickened with powdered *cèpes*. The middle menu rises from the bargain basement, starting off with a medley of crustacean meats (lobster, crab, shrimp), with a cucumber-curry sauce and shrimp tempura on the side. Then you have your choice of truffled risotto or a "pillow" of snails and frog meat. (That course puts me off this menu.) After that you would choose between goose steak and roast lamb, each with imaginative vegetables— cream of white corn with truffles, or spinach canneloni with tomato sauce and basil. The top menu has no choices—just one perfect course after another. Seaweed creamed with saffron whets the appetite for a thick slice of roast *foie gras de canard* served on a bed of caramelized fruit. The *terrine* that follows is appropriately not meaty but a slice of a light loaf made from *cèpes*, vegetable stock, garlic, and parsley. Now you are ready for a little pot of lobster meat bathed in a bisque of lobster stock and Lillet (a wonderfully aromatic apéritif, usually encountered chilled, before dinner). Then comes the main course—just the white of the chicken breast, rolled round a thin stuffing of truffles and chicken liver. Finally the meal ends, like the other menus, with selections of cheese, a chariot of elaborate desserts, and petits fours with your coffee. Whichever menu you choose, black-tied waiters bring everyone's silver-domed dishes at once and, following some invisible signal, lift the covers in synchrony. The choreography never fails to impress. Neither does the bill.

According to the *Michelin Guide*, which awards it two stars, le Centenaire is tops in the region. That's a fair call, if you take into account service, complexity of cuisine, and presentation. However, we have a restaurant that we like even better. When Henry Miller visited the Dordogne in the 1930s, he marveled at the scenery but singled out one locale for particular praise. He stood at the bluff of Domme and later wrote that the view of the dark river winding below was something to be grateful for all one's life. Today at this spectacular lookout stands the Hotel-Restaurant l'Esplanade, with its windows edging the cliff. Inside, the decor is French provincial, with mustard-yellow table cloths and dark blue curtains sporting yellow *fleurs-de-lis.* Huge floral bouquets adorn pedestals placed throughout the room. Floor-to-ceiling windows give out on a view of the Dordogne winding through lush green corn fields in the distance below, and if clients prefer, they may eat outside on the terrace, which overlooks the valley. Like le Centenaire, this is one of those restaurants where waiters come to your table in teams bearing the food on silver platters. Yet at heart, l'Esplanade (which has one Michelin star) remains a country restaurant, with local staff, local cuisine, and local clients, their numbers swelled in season, to be sure, by tourists.

Local cuisine, yes—*foie gras,* duck, goose, lamb, pork, and beef, done with truffles, *cèpes, girolles, morilles*—but exceptionally prepared and garnished with inventive touches. There's a sensational variety of goat cheeses for the end of the meal—small round cheeses of many hues, topped with every imaginable spice or herb—and an opulent wagon of world-class desserts. Because we are frequent clients, madame knows us by name and usually reserves one of the best tables for us by a window, so we can enjoy the sunset and the view of the valley while dining. Here is the menu for one particularly memorable dinner:

*Le Medaillon de Foie Gras de Canard du Crème de Noix*
(Duck Liver Pâté with Walnut Sauce
—Betsy's entrée)

*Les Escalopes de Foie Gras de Canard Grillés aux Framboises*
(Whole Liver of Duck Grilled with Raspberries
—Michael's entrée)

■

*Le Filet de Barbue au Beurre Truffé*
(Filet of Brill in Truffled Butter Sauce
—Betsy's fish course)

*Les Rouelles de Lotte Sauce Bordelaise*
(Monk Fish in a Bordeaux Red Wine Sauce
—Michael's fish course)

■

*Les Noisettes de Filet d'Agneau aux Truffes et la Sauce Périgueux*
(Lamb Chops with Truffles in a Madeira/White Wine/Truffle Sauce
—Betsy's meat course)

*Le Confit d'Oie aux Cèpes*
(Preserved Goose with Cèpes Mushrooms
—Michael's meat course)

*La Selection de Fromages*

*Le Chariot des Desserts*

The relative simplicity of these courses belies the skill involved in serving them perfectly. In many years of dining, we have never received a disappointing dish from chef René Gillard's kitchen. We've celebrated birthdays, anniversaries, and the presence of friends, and the meal has always been up to the occasion. Both sets of parents have stayed at l'Esplanade and pronounced its dinners unbeatable.

There was one evening the first summer that Michael's parents visited that was truly memorable. We four were in the dining room, just finishing our appetizers when, out of a vaguely threatening sky, a violent tempest suddenly roiled through the valley. These dramatic thunderstorms are fairly common during the hot summer months, but we had never seen the likes of this before. It blew up with scarcely any warning and sent things flying. Trees were uprooted in seconds; before our eyes, a huge pot housing a mimosa bush blew right off the terrace and over the cliff. At the terrace tables just outside our open window, napkins and glasses were hurled from their settings, and the astonished patrons outside grabbed their belongings and dashed inside to escape a drenching. With a minimum of fuss, they were reseated in the interior. Inside, windows were closed and shutters were pulled shut to protect the windows. The winds continued to howl, and a few minutes later, the power went. The entire restaurant was plunged into darkness, and it stayed that way for the remainder of the night. Michael's mom was unsettled and worried. We murmured calming words and reasoned that the safest thing was to keep our seats in the darkness.

Without breaking stride, the waiters distributed candles for each table and went on to serve dinner to a packed restaurant. We could see the chefs scurrying behind the kitchen doors in candlelight, intent over their gas stoves, turning out dish after dish of wonderful food. Thousands of dollars' worth of meat and produce were sitting in failing freezers and refrigerators, but the meal proceeded with stately measure, dish by dish. Outside, branches were hurled through the skies, and screaming winds lifted tiles from the roofs of houses. Inside, sipping our wine, we moved leisurely in candlelight through our fish course, meat course, and cheese course. The noble *chariot des desserts* rolled on its appointed rounds. Mom, mellowing and holding her wine glass delicately by the stem (at home she rarely takes a drop), announced that she was tipsy. She opined that we could always sleep on the floor of their room upstairs if the roads home were impassable. By eleven o'clock the storm had abated and the coffee had been served. M. Gillard emerged from the kitchen wearing his white apron and toque, and the roomful of patrons broke into applause. Everyone lingered over coffee as the valiant chef moved from table to table, shaking hands with customers as he accepted their compliments. Finally, we took a candle from our table, walked Michael's parents to their room, and left the darkened restaurant for home. We have had many delicious dinners at l'Esplanade, but none to match that evening of tempests and truffles.

In fairness, you can eat well in every region of France. But in the Dordogne, it seems the soil is more pungent, the dishes heartier, the cooking as fine as *haute cuisine* can get without losing its ties to local tradition. "In the Dordogne—there they eat well." It's true.

# 10

## MONSIEUR CRO-MAGNON

Since coming to the Dordogne, we've become interested in everything concerning the Stone Age, especially Paleolithic art (*paleos* from the Greek, meaning "old," *lithos* meaning "stone"). Some of the world's best examples of Stone Age art are located within an hour's drive of our house. Dozens of sites are clustered around the village of les Eyzies, which bills itself as "the capital of prehistory." At the entrance to the village, there is an unintentionally comical statue of "Primitive Man" set high into the cliffs. The hulking statue has been criticized as being far too apelike to reflect the actual appearance of our forebears, but children love posing next to it, and the statue has become a gathering point for family snapshots. As for so-called "Primitive Man," the current thinking is that he (and she) looked rather like us. "Dress him in modern clothing," the saying goes, "place him in the Metro, and M. Cro-Magnon would be indistinguishable from the average commuter." Perhaps he would be in less of a hurry.

We've developed a soft spot for "M. Cro-Magnon," which is how the locals playfully refer to their distant ancestor. "Cro-Magnon" is the place name of a site on the outskirts of les Eyzies. It was on this spot, where the Hotel Cro-Magnon stands today, that the bones of "Monsieur" were discovered in 1868 while workers were digging to lay a railroad track. It turned out that the bones were much older than anyone thought; they dated back thirty thousand years to the Second Ice Age, when bands of resourceful hunters followed migrating game south to escape the cold. When these hunters arrived, they appropriated natural rock shelters that were then occupied by the Neanderthals. One of these sites, the settlement of la Roque Saint-Christophe, can be visited today: the rock overhang juts out from a natural horizontal gash cut high up into the cliff. No one really knows what became of the Neanderthals after the Cro-Magnons arrived. They may have been exterminated; they may have fled; they may have intermarried with the newcomers and melted into the gene pool. Their traces speak only indirectly about who they were. The Cro-Magnons, on the other hand, left their mark, literally, on the valley they occupied.

The valley was a perfect refuge for these new arrivals. To the north, the mountains of the massif Central stood as a barrier against the ice. Game was plentiful, the rivers yielded fish, and the setting was—and still is—beautiful, a factor that must have been important to a people awakening to art. For it was here that European art was born. First came small, portable objects carved on bone, then symbols and handprints painted on cavern walls. What followed later are the masterpieces of Stone Age art, the famous murals that attract thousands of visitors here each summer.

Prehistorians divide the Upper Paleolithic Era into four periods: the Aurignacian (c. 30,000 B.C.); the Gravettian (27,000–18,000 B.C.); the Solutrean (c. 20,000–15,000 B.C.); and the Magdalenian (15,000–9,000 B.C.). Art was produced continuously, but it was only during the last period that the most important cave paintings were done. When the climate warmed, the herds drifted back to their old habitats in the north, and again the hunters followed. After 8,500 B.C., all traces of the Magdalenian culture vanish. When art appears again in Neolithic times (the "new" Stone Age), several millennia later, it seems to have a second start, from scratch.

These epochs are fascinating because nothing in modern history offers a remotely parallel time scale. Imagine: when the Magdalenian Age ended about eleven thousand years ago, it brought to a close a school of art that already had been in existence for *two hundred centuries*—more than twice as long as recorded history. How is it possible that an unbroken tradition could have endured over such an enormous stretch, when art in recent times seems to change its conventions every few decades? Of all the astonishing facts about Stone Age art, this is the most intriguing. If the prehistorians are right about the dates, no other time frame in human experience can compare with the long, slow passage of Paleolithic art.

As for the paintings, they are remarkably sophisticated. They generally are hidden deep inside the caves, often at great distances from the openings, which suggests that the sites probably were used as shrines or sanctuaries. Contrary to popular belief, the "cavemen" didn't live in caves. No traces of cooking or any domestic artifacts have been found at these sites, only remnants of the artists' craft. From these traces, scholars can tell a good deal about the painters' techniques. First, pigments were ground and mixed: iron oxides, ocher for reds and yellows, manganese for blacks and browns. Then the pigments were pounded into powder and blown through hollow reeds, or hardened into sticks like crayons, or mixed with water and binder before being applied with fingers, feathers, or even a kind of brush made from horses' hair. The cave artists also mastered relief sculpture and engraving. They used sharp, pointed flints to carve images, and they sometimes spread a film of wet clay on the wall, which enabled them to trace outlines on a surface that quickly hardened.

The most magnificent cave paintings in the region are found at Lascaux, which lies only twenty miles to the northeast of les Eyzies. The cave was discovered by four French teenagers in the summer of 1940 and opened to visitors after the Second World War, when it became a sensational attraction. Ironically, the popularity of the cave soon became a threat to its preservation. By the time Lascaux was closed to the public in 1963, a million tourists had crammed into its narrow confines, carrying bacteria and exhaling carbon dioxide that began to destabilize the cave's chemistry and to degrade its art. Now the gallery is carefully monitored. When we saw it in 1987, only five visitors a day, lingering no longer than thirty minutes, were permitted entry. We wrote to the National Director of Prehistoric

Antiquities on university letterhead, described our interest in seeing the art, and were granted permission, though we waited more than a year for an appointment.

On the specified day, we presented ourselves at the gate, dipped our shoes in an antibacterial solution, and followed the guide, who, we were surprised to learn, was Jacques Marsal, one of the original discoverers of Lascaux and by that time a man in his sixties. Marsal led our small party of five through a dark passageway and then dramatically, without warning, threw a light switch. The experience was startling. Imagine groping through a low, damp chamber in pitch darkness, which suddenly is illuminated by floodlights to reveal one of the great art treasures of the world: You are standing in the Hall of Bulls, where every wall is covered with magnificent murals of animals at the gallop—the impression of movement is uncanny. The creatures are brought to life with sure strokes and brilliant colors that still gleam on their crystalline surfaces after seventeen thousand years. Bulls, horses, bison, wild oxen, stags, deer, and one curious beast, part human and part animal, with a unicorn-like horn, make up a cavalcade of figures leaping in a fantasia across the gallery walls. The colors are expressionistic, with red cows and yellow horses, and the figures are stylized according to a plan.

The animals have abnormally small heads and shortened legs, with abstract ovals suggesting hooves. By contrast, their bodies are massive, creating an impression of grace and solidity. The artists (at least eight different hands can be distinguished) used a common device that is the signature of their style: they left a subtle gap where the legs of the animals are joined to their trunks. The method suggests not only movement, but also depth. The overall impact is cumulative, stunning. Everywhere, majestic animals appear to take flight as in some reverie by Chagall. Leaping over imaginary boundaries or striking off in opposite directions in a flurry of overlapping limbs, these animals possess a stately charm. To enter Lascaux is to enter the vivid dream world of our distant ancestors and to share their unsettling sense of the mystery of the world around them.

Twenty years after Lascaux was closed, to satisfy the demands of the public, the French government created a facsimile of the cave called Lascaux II, located only a few miles from the original site. Out of curiosity, we decided to visit the replica immediately after seeing the original. From a technical standpoint, Lascaux II is an impressive achievement. In this underground gallery, eighty meters long, made of concrete and polyester resin, the Hall of Bulls has been faithfully replicated down to the last centimeter. But somehow as art it is lifeless. Lascaux has been called "the Sistine Chapel of Prehistoric Art." If so, then Lascaux II might be compared to the copy of Michelangelo's ceiling frescoes in the movie *The Agony and the Ecstasy*. I thought when I first saw it that Lascaux II had the feel of a Hollywood set.

On a second visit years later, with the impact of the real Lascaux a fading memory, I came away with a more nuanced opinion. In favor of Lascaux II it can be said that the reproductions are convincing and that the images are displayed in their proper spatial arrangement, which is something no book of photographs can convey. Yet the experience remains artificial. This facsimile cave—it wasn't formed naturally but was dug out of the ground— has become one of the most popular tourist attractions in France. For tickets, you drive into Montignac, where signs and banners direct you to the ticket booth in the center of town. Parking is a nightmare, and there are long lines. Tickets are bought for tours with starting times specified by the hour. At the site, concessions predictably cater to the waiting throngs, who are ushered in and out of the man-made chamber with dispatch.

The irony is that within an easy drive of Lascaux II there are a half-dozen genuine caves with authentic Stone Age art still open to the public, and today these originals are visited less frequently than the copy. For example, Font de Gaume, on the outskirts of les Eyzies, is a treasure containing wonderful frescoes, some of which rival the masterpieces of Lascaux. A frieze of bison is beautifully painted, as are a pair of deer gently nuzzling each other, with heads bent as if to drink from a river. Deer, mountain goats, and horses lead the eye to the final and most striking grouping—six huge bison painted on a concave domelike formation. Recently there has been some talk of closing Font de Gaume for much the same reasons that required the closing of Lascaux, but for now, the cave can be seen.

At Rouffignac, ten miles to the west of les Eyzies, an underground electric railway carries you several miles into the depths of an enormous cavern. The ride itself is worth the visit—and for those who can't walk so well, it's the best way to get into one of the great caves of prehistory. At the end of the track, in a large circular hall, a jumble of mammoths, ibex, horses, and bison cover the ceiling. The figures are drawn in black charcoal line and overlap each other in a confusing array. Some of these drawings are thousands of years older than those found at either Lascaux or Font de Gaume.

No matter how hot it may be outside, it is always chilly and wet in the caves, and visitors need a jacket or sweater. That's why the best time to visit a *grotte* is on a blazing hot day, when the experience is the reverse of a sauna. We chose one such day for a visit to la Mouthe, which is omitted from most tourist guides. The cave is owned by the farmer on whose land it was discovered, and now that he is retired, he acts as guide. He has left the cave unelectrified; its only illumination is his bouncing flashlight. The cave's most interesting feature is an image interpreted to be a human habitation, the only painting of its kind from this period. The hut, if that's what it is, looks like a Native American tepee, made of sticks and hides. On our way out of la Mouthe, an accident made our visit especially memorable. The farmer's flashlight conked out, and we had to search for the remaining paintings (and find our way back to the entrance) by candlelight. Cave art was meant to be seen under such conditions; suddenly, vague outlines stood out in bold relief.

It is still a mystery why these images were painted. The early explanation of Ice Age art was based on a theory of hunting magic that assumed that the figures were painted in order to "capture" the spirits of the represented animals, so as to ensure success in the hunt. But the number of animal images associated with spears or arrows is very limited; only a small percentage shows indications of wounds. Many more are shown in attitudes that suggest nothing to do with hunting, such as the deer tenderly nuzzling each other at Font de Gaume. Theories abound to explain the cave murals and their symbols, but after a century of analysis, no one has cracked the code.

Whatever may have been the purpose of Stone Age art, préhisto-tourisme has become big business in the Dordogne. Besides the caves, there are numerous archeological sites around les Eyzies that are heavily promoted. A certain degree of exploitation was inevitable. There are now various brands and shops bearing the Cro-Magnon name, and at the high-toned restaurant le Centenaire in les Eyzies, the menus are named for local caves in ascending order of magnitude: the relatively modest Menu la Mouthe, the impressive Menu Font de Gaume, and the staggeringly gastronomic Menu Lascaux. The main street of les Eyzies is crammed with shops selling books and postcards on prehistory, tee shirts emblazoned with bison images, and prehistory car decals, key chains, and coffee mugs. You can buy stone clocks decorated with Lascaux horses, cave-art caps, and Cro-Magnon shopping bags. There are mineral shops throughout the region and a lively commerce in fossils as souvenirs. There is even a *Camping Naturiste Cro-Magnon*—a Cro-Magnon Nudist Camp—and no, I'm not making this up.

And yet, for the most part, the hoopla and exploitation are good-natured if not tongue-in-cheek. Usually, in fact, underneath the catchy publicity there is a site with real interest and integrity. The outdoor Museum of Prehistory at le Thot is a good example. Children can amble from exhibit to exhibit and observe free-ranging animals of the same species as those that are represented in cave art (with the exception of species that are now extinct). Indoors there are educational exhibits and life-size photographs of the most important cave images from around the region. Yes, there is the predictable theme park, too, and no one does theme parks as goofily as the French.

This one's called Préhisto-Parc, offering low budget dioramas of Neanderthal and Cro-Magnon drama. You wander along a marked trail through the woods and come upon clearings with scenes of men and beasts having at one another. Example: a group of Neanderthal hunters with spears menace a hairy mammoth (looking like a beast from a Thanksgiving Day Parade float). Préhisto-Parc is no le Thot, but even it has an educational component, and for small children, it can be entertaining. Our nephew, though, who was nine at the time, was not impressed with Préhisto-Parc. Raised in Los Angeles, he had already seen Universal Studios.

New caves are still being discovered. One summer we were invited by M. Meunier's son-in-law to explore a cave that he had come across somewhere in the hills surrounding Castelnaud. It was a very small cave, he informed us, with no art but with some unusual concretions. Having learned of our interest in caves from a conversation with Michael, he thought we might like to see an untouched example. Here was our chance to relive the discovery of Lascaux, to enter an unknown cave and find who-knows-what within. We made our date for three the next afternoon.

Not being much of a physical adventurer, I was nervous about this expedition, but I channeled my anxieties into arranging a great outfit: my new Ralph Lauren jeans (I was waiting for an occasion to break them in), my white walking shoes (well proven to resist blisters), and my red and white University of Wisconsin sweatshirt (warm enough for the deepest cave). In other words, I had no idea what we were getting into. I am sure that when we arrived at M. Pasquet's doorstep, he could see that at a glance, but he said not a word as he ushered us to his car.

M. Pasquet was married to Claire, the Meuniers' daughter. He was a slim middle-aged man with fair hair, pale eyes, and a pout, which kept his eyebrows locked in a circumflex position. He seemed constantly bored in Castelnaud. As we drove along back roads, then a dirt road, toward the site, he talked animatedly about his work as a high-school biology teacher in Arras in the north of France. Every summer (rather reluctantly, we guessed), he brought his family down to stay with his in-laws for several weeks. His passion was science, and he was more comfortable outdoors. After he parked the car and got us walking on a trail, M. Pasquet was bursting with energy, pointing out this or that geological feature, plant, or tree. Indoors, *en famille*, he slumped into lassitude. He liked to go off by himself on day-long hikes, and it was on one of these that he had literally stumbled across the opening of a cave hidden by a tangle of underbrush on a path along the ridge of a cliff facing Castelnaud.

There we were now. As we looked across to the cliffs opposite, we could see not only Castelnaud, but, nearer, the Château of Lacoste.

"Are we on the ridge they call le Conte?" I asked.

"Yes, but at its far end. As you'll see, this little cave has had the luck to be out of the way and well camouflaged. You'll see why the experts never found it."

M. Pasquet led the way. Michael gamely followed. And I trailed, hanging onto slim tree trunks as we descended steeply down a dirt path in the wood that tops the cliff. As I clung precariously to a sapling not much bigger than myself, I saw the two men halt. A grinning

M. Pasquet pointed at his feet. *"Voilà!"* The cave entrance was no bigger than an animal burrow, blocked by a heavy rock wedged alongside an oak tree.

*"C'est moi qui l'ai placé,"* M. Pasquet informed us, as he rolled the rock aside.

With surprising agility and no additional explanation, he hoisted himself down, resting his weight on his palms until his legs and torso disappeared into the hole. Then he dropped from sight. We were expected to follow. Michael went first and called up to me from below that the drop wasn't bad. My inclination was to skip the experience and wait for the men topside, but that wouldn't do, since M. Pasquet had arranged his entire afternoon to accommodate us. So I squeezed in, feet dangling, then dropped into darkness, a distance of four or five feet. I landed in soft wet clay, splattering mud over my shoes and jeans; Michael steadied me by the elbow. In another moment M. Pasquet had illuminated a powerful lamp attached to a battery pack in his knapsack, and we could see where we were. We were standing in a rocky chamber about ten feet in circumference with enough headroom so that it was possible to remain upright. Above us, with blue sky showing, was the ragged entrance hole. A low, narrow passageway ahead of us led into the bowels of the earth, our next destination.

M. Pasquet dropped to his hands and knees and crawled through the passage, taking the light with him. There was no option now but to continue. Michael went next. I followed. After a dozen yards or so, the ceiling of the corridor lowered, and we were reduced to crawling through mud on our stomachs, pulling ourselves forward on elbows and knees.

"*Ce n'est pas loin,*" M. Pasquet called back in encouragement. "It isn't far."

He was already in the next chamber, shining his light back at us to show the way. I had resigned myself to the loss of my jeans, but suddenly the question became whether I was going to keep my hips. I was stuck—at the wide point of the *derrière.* Michael had squeezed through successfully behind our guide, but I was wedged tight against the constricted walls of the passageway and couldn't budge. The men reached back, each grasping one of my hands, and pulled. With rips and scrapes, I was dragged indecorously into the chamber of miniature stalactites that was the object of our expedition. There was room only to kneel, but inches above our heads in the low, wide chamber was a glistening ceiling of delicate stalactites, each no longer than a finger, glowing white and translucent in the beams of the lamp. There were countless numbers of them hanging as if from the sole of some celestial golf shoe, left undisturbed for ages. One by one the needles of solid light caught our attention. Then suddenly they merged into an otherworldly cocoon in which we floated, in awe.

Too soon, it was time for the return journey. Michael followed behind me, with M. Pasquet leading the way, so that one could push from behind while the other tugged. It proved a successful strategy. Back at the first chamber, M. Pasquet pulled himself up into daylight, with Michael boosting me again from behind, until my head and arms cleared the circumference of the entrance hole. Caked in mud and covered with bruises, I regained my feet but suddenly felt unsteady in the afternoon heat, for the sun was still strong and the damp cave had been dramatically colder. Michael looked a bit pale himself, but we gave ourselves a shake and declared ourselves successful spelunkers.

The next day we dropped by M. Meunier's house with a small gift for M. Pasquet as a way to thank him for his efforts, but he had gone off on a walk and was late in returning. No matter: M. Meunier would keep us entertained. We commented on his son-in-law's generosity in giving up an afternoon to lead us to the secret cave.

"*Eh oui, il est gentil,*" M. Meunier allowed, but this commendation was surprisingly grudging, accompanied by a puffing of the cheeks and a shrugging of the shoulders as if to indicate something amiss. Noting our puzzled reaction, M. Meunier explained: "*Il n'est pas d'ici.*" He's not from here.

"He's from the north," he added, as if that should suffice as elaboration. To M. Meunier, born and raised in Périgord, anyplace north of Limoges was beyond the pale.

Realizing that he might have appeared disloyal to his daughter, M. Meunier caught himself and allowed of his son-in-law: "*Mais il est intéressant.*" Yet this, too, was an ambiguous signal. "Don't play at being interesting" (*"ne joue pas l'intéressant"*) a parent might say to a child who is clamoring for attention or to a teenager straining for originality. For those who earned his unqualified approval, M. Meunier's adjectives of choice were *brave* or *sérieux*. To be called *un homme sérieux* was praise indeed. But *intéressant!* Obviously there was something about his son-in-law that gave M. Meunier pause. He seemed to be debating internally whether to share his feelings with us, and then, with a nod of his head, he made up his mind.

Would we like to see M. Pasquet's collection of crea-tures? (Had we heard correctly? Our expressions must have seemed quizzical.)

*"Voulez-vous voir ses bêtes?"* he repeated with a conspiratorial grin.

Now we were at a loss. *Bêtes* means animals. Farm-ers talk of feeding their livestock: *il faut nourir les bêtes*. But M. Pasquet could not have brought cattle with him on vacation, so what was M. Meunier talk-ing about? And why the mischievous grin, as if to say, "you're in for a surprise"? The answer revealed itself when M. Meunier led us to the barn, where his son-in-law had parked his trailer. There, ranged along the stacks of hay, were rows of small chicken-wire cages containing an astounding array of giant insects. We rec-ognized the praying mantises but could only guess what some of the other exotic species were, which looked like (and turned out to be) monsters from the Amazon rain forest. This strange zoo certainly looked incongruous alongside the farm machinery in M. Meu-nier's barn.

As M. Pasquet later explained to us, the rare insects belonged to his biology department and were his re-sponsibility. They required special care, and not willing to entrust the task to anyone else at school, he took them with him when he left on vacation. It was a per-fectly reasonable explanation, but M. Meunier pre-tended to be flabbergasted. Bringing bugs, even fancy ones, on a visit is not something country folk do. "They're for spraying, not feeding," he muttered, chuck-ling at his own joke. "Up north, things are different," he added with a shrug.

We think of that incident now whenever we see M. Meunier, for a year later Mme. Meunier died, and although it took some convincing, M. Meunier agreed to move in with Claire, the grandchildren, and M. Pasquet in distant Arras. Now, like us, he's only a seasonal visitor. He comes back to Castelnaud in the summer, part of a caravan led by M. Pasquet's trailer—with its *bêtes*.

"*Comment ça va?*" we ask when we see him. "How are things in the north?"

"*C'est différent,*" he shrugs, looking disconsolate. But what can you expect?

"*Que voulez-vous? C'est le nord.*"

# THE BATTLE OF
CASTELNAUD

## CLOSINGS

There is a seasonal rhythm to owning a vacation house that makes us feel all too keenly the passage of time. Summer's end brings with it a round of closings. It begins with the closing of the house, which we have to batten down for a long absence. Then there is our wistful circuit of goodbyes. We have developed a ritual of farewells that once established cannot be broken without hurt feelings. We visit our friends and neighbors, clink glasses, and wish them health and a happy new year in advance. There are going-away presents for the young. "Until next summer!" we say. With the old there are hints of melancholy as we talk confidently about next year's return.

We begin the countdown to departure the afternoon before we are to leave. I start by defrosting the refrigerator, which entails controlled flooding in the kitchen over several hours. I pack away dishes and silverware and jettison foodstuffs, while Michael tidies up outside and hauls away garbage. The night before, we pack our suitcases, shower, and eat a late dinner out, leaving the mechanical work for morning. As we mount the path to the house, we take a last look at the castle at night, illuminated against the inky sky.

After a quick breakfast in the morning, Michael packs the car, while I finish stowing the kitchenwares and empty the flowerpots outside so the earth won't hold water that could freeze and crack them. Then we start at the top of the house and work our way down by floors. In the attic we strip the bed, leaving a thin, washable bedspread on top to catch droppings from visiting mice or bats. Pillows go into the bureau drawers, where they will stay dry over winter. The screen for the large window comes in, and we pull tight the shutters, lock the casement into place from inside, and unplug the lamps and fan.

Then it's down to the *séjour* for a similar routine. The sheets from the bed go over the couch and armchair to protect them from dust. Cushions go into the armoire, on top of the blankets. Whatever is outside comes inside, including the picnic table and chairs, parasol, ladder, flowerpots, and gardening tools. We wedge a board into the fireplace chimney to block birds and animals that might try to enter. Everything but the phone is unplugged. We lock the shutters and panes and pull closed the outside door to the terrace, which is solid wood and bolts into the stone door frame. As we do so, the room suddenly goes black. This moment always feels threatening to me, as if we're losing our home, along with the light, forever. We close and lock the interior door. Feeling our way to the stairwell, we descend to the *cuisine*.

There, water control is the principal concern. The only time we've had a problem was one winter when our water pipe and water heater froze because they hadn't been properly drained. Now we have a clipboard outlining a set of steps that we check off meticulously to prevent a repetition. A single narrow pipe carries water into the house from a distribution box outside connected to the town's supply. In the kitchen, it branches off into the sink and water heater on the wall above it, then continues through that wall into the bathroom, where it branches again to serve the sink, shower, bidet, and toilet—simplicity itself as far as plumbing goes. The house-closing strategy is to drain the main pipe thoroughly and then dry out the traps of the receptacles.

The operation is carefully synchronized. I turn on all the taps at once while Michael goes outside and around the house to the stone water box. With the precision and drama of a space launching, we shout signals at each other through the kitchen window. When all the taps are running, Michael smartly cuts off the water from the outside main, and the flow trickles to dribbles and drops until the taps are dry. Next we pour *alcool à bruler* (white spirits) into the drains, to help evaporate water remaining in the traps and to work as antifreeze during the winter. One final step—the water heater above the sink gets special treatment. There's a drainage screw at the bottom of it that opens to clear the coil inside, which is connected to the pipe branching into the sink. (When the hot water tap is turned on, the heater flames up and heats the water flowing to the tap.) The idea now is to blow through the faucet to force out water remaining in the unit's coil—a ridiculous posture in which to be observed, but we were instructed by M. Meunier as to its necessity. After one attempt at pursing his lips over the grungy faucet, Michael invented another method. To the faucet he attaches a plastic foot pedal pump, the kind used for blowing up bicycle tires, and he pumps away. Sure enough, water dribbles out of the heater's drainage spout. As an extra precaution, he insulates the exterior water main with straw before replacing the stone lid, as is the local custom.

We are almost done. The kitchen shutters are clamped, the windows are locked, and the peephole on the medieval wooden door is hammered closed for the season. The last thing to do is to shut off the electricity. If we forget, we will be paying extra bills all winter long. A flick of a lever in the food pantry does it; then we turn the key and are out the door.

But not out of town, for now our round of goodbyes begins. We knock on the doors of our immediate neighbors, then drive over the crest of the hill to say goodbye to Anne-Marie and the girls and to the Delechaux family, who live nearby. The protocol for these visits entails an apéritif. Then it's down the hill to bid goodbye to M. Meunier and to commiserate with him about the winter he's spent in the north. We assure him that Wisconsin winters are worse. If M. Pasquet is out walking, as he usually is, we joke about the insect menagerie in the garage. It is impossible to escape without another apéritif, and on more than one occasion, we have pulled out of town half potted, facing a drive to Bordeaux in the noonday sun.

As long as Mme. Boucher was alive, our last visit was reserved for her, and over the years we developed a precise ritual for parting. In the beginning she, too, would insist on offering us an apéritif. When we explained our dilemma, she invented a compromise. She would make a *bon café* to keep Monsieur Michel sober for the road. However, to accompany the coffee there would be biscuits and the familiar jar of prunes steeped in liqueur. So now, added to the obligatory drinks on our previous stops, we would be fêted with alcohol-soaked prunes followed by black coffee that was as thick as caulk. I never drink coffee, and Michael doesn't like it without cream, but in France *café au lait* is restricted to breakfast. To ask Mme. Boucher for milk would have implied that her coffee needed improvement, and since she prided herself on her brew, we couldn't do that. So we would drink it straight, or rather, Michael would, while I toyed with my cup and ate my prunes.

Then it would come time to exchange gifts. From home I would bring fine stationery, or a shawl or kerchief, something lightweight that could be nicely wrapped. "We hope you will wear this in the winter and think of us," I might say. In return, Mme. Boucher would bring out some delicacy that she had made or that her daughter-in-law had brought for her, perhaps a jar containing an entire *fois gras*, homemade. This potlatch ceremony grew more elaborate every summer until it threatened to deplete our neighbor's larder. We would stay for at least an hour, and Mme. Boucher would stand at her window, waving, as we drove away. Each year she would say, "Perhaps I won't be here when you return." For a dozen summers the inevitable prophecy was forestalled.

It's a half-hour's drive, hugging the Dordogne, to Bergerac and then a straight, two-hour run to Bordeaux.

After Bergerac, the road is flat, hot, and dusty for most of the ride, until all at once the famous vineyards appear, and the sprawling city of Bordeaux rises in haze above the horizon. Because our flight from Bordeaux to Brussels departs early in the morning to make its Chicago connection, we usually stay overnight at an airport hotel on the city outskirts. After installing ourselves, we have one more visit to make. Our friend Yvette, who is ninety-two years old, lives outside Bordeaux, and we have made it a tradition to dine with her on the eve of our departure.

It might seem odd that visits to elderly women would bracket our final day in France, but that is how it was while Mme. Boucher was still alive: coffee with Mme. Boucher in Castelnaud and dinner with our friend Yvette outside Bordeaux. Although the two women had much in common—both widowed, both without children to look after them—these friends of ours were quite different in outlook. Whereas Mme. Boucher careened daily between delight and depression, Yvette's disposition is sunny and stable. In parting, Mme. Boucher grew sad, ending often in tears. Yvette's goodbyes, in contrast, have always been bright, like her personality. Not that her life has been trouble-free. Like us, Yvette lives next door to a castle, but until recently she lived inside it.

Michael has known Yvette longer than he's known me. Years ago, when he was a young assistant professor driving through the Dordogne, he met Yvette's husband, Pascal Dupré. Out of a chance encounter grew a friendship. Michael had stopped at a picnic site by the side of the road when he noticed a pair of elderly men preparing lunch. Formally dressed in three-piece suits displaying their World War I decorations, the old gentlemen had set up a folding table with camp chairs and were pan-frying fish over a portable propane stove. Michael was kneeling by a brook to wash some cherries when one of them, Pascal, hailed him and invited him to lunch.

Pascal was a retired *fonctionaire* who as a youth had dreamed of becoming a writer. But when he returned from the Great War, he was offered a secure position in the bureau of taxation and so spent an uneventful career toiling at numbers in a provincial town. At night he wrote for his own pleasure. Now in retirement he devoted himself to his muse and to good food, as well as could be managed on a skimpy pension. Once a week without fail, he and his old comrade in arms, M. Émile, lunched together sporting their military ribbons. In good weather they embarked in Pascal's doddering Citroën in quest of the perfect spot for a *déjeuner sur l'herbe*, where Pascal would recite his latest verses to his friend. M. Émile was much frailer and barely spoke, except for an encouraging *"C'est ça."* On this occasion Michael doubled Pascal's audience, and when it was learned that he taught literature at an American university, albeit from a state with an unpronounceable name *("Suisse Consine?")*, Pascal became animated. They discussed writers and agreed to correspond. Michael continued on his way and had almost forgotten the encounter until he returned home to find several packets waiting for him containing the collected oeuvre of M. Pascal Dupré. What did the young professor think of his poems, and was the work publishable?

The poems were charming in the style of another age: melodious verses in careful rhyme praising the beauties of nature. With an affectionate respect for the tender poet, Michael translated several and contacted a few small presses, but to no avail. In the end, he chose one of his favorites, had a broadsheet printed privately with the original and an English translation alongside it, and sent copies to Pascal. It was a long poem about a flowering shrub in Pascal's garden that had been blown down by the wind, ending:

> *Car lorsque meurent tant de choses!*
> [For so many things must die]
> *Que s'effacent les souvenirs,*
> [Erasing memories—and yet]
> *Je vois un grand bouquet tout rose*
> [I see a great pink bouquet]
> *Et que rien ne pourra flétrir.*
> [And nothing can wither it.]

A letter came back from Yvette describing how Pascal had been touched and delighted. The correspondence with the Duprés continued, and the next time Michael was able to visit France, he was invited to dinner.

I've seen photographs of that visit and find it remarkable that Yvette seems to have aged so little in the decades since. Even then her thick hair was pure white—not gray, but white. She had a sweet, natural smile and dancing blue eyes—as she does today. She doesn't speak much about her youth, but we have gleaned that Yvette grew up as the only daughter in a large Basque family near the border town of Saint Jean de Luz. Her mother died young, leaving Yvette with the job of raising her brothers. As the years passed, she watched as, one by one, the boys married and moved away while she stayed on in the house as the caregiver for her father, who by then was ill. When she and Pascal met (both on vacation, walking their dogs on a quay in Bordeaux), she was already past fifty and had never married. He was much older, a widower. Pascal tipped his hat, and a few months later they were married.

On Pascal's pension the couple rented a one-bedroom cottage in a hamlet near Bergerac, where they were living when Michael visited. It was a romantic little house, although conditions were primitive. Not only did the house have no heat except for a fireplace, but neither had it a bathroom nor any hot water. Yvette did the dishes in cold water in the small kitchen. There was a toilet in the shed that served as the garage; to use it you had to squeeze into a closet next to Pascal's antique Deux Chevaux. The water in the toilet sometimes froze in winter, which is why there was an ice pick hanging from a hook next to the bowl. Yet Michael saw that Pascal and Yvette were as happy as songbirds there. After dinner, they all sat around the table and listened to Bizet's *Carmen* on Pascal's antique phonograph.

When we married, I received a sweet letter from Yvette congratulating us and hoping that we all could meet. But within months there came news that Pascal had passed away, dozing in his chair while listening to his favorite recording.

"He had a happy life and a peaceful death," Yvette wrote. "How I will miss him!"

She announced that she had received an invitation from her widowed brother to come live with him and her nephews in a suburb of Bordeaux. What Yvette didn't mention was that she was moving from a cottage to a château. For that indeed is where we discovered her at the end of our summer of house hunting when we called at the address she had given us.

I thought we had mistaken our directions when we pulled up in front of a spear-pointed gate and high stone wall stretching out of sight, enclosing vast hectares of forest. The gate had been left open, so we drove through, following a long, winding path through the dense trees. At the end of the *allée* was a remarkable vista: a pale white château in the Empire style built on one level with a portico in front resembling the White House and two long flanking wings on either side. Beyond the dramatic slope on which it stood, the city of Bordeaux spread out in the distance, sunlight sparkling gaily on the Garonne as the wide river curved under a series of bridges. We were sure we had blundered into the wrong property. Two watchdogs bounded out to accost us, but they were collared by a good-looking older man with white hair who rushed out to restrain them, followed by a smiling Yvette. This was her brother, Robert, who greeted us warmly, a Gauloise dangling from his lip. With a courtly gesture, he waved us up the two short steps and through the arch of the wide doorway.

The entranceway opened into an enormous hall that in a former age must have served for lavish receptions. On the walls were tapestries and museum-sized paintings, mainly Spanish religious and mythological works of the eighteenth century. There were carved ceiling moldings painted in gilt. The floor had exquisite parquet work, and I pictured musicians and masked balls, with ladies in sweeping gowns gliding toward the veranda.

Off the great hall were dining and sitting rooms and two long corridors containing the bedrooms. Robert ushered us into a room walled with old blackened mirrors and presented us with *kirs royales*, flutes of champagne flavored with *crème de cassis*. A most gracious host, he saluted us with his favorite toast, which we since have adopted as our own: *"À vos désirs!"* To your desires!

Robert obviously relished our surprise at finding his sister in such opulent surroundings. Before dinner, our expansive host gave us a tour and historical sketch of his domain. The château had been built during the reign of Napoleon by the chief military engineer of Bordeaux, who had been deeded the land by the Emperor himself as a reward for service. This engineer was an ancestor of Robert's late wife, to whom the estate had descended through a circuitous route. Robert's two sons would be the heirs when he was gone. Now, father, sons, sister, and an assortment of guests and relatives occupied the premises, which had sixteen bedrooms. Yvette showed us her quarters at the end of one of the long corridors. It was large enough to be a small apartment, with a soaring ceiling, oversized windows covered by damask curtains, and a fanciful canopy bed. She seemed very much at home and, despite her loss of Pascal, happy to be reunited with her debonair brother, whom she adored.

Dinner was served in an oak-paneled dining room ringed with the mounted heads and antlers of local game, which in former times roamed the estate. We were joined by Yvette's nephews, Philippe and André, then in their twenties, the one wry and clever, the other quiet and kindly, observing his aunt attentively and anticipating her need to fetch this or that from the kitchen. As I gazed around the dining room, it gradually occurred to me that the family might not be as wealthy as appearances indicated. The upholstery of the chairs was a bit worn, and if you looked closely, the mounted animal heads were flea-bitten; little bare patches were interspersed with the fur. The walk to the nearest bathroom was a good distance, and when I repaired there, I saw that the plumbing was antiquated and overdue for renovation. Plaster was cracking in a few corners, and we heard that the roof leaked.

It is one thing to inherit a castle; it is another to keep it up. We later learned that the great engineer's fortune had dwindled through the generations until there was barely enough left to pay the tax man. Robert's side of the family came from a line of shopkeepers in Bordeaux—there was no money there. And sadly, over the next few years, he was forced to sell off sections of the park to meet expenses. Each summer when we returned for our annual visit, the woods surrounding the château would shrink, to be replaced by tracts for public housing. Our dinner parties in the panelled dining room were always gay—plenty of good Bordeaux wine and food, and always an abundance of lively conversation—but sometimes a current of anxiety rippled the air. Yvette hinted that things were precarious, and then disaster struck.

Robert was felled by a stroke. Yvette's letters during that winter were grave. First Robert was bedridden, then hospitalized, then removed to a nursing home, then gone. When we visited Yvette the following summer, the château was in turmoil. Half the surrounding forest had disappeared, sold off to pay the estate taxes. A low-income housing division was going up on land that once had been the property's hunting grounds. Some of the rooms were empty—major pieces of furniture had been sent to auction. In desperation, Philippe and André concluded that the only way to keep their inheritance was to turn the château into a luxury hotel. They aimed to join the prestigious Relais et Châteaux chain. Member hotels, they explained, could be extremely profitable. Their site was superb, the façade of their building impressive, the interior roomy. Of course, a major renovation would be required. The bedrooms would have to be redone, the roof repaired, the kitchen gutted, the plumbing modernized, the wiring brought up to code, the dining room reconfigured, walls removed and added, a swimming pool installed. Philippe would live in the main building and manage the enterprise; André, who was looking for a position teaching horticulture, would live away. What about Yvette? The devoted nephews had not forgotten *Tati*—Aunty—who was beloved not only for her sweet self but as their only living relative. Their plan was to renovate a section of the elegant white-stone racing stables and create several apartments. One would be for Yvette; others could accommodate staff for the proposed hotel.

The brothers started with the stables and managed to get as far as finishing Yvette's apartment. Then they began demolition work in the main building. At that point, things went awry. For capital they were counting on revenue from the land sale. They also were relying on a large bank loan, but either the taxes or the construction costs were higher than anticipated, or perhaps the bank loan was denied—we never learned the full story. In any event, they emptied their pockets halfway through the demolition and were left with an accusing pile of rubble in the interior of one wing. Plans to open a hotel were abandoned. Philippe took a job in town, married, and installed his young family in the one habitable wing of the château. André was offered a lectureship in Paris and moved there. Yvette, constantly cheerful, settled into her modernized apartment in the stables facing a cobblestone courtyard, and that is where she receives us.

For our dinner parties she usually has on hand several old family friends. Nathalie, with a Talulah Bankhead voice and a cigarette always in hand, likes to match wits on literature. Her favorite novels (in French) are by Samuel Beckett, a sophisticated choice. Victor, a retired journalist, reminisces about the visit he paid to New York in the fifties. His wife Odette brings every conversation back to pets—her dogs (brought with her, of course), her cats, a friend's monkey, the inhospitable reception of pets in Italy. Each year we rehearse old scripts for a while and then, after a glass of wine, try to embark on new topics. Like Yvette, the friends are aging; each year they seem more frail. We lift our glasses in memory of Robert and toast: *"À vos désirs!"* But now, on the eve of our departure, we arrive at Yvette's doorstep with concerns about her health and her ability to continue alone in her isolated apartment.

The parable of the brothers' failed hotel is symbolic of a larger drama: the struggle of the French to preserve their country's heritage through tourism—if possible, without wrecking it. Some families find that the only way they can hold onto their land is to develop it. Others save their historic buildings by opening them to the public, but that changes their character and function. The motivation behind these measures is understandable: the French economy is in transition. One of the reasons France remains so beautiful is that 90 percent of the country is still rural, but the agricultural base that supports this way of life is under threat. The young are deserting the farms and villages where they grew up. The number of working farms in France has been cut in half since the 1930s, and as a result, many of the rural villages that visitors find so picturesque are dying. As population flows out of the countryside, the shopkeepers in surrounding villages lose their customers. Shops close, then schools. Pensioners hang on, but as they die, city folk (or foreigners like us) buy these houses for vacation homes, and a living village becomes a summer colony where half the houses are shut up in the winter, rather than a community of mixed generations living and working year round. The new jobs that are created cater to this replacement population, and the tourist industry—with its hotels converted from châteaus, its restaurants and impulse-buying shops (crafts, souvenirs, tee shirts), and its attractions to keep children entertained—displaces agriculture as the economic base. Yet the alternative is to let these villages die. If there are going to be jobs in rural areas to convince the young to stay, how else will they be generated but through tourism?

No doubt, the growth of tourism is inevitable. The Dordogne is far from spoiled, but some of the changes we have witnessed have been disheartening. During our first summer in Castelnaud, when Michael floated for miles down the river on a swimming-pool air mattress, there was hardly a boat in sight. Now the river is crowded with rental canoes and flat-bottomed motor barges (imitating the old cargo barges that plied the river in the nineteenth century), ferrying tourists to no destination and back. Along the banks of the river where corn and tobacco used to grow, fields have been transformed to rows of *campings*. Tents dot the shores, and recreational vehicles snarl traffic on the narrow roads because a season of camping can be more profitable for some farmers than a season of crops.

All the shops at the foot of Castelnaud owe their existence to the summer trade. Where there once was a cornfield, now we have a butcher, greengrocer, hair salon, and outdoor café, and there are expansion plans under way to include a bakery and a hall for social events. The mayor of Castelnaud takes pride in this economic growth and has turned an enterprising hand to encourage it throughout the village. On his own sprawling property on the outskirts of town, he planted a grove of walnut trees and opened a walnut museum. Visitors pay to walk around the walnut grove and to enter the barn to see exhibits. At the entrance to his driveway the mayor installed a row of sculpted walnut shells the size of boulders, molded out of white cement. All over the valley, road signs direct visitors to Castelnaud's famous "Ecological Museum of Walnuts," as if it were the Louvre.

Just as during the Middle Ages, our village still depends on its castle for survival, only now it is tourism rather than arms that provides a livelihood. Although our house is sheltered on a side lane leading off the main path, there is now a constant blur of movement on our periphery, punctuated by delighted shrieks of schoolchildren on their way to visit the castle's museum. Occasionally tourists stray down our lane and wander around the side of our house. However, once they realize they have gone off track, they usually lower their voices and retreat.

We have adjusted to the flow of foot traffic. The visitors are amiable, and there's something charming about the chatter of children in French. It's the automobiles that have caused a problem. Mme. Boucher, whose house gave out on the square, used to complain of car doors slamming *pam! pam!* as people parked and got out, a sound she never used to hear. Fortunately, cars have no access to our little *quartier*—once past the *Mairie*, only pedestrians are allowed. But just one narrow road leads into the village, often making it difficult for residents to get in or out. The commune's solution several years ago was to reroute traffic to the west end of the village, leading the cars to fields that were flattened into parking lots. First one field became a parking lot, then a second, then a third. The lots were graveled, and finally parking meters were installed. Parking meters in a medieval village? Those visitors who are obedient follow the signs, park in the lots, then walk into town, pass through the square, and march up the footpath to the castle. Only locals (*"sauf riverains"*— that's us) are supposed to use the entry road and park in the small lot reserved for their convenience near the square. Of course, not everyone observes the rules.

There was a single café in Castelnaud when we arrived, M. Daniel's, and few regular customers besides M. Crotté. Now there are five snack bars, including one at the castle, each with its rack of postcards. In Mme. Boucher's former gardening shed, just off the square, a couple has set up a regional products shop. And now that she is gone, what will become of Mme. Boucher's house? For the time being, her granddaughter is using it as a weekend getaway, but eventually it may be converted to commercial use. Already portable stands are set up around the square, all selling local merchandise: *fois gras*, walnut specialities, *eau de vie* distilled in Sarlat, fruit jams from the village. One boutique sells women's scarves and hats; another, across the street, offers summer skirts and blouses. There is a bookstall with old and new publications on local history and now an atelier that makes miniature châteaux, which fascinate the children. It is true that these *petits commerces* are owned by local artisans and stocked largely with their own handicrafts. It is also clear that the little businesses around the *Mairie* provide a livelihood for a dozen people, about half from the village and half from nearby towns. Nevertheless, things are changing in Castelnaud. And that unsettles us, particularly as we make ready to leave at the close of summer. It is then that we take stock of every incremental change and feel most vulnerable to their collective impact.

# 12

## THE BATTLE OF CASTELNAUD

KRASSHOOM! The terrifying roar jolts us from our chairs and sends us scrambling out of the house in panic. "What the..." Michael begins, but he doesn't need to finish his sentence. We both see what has shaken the walls: a fast-disappearing fighter plane so low on the horizon that it must have singed the castle keep as it screamed by. These mock attacks have become part of the summer scene. The fighters are Mirage jets based at a military airport outside Toulouse, a hundred miles away. The hotshot pilots love to test how close they can come to the castle without knocking it down. They come in low on practice strafing runs, ripping down the middle of the valley. Flying faster than sound, they are undetectable until right on top of us. Suddenly, there will be a nerve-shattering crash overhead, a rush of shadow, and a retreating roar as a Mirage buzzes the artillery tower and vanishes. When we heard the news a few years ago about an American fighter on a training run that accidentally severed the lines of a cable car in Italy, we immediately identified with the victims. It was all too easy to picture a jet smashing into the castle above us and sending tons of stone tumbling down on our house.

Castles are built for defense in anticipation of war, so perhaps it is fitting that Castelnaud still plays a military role, if only as a practice target for the French air force. What is more troubling is that another kind of struggle is being waged around its parapets, and we are on the front lines. In the old days, peasants living close by the castle's walls could not expect to avoid its quarrels. We find ourselves in a similar position; not much has changed regarding the perils of proximity. In the past several years we have been assaulted by construction clatter, medieval music piped over a sound system, greasy exhaust from a restaurant ventilation fan, and even ballistic missiles from a pint-sized catapult. More than once we have found ourselves under siege from the castle in our backyard.

We have had to remind ourselves that a fortified castle isn't a monastery. You don't go there for peace and quiet. A castle's stone courtyards are meant to ring with the noise of purposeful activity, and they do today, but with a difference. The turnstile for the Museum of Medieval Warfare never stops clicking. Visitors enter through a door at the base of the round artillery tower and climb a winding stone staircase to the *corps de logis*, which housed the living quarters of nobles in the fifteenth century. From there they follow a self-guided tour through several levels of halls, keeps, bastions, and courtyards, exiting at the *basse-cour* with its spectacular view of Beynac Castle and a stunning panorama of the Dordogne and Céou Valleys. Along the way you can visit collections of medieval armor and weapons, pass wax figures of soldiers manning canons and engaged in other chores of combat, admire dioramas depicting sieges, and fiddle with computer games using medieval themes. Throughout the interior there are television monitors tracing the castle's history and stages of construction. Outside on the grounds are full-scale models of ancient war machines: giant catapults, cannons, and something called "the organ," a killing machine made up of a cart on wheels with twelve musket barrels that could fire simultaneously. It is all quite educational and bloodcurdling, a winning combination for parents and kids. We knew we were in trouble when a story about the museum appeared in the *New York Times* and a color photo of the castle (with our house visible below it) entered the *Michelin Guide to Périgord and Quercy.* Yes, it was thrilling to see our house pictured in the *Michelin Guide,* but we knew what was coming. Today *le Château de Castelnaud* is the most visited castle in the southwest of France.

On the tour, visitors learn that the castle's first foray into military history occurred in 1214, when the fearsome Simon de Montfort led his crusaders against the local strongholds of the Cathars. Castelnaud was a powerful fortress in the hands of the heretics; by then it already had been standing for a century. ("Castelnaud" or "Castelnau" translates as "new castle" in the old *langue d'Oc,* and it seems that its first owners adopted "Castelnaud" as their family name.) Under assault by the bloodthirsty Simon, the heretics fled. Simon usually razed defeated citadels, but in this case, he preserved Castelnaud for his headquarters. The hounded Cathars retook the castle in 1215, but within another year the castle was seized again and burned by the Archbishop of Bordeaux. This pattern of destruction and rebuilding continued in succeeding centuries.

During the Hundred Years War the castle changed hands repeatedly, and it became a site of conflict yet again in the sixteenth century during the Wars of Religion. The Caumont family, who then owned the castle, were Huguenots (French Protestants). Their most famous champion was Geoffroy de Vivans, born in Castelnaud in 1543. His military exploits were legendary, such as his scaling the sheer bluff of Domme in 1588 in the dead of night with thirty soldiers to capture the Catholic garrison. Castelnaud remained in the possession of this family for the next two centuries, but it was inhabited only episodically and fell into disrepair. Finally, the castle was abandoned during the French Revolution, when it reverted to the state. For a period the castle complex served as a virtual quarry, as sections were demolished to obtain building stone for public works and private houses. By the end of the nineteenth century, little was left but a romantic ruin.

And so the castle remained, slowly decaying, its towers roofless with trees growing from the vestiges of collapsed walls, until 1966, when it was purchased by its current owner. The scion of a wealthy family and himself a military engineer, the new proprietor aimed to restore Castelnaud to its former glory and at the same time create a setting for his personal collection of medieval arms. That same year, the state declared the ruin a historical monument, and restoration work began.

Of course, when we bought our house we knew that the castle was undergoing restoration, because we could monitor the activity from our terrace. The massive, steeply-pitched *lauze* roof on the keep (*le donjon*) was obviously new, and it was easy to see where lighter colored stone had been used to bridge gaps in the old walls. The upper section of one façade was clearly restoration work. There were workers cleaning vegetation from crannies and masons on scaffolds hauling themselves up and down towers. Occasionally the sound of hammers chipping away on stone was distracting, but the bustle was agreeable. After all, our view was being improved. We were living right under an historical monument—what could be safer? It wasn't until the third summer that we began to feel apprehensive. A ticket booth and turnstile gate appeared at the end of the lane leading up to the château. The museum had opened. At first, this was fine, too. It was exciting to see the inside of the castle, which had been closed to the public. Pedestrian traffic was light. In the evening, the ticket booth closed, and we were free—as we still are—to duck under the barrier and roam around the grounds.

However, by the fourth summer, the buzz of tourists began to register, and by the fifth, we were fretting. That was also the summer of the grease fan. Every day, beginning at noon and lasting until two o'clock, the overpowering smell of onions and cooking grease blew onto our terrace while we were out eating lunch. It didn't take long to track the source: the castle had set up a little restaurant on its grounds. The restaurant wasn't in our line of sight, but it certainly was in our line of smell. Its kitchen had been installed in the rectangular tower, and the vent from the stove's exhaust fan was so positioned that it blew the smoke directly into our yard. We bore the annoyance for a week or two, becoming increasingly irritated. At lunchtime Michael took to lurking about the post to which the restaurant's menu was affixed. As tourists paused to scan the menu trying to decide whether to stay for lunch or leave, he would shake his head gravely and wag a sepulchral finger like the ancient mariner in Coleridge's poem, stopping one in three—not to tell them a tale but to wave them off. He uttered no word, but his finger wag never failed to alarm potential clients. The typical response was for the startled tourist to mimic the wag with raised eyebrows, as if to ask: "no good, eh?" A conspiratorial nod confirmed the worst. Off the pale tourist would go as quickly as possible, grateful for the tip. However, Michael couldn't haunt the premises every day, and some customers ran the blockade anyway. Business couldn't have been very good up at the restaurant, but the grease fan kept blowing. It was time to complain.

In August we learned that the proprietor of the castle, who spent most of the year on his estate near Paris, was scheduled to make an inspection visit. We requested a few moments of his time and met with him in front of our house. This, by the way, was the only time we have seen M. le Châtelain in the flesh. He was younger than I expected, casually dressed, lean and tall to the point of awkwardness. He wore thick, bottle-lens glasses and seemed to have trouble focusing. The image he conveyed was that of a computer programmer rather than a suave aristocrat. We walked him around back and up the stairs to our terrace. Monsieur's manner was reticent, but he listened to us politely, nodding. *"Bon,"* he said at last and agreed to have someone look into the matter during the off season. Indeed, when we returned the following summer, the malodorous draft had been redirected.

Only now we had a more serious adversary: Éléonore d'Alambert, who was the new manager of the restaurant and who, like the town's enemies of old, seemed bound and determined to drive out the inhabitants. Her siege weapon was a cassette of medieval music featuring a high-pitched soprano soloist chanting liturgical hymns—one tape played over and over on a loud speaker, maddening, repeating endlessly on a loop. The broadcast started at lunch and continued throughout the afternoon and on into the evening as a lure to attract clients to the café. Very few came. Perhaps they were repelled by the lugubrious music. Being so close to the castle, we, of course, could not escape, nor could the other victims, our neighbors.

There was only one person in Castelnaud who could abide this mechanical moaning, and that was Éléonore. She reveled in it. A former cabaret singer from Marseilles, she was now past her prime but remained proud of her youthful career as an *artiste*. For her, the chanting was more than an advertisement for the café; it was a reminder of her bygone days in show business. And, she thought, the medieval singing added a touch of class to the establishment. We complained about the music to the castle's manager at the ticket office, to no effect. We wrote to the owner, who replied that he would caution her. The situation only got worse. M. Meunier counseled patience. Better not make an issue of it, he suggested; she couldn't last long at the rate she was going. The neighborhood was getting fed up with the situation. "Wait it out," was his advice.

In college Michael had read Jean Giraudoux's play *La Folle de Chaillot* (*The Madwoman of Chaillot*), from which he constructed a useful epithet. He began calling Éléonore *"la folle du château"* to vent his irritation. We tried ear plugs to block out the music, since it was always too warm at night to keep the windows closed, but the high-pitched perpetual moaning came through. Mme. Boucher complained to us that she no longer was able to sleep as a result of the disturbance. One night it was well after midnight, and the music was blaring. Michael strapped on his armor (at any rate, threw a robe over his pajamas) and sallied forth to joust with our antagonist. When he arrived, he found the place deserted, with Éléonore sitting alone at a table, clinging to a wine bottle. The restaurant had been empty, probably since lunchtime. At close range, the music was deafening, but Éléonore seemed oblivious. Michael tried to rouse her, but scarcely had he begun when *la folle* sprang to life and suddenly took a swing at him with the bottle. How dare a foreigner tell her what to do, she cried, her face contorted with rage. What business was it of his that she played her music? She intended to smash him in his dumb face (*dans la gueule*) if he didn't get out of there, and she knew how to do it too! Éléonore spat forth this rant as she advanced unsteadily, brandishing her weapon. Michael was backed against the parapet. He could see that there was no reasoning with the woman, at least on this occasion, so he slipped away into the shadows. Defiantly, *la folle du château* kept the music going all night.

In the morning we went to see the mayor and found him surprisingly sympathetic. He admitted that most of the other villagers living within earshot of the castle had complained too. "Don't worry," he told us, "the situation will be resolved." He assured us that Éléonore was going bankrupt, and that her lease at the restaurant would not be renewed. Sure enough, when we returned the following summer, a different manager had been given the concession. We neither saw him nor heard him; there was no exhaust smoke to trouble us, no music, no annoyance from the restaurant at all. The café did a quiet little lunch business with visitors to the castle, sold cold drinks in the afternoon, and closed in the evenings. We thought that at last we were safe.

By now we had fallen into the habit of reconnoitering each summer as soon as we arrived. Even before unpacking our bags, we would check the perimeter for threats. What was new at the castle? What provocations loomed? Upon our arrival one year, we found that Fernando, the caretaker of the castle, had planted a pole with a television satellite dish in our yard with a long cable leading to his house. He explained that the owner of the castle would not let him put the dish on his own roof because it clashed with the medieval setting. It didn't last long in our yard, either. All in all, in the several years following Éléonore's defeat, such enemy advances were containable. We weren't prepared for the main assault when it came.

It was in the summer of 1996. We knew as soon as we arrived that something spectacularly bad was afoot. As we watched, disaster unfolded on the little plot of land above our terrace, where the Crottés had once had their garden. The land went back a short distance before rising to join a series of stepped walls leading up to the castle. In this elevated space, someone had constructed a flimsy movie-set façade of a *château fort*. About ten feet high, it was propped up from the back with wooden slats, while its blocks were made out of Styrofoam. What was this tomfoolery? We tried to rationalize the situation and invent scenarios. Maybe Castelnaud was having a fair. This—whatever it was—had to be temporary, or else the model would have been more solidly built, right? It looked like it could tip over at a touch. Yet what was it doing behind our house? And how long would it remain?

Our hearts sank during the week as we watched workers pour a cement foundation into a little moat dug in a semicircle around three sides of the mock castle. Into this foundation they stood eight iron masts each about fifteen feet high, and between the masts they proceeded to hang a sturdy net. Now we were gaping at a Styrofoam castle surrounded by shiny iron poles and what looked like a soccer goalpost. We were completely perplexed until the day that Michael removed the screen from our bedroom window and leaned out far enough to see what was happening at the other end of the grassy corridor, where a small crowd was assembling. It was as if he had been thrown back in time. For there, being dragged into place by a team of soldiers in period costume was a replica of a twelfth-century catapult, built to 25 percent scale. No, it was more than a replica—this was a working model, for it was being cocked and loaded and aimed our way! A docent was giving a lecture on medieval war machines. Children pushed to the front to witness the exciting demonstration. SSPRONG! snapped the arm of the contraption, and THWACK! went the plastic ballistic missile as it struck the little Styrofoam castle and sent its blocks flying into the net. An attendant ran down the firing range and reassembled the breached castle for another round. This second salvo missed the target, including the net, and sailed into our yard, striking the picnic table.

"Can you see what's going on up there?" I called up to Michael, who was sitting in the open window.

"My God, we're being bombarded!" he cried. "It's war!"

Indeed, it was. In its eagerness to boost attendance, the castle kept mounting new attractions, and this one, *le champ de tir au trébuchet*, or catapult range, was destined to become its most popular show. During the high season there would be demonstrations on the hour, included in the price of admission. It was small comfort to say that we had the best seats.

That evening Michael muttered disconsolately, "We'll have to sell the house."

"There must be something we can do," I urged.

We began by summoning the mayor. By now he and the owner of the castle had had a falling out, which we thought might aid our cause. The previous year the mayor had infuriated M. le Châtelain by supporting a plan to build a highway through the center of the valley, which would have been an eyesore. (On this issue we sided with the castle, though we saw no reason to mention that to the mayor.) The castle, in response, hung out a huge banner across its façade, visible for miles, proclaiming "No to the massacre of the valley!" The campaign generated enough opposition to get the project shelved. The mayor had never forgiven monsieur for embarrassing him, so now we offered him the opportunity for a counterattack, a chance to accuse his adversary of a similar breach of aesthetics by cheapening the village with a sideshow. Unfortunately, he seemed disinclined to take up the cudgels on our behalf.

"Yes, it's ugly," the mayor agreed as he stood on our terrace looking up at the pretend castle and its soccer net. *"Et en plus, ça va rouiller,"* he added, gazing at the gleaming poles ("and what's more, they are going to rust"). That hadn't occurred to us, and it made us feel even worse. But the castle's property was not under his jurisdiction, and he could do nothing. He suggested that we write to the national organization governing the protection of historical monuments to see whether such a construction was against the rules. That sounded promising; at least it gave us hope.

While we were in the midst of this conversation, M. Meunier arrived. He had heard of our distress from Anne-Marie.

*"Mon Dieu!"* he exclaimed when he saw what had stirred our wrath, puffing his cheeks to expel air and flapping his arms outward from his sides in a gesture of disapproval. "What *is* that contraption?" he growled. Then, switching to the habitual assessment mode of an old real-estate agent, he surveyed the impact on our property and observed: *"Çe n'est pas gentil du tout."* No, not very nice at all.

He exchanged a few comments with the mayor and then turned to us with an idea. M. Meunier's view was that we should consult with the notary who had shepherded us through the purchase of our house. Perhaps he could find some clause in the building code that could be invoked to redress our grievance. Notaries were often called in to settle property disputes between neighbors, and as former clients, we were entitled to his opinion. We all agreed it was worth a try.

It had been ten years since our visit to the notary's office, up two flights of creaking wooden stairs above the library on la rue de la République, but he remembered us. He didn't say so, but how could he have forgotten the nervous American who had a panic attack and lost his ability to speak French when it came time to sign the contract to buy his house? He came out from around his desk, shook hands, and motioned us to take seats. He himself had aged considerably in the interim, his hair now gray and his movements measured. His mind, though, was still sharp. His worldly mien proclaimed that nothing human was alien to him, no chicanery, subterfuge, or bald effrontery too surprising to a man of his experience. During his years in the profession he had seen it all. Settled deep into his leather armchair, he listened indulgently to our story and then, in his elegant French, brought the interview to a close with a series of staccato questions.

"Tell me this, Monsieur. Is the annoyance you speak of located entirely on the property of your neighbor?"

It was.

"And is this annoyance located within three meters of the boundary of your own property?"

No, it was further back than that.

"Then, unfortunately, Monsieur, there is nothing you can do except to plead with your neighbor to remove it. But he is under no obligation to do so, and I doubt he will."

"I see. So we have no grounds to file a legal action?"

"Monsieur." Here a brief pause, the notary staring at his clasped hands on the desk. "Your adversary comes from a family reputed to possess the second largest fortune in France. A legal action is not recommended." Notaries are nothing if not realists. We took his point.

Back at the house, armed with a dictionary and a handbook on how to write successful business letters in French, Michael set about drafting two epistles, one to the owner of the castle and another to the Agence des Bâtiments de France in Périgueux, which has oversight of historic monuments. To the owner of the castle he wrote:

"Monsieur:" (Salutations are jarringly abrupt in French business letters—no "Dear Mr. So-and-So—just a formal "Sir" followed by a commanding colon. Gestures of ingratiation are reserved for the closing, which requires sycophantic groveling—see below.)

Sir:

Permit me to call your attention to a grave inconvenience resulting from the proximity of a model castle serving as the target for the firing range of a catapult that has been installed on your instructions close to the terrace of our house in Castelnaud. [The reader will gather that this is a literal translation; it sounded just as awkward in French when Michael read it to me, but even after four drafts, it was the best we could do.]

We appeal to you, Sir. We have been living in Castelnaud for ten years, and the principal charm of our house has been its magnificent view of the castle, which dominates our terrace. But now you have interposed between our house and the castle an affair that can only remind one of Euro-Disney. It is necessary to say that this carnival contraption [machin de carnival] does little justice to the site. [I advised against this flourish, but let it go.]

Therefore, Sir, I wish to thank you in advance for your good will and ask that you consider dismantling the model or moving it to some other location.

In awaiting your response, I beg you to believe, Sir, in the expression of my most distinguished sentiments.

And to the Agency of Buildings of France, he wrote:

Sirs:

Following the advice of the mayor of Castelnaud, I am writing to call your attention to a new construction of questionable taste that threatens to ruin the façade of the Château of Castelnaud, which is a protected site. The proprietor of the castle has installed a carnival game that surely must violate the rules governing an historical monument. The game consists of a model of a castle, which is the target of a catapult. The model is enclosed in a net supported by large ugly metal poles, and all of this is in plain view as one enters the village.

Sirs, I appeal to your pride in French history and architecture. I enclose a set of photographs for your consideration and ask whether this construction is in accord with the rules. I believe not. Therefore, I call upon you to take the necessary steps to remove it.

I beg you to believe, Sirs, in the assurance of my most devoted sentiments.

It took the better part of an afternoon to get the letters into shape. There was no immediate reply, nor any eventual reply for that matter, to either. For the next few weeks we sat on our terrace and brooded. We had fallen in love with our house because of its romantic setting. Now that setting was debased by a tawdry exhibition that seemed to mock us whenever we went outdoors. Before, we had a castle above us. Now, we had Château-Histo-Parc. Michael was beside himself and grew more morose each day. We took to eating our evening meals in the kitchen rather than subjecting ourselves to the spectacle outside. Each day we checked the mail in vain, hoping for some response to our letters.

After the initial testing of the catapult, we had been spared further aerial bombardment until one late afternoon toward the end of our stay. I had been bending over my flower bed doing some gardening when a plastic projectile caromed off the top of a pole, looped into the air, and actually bopped me on the behind, causing minor damage to my dignity and collateral damage to my lavender. Michael, who had been watching from the doorway, danced out in a pique.

"That does it! We'll sue them for battery!" he barked. It took me a while to calm him down. To sue the second largest fortune in France for being hit in the *derrière* by a plastic cannonball was not—was not, I repeated—a practical plan.

"Forget about lawsuits," I told him. A better idea had occurred to me while gardening. "Look, what did people like us do in the old days if their house was under attack?"

"I don't know, " Michael replied in an exasperated tone. "They ran—into the castle, behind a moat, behind a wall as far away as they could get behind some barrier."

"Exactly!" I said. "What we need is a barrier between us and the catapult."

Michael sighed. "If we tried to build a wall against the back of the terrace it would have to be thirty feet high to block our view of the damn thing. I've already thought of that."

"I'm not talking about building. I'm talking about planting, planting a barrier hedge *above* the terrace between us and the net." Michael looked skeptical for a moment, then his frown softened. He surveyed the hillside and tried to picture a flourishing hedge.

"Maybe. But we would need to get permission from the castle to plant up there." He looked up again, and his tone turned caustic. "Then we would have to wait umpteen years for the hedge to grow before it made a difference. Other than that, it's not a bad idea."

But I knew that it wouldn't take forever to grow the hedge if we could plant *lauriers*, which are fast-growing laurel shrubs that reach the height of small trees in almost no time if they aren't cut back. They grow everywhere in the Dordogne and spread laterally to make terrific privacy hedges. We had planted a couple at the side of the house a few years ago and they were already eight feet tall and going strong. Here and there along the roadside we had seen stands of *lauriers* that were twenty to thirty feet tall. Yes, it would take some time to give us coverage, but given the angle of vision from our terrace, if we had a stand of *lauriers* separating us from the target castle, they would hide it in a few years and provide a defense against incoming ordinance. There was just one catch. We needed the castle's permission.

Michael was convinced that it was worth a try. The next morning he ventured forth again, armed with the evidence of the violation of our air space and bearing the offending missile under his arm. He marched to the ticket office and asked politely to speak to the castle manager, a Parisian dyed blonde who was always impeccably dressed. Apparently she had been expecting him, for she apologized for the errant bombardment and, to his amazement, acceded at once to his request.

"Yes, I give you authorization. There is no need for me to confer with the proprietor."

This meant that she had conferred with the owner already and that they had decided on some accommodation. Perhaps they were waiting to see whether we would ask them to build a fence around the target, or require them to landscape at the castle's expense. If so, our demand seemed modest, for we offered to bear the cost of the planting and to make the arrangements ourselves. All we were asking for was permission to plant on the castle grounds.

Michael returned with the good news that our plan was approved, and we immediately drove into Sarlat to make arrangements with a nursery. The gardener followed us back to check the site, verified that we had the castle's authorization to plant *("pas de problème"),* and promised a robust series of shrubs along the strategic line that we had indicated. The planting would take place in October, while we were gone.

Meanwhile, Michael had been mulling things over and had a proposal of his own to make to me.

"What do you say that we take next summer off? It would give the *lauriers* time to get established, and after all that's happened, we need a break."

He had been thinking of a house exchange. His brother David and our sister-in-law Lucie had joined a vacation exchange club a few years earlier, had traded their house in Los Angeles for a house in the Alps for a month, and it had worked out well for them. We could try the reverse—offer to trade our house in France for some other vacation site. A year away after the trauma of this summer might be just the right thing, Michael argued. When we returned, the camouflage hedge would be two years along, and we could gauge the success of our strategy. And wouldn't it be interesting to discover how much we missed France when we were elsewhere?

My immediate response was discomfort. We had built a sense of continuity and commitment with our village neighbors and friends, and they might question our loyalty if we failed to turn up next summer. But then, those very friends could be marshaled to our side if we told them the whole story and asked them to help with the plan, monitoring things for us during one summer of strategic absence. Perhaps we did need a break.

We continued the discussion over dinner. What really worried me was that Michael seemed to be distancing himself psychologically from Castelnaud. If this were the beginning of the end, I wasn't ready for it. My suspicion was confirmed when he remarked with a touch of irony that none of this would have happened if we had bought *Cent Étoiles*.

"Without a bathroom or a stick of shade? Yes, and by now they would be treating me for sunstroke and you for constipation," I retorted.

He laughed, breaking the tension.

"Okay, a low blow. But look, we do need to take time out, don't you think? One summer away, and then we'll come back. I'll feel better when that piece of junk is even partially hidden by the shrubs."

He persisted, assuring me that he really wasn't ready to sell the house and no, he wasn't sorry that we bought it. All right, then, that was the plan. But as we got ready to close the house that summer, I was troubled by uncertainty. I had no idea where we would be next year or how I would feel in a different place.

That night I dreamed that we were living in the Middle Ages and Simon de Montfort and his army were attacking the village with giant catapults flinging boulders the size of wagons. A huge stone crashed into the tower above us, sending tons of debris down on our house. I was buried in rubble, unable to breathe, gasping for air.

"Wake up," Michael shook me, "you're having a nightmare."

I opened my eyes to the familiar roof beams over my head and felt a rush of relief.

"I love this house," I said to Michael. "We're not giving it up."

## 13

EXILE AND RETURN

Before closing up for the summer, we scrambled to take photographs, estimate the size of rooms, inventory house contents, and record the procedures of opening, closing, and upkeep. We would need this information for an ad in the house-exchange booklet, a promotional letter to send prospective exchangers, and a file of house information for eventual tenants. As we compiled the materials, I found myself reminiscing about where and why we purchased the armoire, the writing desks, and the tawny leather chair that we regularly vied over. I wrote instructions on how to close the armoire without stressing its delicate panels and considered whether tenants should be asked to apply beeswax by hand, as we did each year. No, they couldn't be expected to lavish love on every item in the house; they would be here for a holiday.

Back in Madison, we dealt with the challenge of constructing the telegraphically short ad in the house-exchange booklet. We were entitled to two short lines, and most people filled these with symbols from a predetermined list. Neither the symbols nor their translations captured the spirit of our house. How were people to know that the house nestled, with complete architectural harmony, within a village built around a medieval fortress? How could we convey the unique beauty of a room with walls of soft-colored stone? Would readers of the catalogue know anything about Périgord—the way of life, the food, the history, the natural beauty, the sweet temperament of the people? There were no symbols for castles, abbeys, caves, prehistoric sites, open-air markets, outstanding restaurants, or fine wineries.

Finally, we decided on this one-line description: "Stone cottage, village, castle view, cave area." Through symbols we indicated the presence of a fireplace, shower, garden, mountains, river, public swimming, hiking/walking, and tourist attractions (right in the backyard if they wanted one, but we did not have the space or gumption to explain about that—besides, our new hedge would diminish the nuisance). A photo would have to convey all else. We chose a shot that showed not only the house but the retaining wall for the terrace and a glimpse of the houses on either side. Our thinking was that people who were looking for rural isolation would be warned off by the evident proximity of neighbors, while those seeking village charm would be enticed by the white hibiscus flourishing by the stone porch and the scarlet petunias decorating the terrace wall.

Working with one of these exchange catalogues is rather like using a dating service. You give information about your house, set dates when you will entertain an exchange, and state your preferences for locations. Our notion was to try a clean break, a vacation as different as possible from those at Castelnaud, and we decided that meant coastline instead of inland, cool instead of hot, modern instead of ancient, and English-speaking instead of Francophone. So we posted GB, CA, US, USNW—Great Britain, Canada, United States, and more specifically the northwest states. We hoped that in one of those locations there would be some couple tiring of misty summers at their seaside cottage and dreaming of inland hill towns, steady sunshine, and French cuisine.

We sent in our ad and waited for replies—any time after Christmas, we were told. Away visiting family in the week before New Year's, we wondered how many letters there might be from exchangers waiting at home in our mailbox. When we returned, we discovered five replies—two from San Francisco, two from Seattle, and one from Vancouver. The hopeful correspondents all sent letters with tantalizing descriptions. We went back to the exchange catalogue to scrutinize the ads, locate the addresses on city maps, and consider the relative merits of neighborhoods. There was a sense of pressure, since we knew that most exchangers sent off multiple feelers and would be eager to make a match as early as possible.

We were elated when our first pick, Vancouver, confirmed by e-mail that an exchange was on. A recently retired math professor and his artist wife were keen on a month in Périgord, and we would occupy their townhouse condominium on the marina opposite Granville Island. We would have views of water, yachts, the island markets, the skyscrapered city beyond the island, and the mountains towering over all. That's all we needed to know. The Canadians were more curious. In response to a steady stream of questions, we acknowledged our reservations about growing tourism in the village but lovingly described our favorite restaurants, outdoor markets, butchers and bakers, grocery stores and hardware stores, historic and prehistoric sites, car tours and walking trails, friends and advisors. By spring we had composed a sheaf of documents on the house and the area and had spent more than a few nostalgic hours remembering our Castelnaud experiences. In June, when we packaged up the big iron house key for mailing to Vancouver, I was a little nervous about parting with our house, even temporarily.

Our first days in Vancouver washed away those misgivings, and a phone call from the Canadians in Castelnaud assured us that everything was fine at that end, too. Ignoring Vancouver's famous drizzles, which greeted us in early July, we started a routine that brought out the best of the city, rain or shine. Mornings I woke to first light striking the water outside our bedroom windows. Quietly, I padded to the wall of glass looking out at the marina and the island. I drew the curtains, so that Michael could sleep a few more hours while I took my usual long morning walk. In this case that meant not the *Grande Randonnée* trails of Périgord but stepping out the door to the boardwalk, which leads to the bay, by beaches, past yacht clubs, through homey neighborhoods, and out to the headland where the University of British Columbia reigns. Other days I would take the bus to the trails through Stanley Park. By midmorning I would be home, tingling from exercise and the misty morning air, ready for breakfast on the tiny terrace overlooking the marina. I would find Michael there, finishing his coffee and the morning paper. Sometimes in our breakfast chats we wondered whether the folks from Vancouver had breakfasted that day on our terrace in Castelnaud and how the *lauriers* were doing. Then we would turn to our day's plan.

We had agreed to work every day from midmorning to midafternoon on a writing project we had taken on together. Before going off to our separate spaces—I to the computer in the math professor's office, Michael to a leather chair overlooking the marina—we would decide on the outing that would provide that afternoon's sight-seeing. With the prospect of a reward dangling before us, we went uncomplainingly to our labors, which bound us more closely to France than we could have imagined, even though we were thousands of miles distant. For the job we had taken on was the translation of a cookbook that had been written by our neighbor Jean-Louis in Castelnaud.

The summer before, in the midst of the catapult campaign, Jean-Louis had come to dinner carrying a present held behind his back. Over *kirs* on the terrace, he presented a small book bound in thick, glossy, maroon red paper, with an inset painting of walnuts and walnut leaves. With pride he watched us start at seeing his name just under the title. To our delight, we discovered that Jean-Louis was the author of a beautiful little book on walnuts and how to cook with them. We had known him to be a marvelous cook, and we had often talked about local cuisine. But he had kept the cookbook a secret from us until it was finished and published (self-published, to be exact).

Over the summers we had grown to appreciate our quiet neighbor's wit and invention. We had observed him daily from our kitchen window—contemplatively smoking his first morning cigarette sitting on his front stoop, talking at great length to his beloved dog, rushing down the hill to make his first appointment for the day, coming back home late and tired, but always with time for *badinage* with the Americans. His remarks stretched our French comprehension to accommodate puns and ironies, and he was able to make us laugh even when we didn't quite get the joke. We had found him a delight since the first day we met. And that was a surprise, for in the beginning we had worried that he would be the neighbor most likely to cause problems. When M. Meunier first showed us our house, we were wary of a little sign posted on a door close by that read *Tourneur sur bois* (Woodworker). We anticipated noise out of that profession, or at the very least, the whine of a lathe. As it turned out, we endured only one day of intermittent screeches of a buzz saw, since Jean-Louis produced his wares in the quiet of winter and sold them in tourist season. He took to the lathe in summer only when he received a special order. Besides, his career as a woodcarver was winding down. The fact was that he could barely make ends meet once he paid for materials, tools, and rental of a shop for summer sales.

In the next few years, Jean-Louis adopted and shed a succession of work identities as a cabinetmaker, canoe-rental agent, kayak instructor, and book salesman. During all that time—without ever mentioning it to us—he dreamed of starting his own press dedicated to publishing books on the subject of Périgord. For several years he bought and sold old books on the region, going from fair to fair in summer and from bookstore to bookstore in winter, developing along the way a network of fellow connoisseurs and publishers. These acquaintances knew of tomes on the life of old Périgord that had gone out of copyright and could be repackaged for a modern audience. A few had notions of books they would write if only there were an interested publisher. Establishing a press would require capital, taste, know-how, and faith. Jean-Louis had all but the first. But his friends in the printing business helped him locate a sturdy old press, which he installed where other Frenchmen put their wine, in the cellar. Booksellers gave him advice on marketing. When he determined that a walnut cookbook would be his first project, an artist friend paid back years of free dinners with some exquisite drawings and an attractive book design. Nadine, the smart and funny girlfriend Jean-Louis had lured from Paris to Castelnaud, proved her worth by volunteering to test the recipes, even though she had previously cooked nothing more complicated than an omelet. In little more than a year from the moment he first conceived his cookbook, Jean-Louis was a publisher, editor, and author, and his first book was on the market. As he sat before us with Nadine at his side and his book in the middle of the table, he looked a very happy man.

For the next few evenings, I worked my way through a batch of Jean-Louis's tempting recipes, finding each more delicious than the other. Then, while savoring a tender forkful of *Dinde Sautée aux Morilles et Noix*, I was accosted by Michael's proposal: "What would you say to translating Jean-Louis's book into English?"

My initial surprise gave way to mounting interest. Michael already had a publisher in mind—a small press in California that prides itself on vanguard taste and high production values. If I would translate a few recipes, he would send them with the original French version to the publisher, whom he knew from an earlier mutual project. All we needed was Jean-Louis's blessing and the conviction that we would enjoy the work for its own sake (in the book business, few should anticipate profit). For Jean-Louis the idea was immediately attractive. It would do his name and his press good to be known in the United States, and with luck there might even be royalties.

By late autumn, contracts had been signed on both sides of the Atlantic, and we were committed. Then, through the teaching year, we prepared for writing. Michael compiled research on U.S. walnut production and on recent medical studies on walnuts and heart health. He located domestic sources for walnut liqueur, and together we held a tasting to determine whether Amaretto, cognac, or sweet vermouth could be used as a substitute for the liqueur in some preparations. I bought a digital scale that converted from ounces to grams and started testing recipes. For the trickier dishes, I asked friends to try out my translations, and they reported back on their results. We had walnut dinner parties. But it was not until summer vacation that we were free to turn our full energies to the project.

On Canada's Pacific shore, far from Castelnaud and walnut groves, we immersed ourselves in French. Michael translated Jean-Louis's introduction, all about walnut production, processing, and sale. He added a section on medical research proving the cholesterol-cutting effects of eating walnuts. Meanwhile, I translated recipes. At first I thought that all I needed to do was translate ingredients and directions accurately, making sure to convert metric measures to cups and teaspoons. That worked for the salads, but for little else. As I translated, I now and again sensed that something was wrong. For example, the temperature, properly converted from French oven settings to the Fahrenheit equivalent, might sound too hot. I would try the recipe out and, sure enough, the walnut cake would overcook. My guess is that the tinny ovens available in rural France leak more heat than their American equivalents, and so they need to be set at a higher temperature. Whatever the reason, each translated recipe had to be tested. Then there was the question of how to handle ingredients not generally available in the states. What would I say could be substituted for *crème fraîche, cèpes,* or *verjus?* French yogurt has a richer taste and a lighter texture than American yogurt, and a cup of American all-purpose flour outweighs a cup of French flour every time. Adjustments would be necessary.

Meeting in the condo's kitchen for a midday snack, we found each other happy and energized. Michael was in psychic partnership with Jean-Louis, struggling to express to an English-speaking audience the meaning of the walnut for Périgord and its people. I was trying to be faithful to generations of Périgordian cooks as I tested Jean-Louis's recipes, using ingredients bought at a Vancouver supermarket. Mentally, we both spent half our days in France. Evenings, we would eat out on our borrowed terrace, looking at boats moored in the marina. The crisp air was Canadian, and so were the ingredients on our plates. But the flavor was Périgordian. With our apéritif we might have Jean-Louis's version of prunes stuffed with chopped apples and walnuts. Our meats were crusted with walnuts and our poultry stuffed with magical combinations of walnuts and fruits. Until I got the directions just right, we had variations of walnut ice cream night after night—coffee-walnut, honey-walnut, banana-walnut, nougat-walnut.

"It feels like Périgord-sur-Mer," said Michael.

Meanwhile, late afternoons we were out in Vancouver, enjoying its modern skyline, the reflections of sun on its mirror-faced buildings, the sparkling interaction of water, glass, and sky, the nearness of refreshing redwoods and rainforest. On cloudy afternoons we were in museums studying Native American carvings, or Northwest oil paintings, or contemporary crafts. On bright afternoons we frequented the city's outstanding zoo, aquarium, beaches, parks, and gardens. The variety of Vancouver kept us stimulated, and the mercury on our pleasure thermometer was soaring. According to residents, midsummer brings the year's only decent weather to Vancouver, but it was midsummer now, and we were thoroughly taken by the city's beauty. In fact, we were having a wickedly good time. Michael began to hatch a new plan: What if we were to sell the house in Castelnaud and buy a little summer getaway here? For a week we toyed with this fantasy but then came back to earth. Property is expensive in Vancouver. And what were we—serial monogamists, ready to give up a decade of emotional investment in France to plunge headlong into another commitment, one that could waver in another ten years? The marital analogy began to take hold. We were in a trial separation from Castelnaud—a pretty risky style of separation, in which you are allowed to date freely. Here we were, getting it on with our first date, Vancouver. Perhaps that was a bad sign—but did it say something about Castelnaud or about us? Had Castelnaud changed so much over the years that we were no longer compatible, or had we just run off for a fling like tipsy conventioneers? It was suspiciously easy to feel happy and free in a pretty place where we had nothing invested and where no one laid claims on us.

The month flew by, and we took our old worries out to dinner with us on our last night. We had spent the afternoon restoring the condo to the Bauhaus spareness favored by the owners, and we didn't want to sully the kitchen by fixing one last walnut recipe. We headed for the Chinese restaurant at the foot of the Granville Bridge. In this city of Asian influx, standards for Chinese cuisine are as high outside Chinatown as within its precincts. The delicate meal should have lifted our spirits. However, end-of-vacation blues and unresolved questions about Castelnaud resisted the upward pull of Ginger Shrimp and Three Delicacies Sizzling Rice. Our Vancouver stay had been idyllic, but as agreed, we were discussing our return to France next summer. As the fortune cookies arrived, I was brooding—remembering our last goodbye coffee with Mme. Boucher and the depth of the affection we shared. Next year would test whether Castelnaud, with all its changes, was still our beloved place.

"Well, what does the fortune cookie tell us?" asked Michael, who had left his reading glasses at home.

Its aptness was uncanny. I got that funny feeling in the chest that tells you something crucial is happening. When I finished reading, Michael said, with a touch of wonder, "You can call that prophetic, all right." And it was at that moment, I think, that he began to move out of reverse and into neutral.

Back in Madison in August, we were pleased to hear that France was about to send us some welcome guidance on our cookbook project. Henri Delechaux, the son of my walking companion, Annie, was an expert *pâtissier*, based at one of the most renowned pastry shops in Paris. Annie had told me that Henri was interested in coming to the United States, so I had given his name to a good friend of ours who had just been appointed manager of the bakery in an upscale food market that was soon to open in Madison. While she was still planning the new bakery and its staffing, she visited France, took a workshop on country breads, and stopped in at the *pâtisserie* on the Left Bank where Henri worked. She was impressed. Within months, in time for the bakery's September opening, Henri and his wife Hélène arrived in Madison. We saw the young couple frequently during that year. Not only did we reap the praises of our friends for helping to bring an authentic French pastry chef to town, but Henri was always helpful as I experimented with recipes for the dessert section of the cookbook. Unfortunately for Madison, visa problems prevented the couple from remaining beyond the year, and they returned to Paris, where they now run their own successful *pâtisserie*.

It was curious to see our Midwestern college town through the eyes of these young Parisians. They loved the placidity, the lakes, the parks, the landscaped university campus, the low cost of living, the variety of housing styles, their apartment's efficient plumbing and air conditioning, their enormous color television, and their second-hand American car with automatic transmission. Conversely, I found myself feeling distant from home at odd moments as I showed them around. Commonly, when we return from France I am struck by the differences in scale between a small city like Madison and the towns of the Dordogne. Some of our side streets in Madison are as wide across as their major roads. Our oversized cars, houses, markets, malls, enormous farms—the sprawl of things, the profligate space of the Midwest—amazes me. But the shock of the unfamiliar wears off in a day or two, and it's France that seems distant and exotic, while Wisconsin resumes its position as the norm. With Henri and Hélène in Madison during the year, I found my thoughts constantly oscillating between our two worlds, keeping me off balance.

Periodically we found it necessary to telephone France with some question for Jean-Louis relating to the production of the cookbook. Michael always seized these occasions to ask about the progress of our *lauriers.*

"*Ils poussent bien,*" Jean-Louis assured us. So they were growing well; that was a good sign.

By Christmas, the completed manuscript went to press, and in the spring, the English version of *The Walnut Cookbook* appeared, garnering a batch of pleasing reviews. As fast as they came in, we faxed them to Jean-Louis. Throughout the spring we were buoyed by the momentum of publication as we prepared for our return to Castelnaud after an absence of two years. A few weeks before departure, we telephoned. Though we had written to let Jean-Louis know our arrival date, we had not heard back from him since his elated reply to our fax of an early and favorable review in the *New York Times*. From his hesitant greeting, "Ah, Bet-sy, Mi-ceuil . . . " we knew there was something wrong, and we both immediately feared damage to the house.

After a few moments of unrevealing chitchat, Michael asked, *"Qu'est ce qu'il y a, Jean-Louis? Quelque chose est arrivée?"*

It was the news of Mme. Boucher's death. It had happened a few weeks earlier, but Jean-Louis had been hesitant to call us, knowing the distress it would cause. Regret rang in his voice, over the transatlantic wires. It seems there had been a storm, and the lights had gone out in Castelnaud for two days. Mme. Boucher had put herself to bed with the aid of a candle, but when she got up in the night she fumbled in the dark, tried to walk across the room, and fell, breaking a hip. From the shock, or from the stress of lying until morning when she was found by a neighbor, she suffered a stroke. A few days later she died, just a week short of her ninety-third birthday.

On our flight to Bordeaux that summer we struggled with conflicting emotions. We were happy about the cookbook and our new connection with Jean-Louis, but beneath the surface we were grieving for Mme. Boucher. And at the same time, we were wrestling with the anxieties that had driven us into temporary exile from our summer home. I wondered how losing our dearest neighbor would affect our attachment to the village. Would we now feel that an era was over and it was time to move on? Or would our mourning show us just how much we were part of the village family? With these questions gnawing at us, we suffered poorly the long night's plane ride, the seemingly endless morning stopover in Brussels, and then, at noon and with jet lag developing, the hot drive from the Bordeaux airport to Castelnaud.

It must have rained heavily in the Dordogne that spring. The river was high, and the valley had never looked more beautiful. Though it was only the twenty-fifth of June, the fields were deep green, thick with corn and tobacco. A great swath of Van Gogh sunflowers greeted us as we made the turn at Vézac and headed down the valley toward our castle.

No sooner had we approached the turn for the Castelnaud bridge than we began to notice the inevitable "improvements." The departmental government had invested in official signage for Castelnaud's tourist attractions. At the corner, stacked neatly one above the other, were uniform arrows pointing the way to the castle, Josephine Baker's les Milandes, her swimming pool, the mayor's walnut museum, and something new, a "museum of rocks." Affixed underneath were smaller plaques noting the names of four cafés and two restaurants. Well, at least there were no new ones, and no hotel yet, either.

As we crossed the river and made the turn to mount toward the castle, we noted that the shops by the river were looking prosperous, with a new common courtyard and lushly blooming flower beds. When we made our turn (with the aid of more new signage), we were dismayed to find that the road up to the village had been widened. We had thought we were safe from such an invitation to more traffic because the hillside was so steep, leaving no room for expanding the narrow road that hugged its side. Modern engineering had solved that problem. I had to admit that the smooth new pavement, the widened road, and the flowering slopes were genuine improvements, but this could mean that buses and trucks, which used to have no access to the village, would now be pouring through it. And what might the village itself look like if the widening extended right up to the castle walk?

We held our breath as we sailed smoothly up the hill, catching the first sight of the castle and the village around it, looking glorious. When we reached the fork where the road branches off into town, Michael made a sudden pull to the left into what used to be the vegetable garden of M. Fauré, our odd-job friend. His half-acre plot had been turned into a parking lot for tourist buses! We were taken aback, caught between dismay at the razing of our neighbor's garden and relief at the fact that the buses were provided a halting place. They were not to enter the village. For we could see that the road from here to the castle was just as narrow as ever. We stepped out of the car and read the signs instructing the bus drivers to turn off their motors and to under no account attempt to go higher into the village. Passengers should dismount and walk the short distance to the castle. I stood there with my feet on the gravel, remembering all the times when M. Fauré, gathering his morning crop of string beans, had risen from his crouch over this ground to call out a friendly greeting. This corner was no longer neighbor's ground; it was now commercial space. That's what my heart said, but my head replied that the village had found a clever way to accommodate the tourist traffic without impinging on the village proper.

We gave each other a nervous look, reentering the car in silence. The drive up the hill was as beautiful as ever—even more so, since the ancient dry-point walls had been restored after decades of tumbling into ruin, and the roadside was weeded and trimmed with a degree of care that the *cantonniers* (the village roadwork men) had never before taken. The village, too, seemed particularly well maintained. The stonework on houses and shops was in better repair. Shutters had been varnished. Windowsills had been painted. Pots of hanging geraniums were everywhere. A recently planted *mai* towered over the *Mairie* with a hand-painted placard congratulating the mayor on his reelection.

As we pulled up next to the *Mairie*, I noticed a new openness about the whole *quartier*. "What looks different?" I asked Michael. "There's nothing new here, but the shape feels changed. Was something taken down?"

He looked around, as he got out and walked back to the trunk to begin removing the luggage. "You're right. There are no telephone poles, no electric poles. They must have put the wires underground."

The whole village looked lovely. The cafés were thriving, with pretty new parasols over the tables, and there were two or three new businesses, tucked into spaces that had been unused. Just inside the archway over the path to the castle and our house, there was a new shop specializing in gourmet cookies. Through the open doorway, it looked as French as it could be, with cookies stacked in neat geometrical shapes on a table dominating the room. I knew that the cookie was thoroughly un-French, a British incursion into continental culinary space, and yet here was the new shop looking elegant and Gallic, and obviously delighting the tourists, French and foreign.

I was smiling now, as I followed Michael, each of us pulling two suitcases up the pathway to the house. Halfway up, Michael dropped the suitcase handles, threw his arms up in the air, and shouted, "Unbelievable! The *lauriers* have hidden the catapult—well, almost." And suddenly he was running up the hill. It was no mystery where he was heading. I knew he would round the house, dash up the steps behind it, and plunge onto the terrace, looking to see how high the *lauriers* had grown in two years. I had to laugh. There I was, with four suitcases in the middle of the pathway, being ogled by tourists passing up to or down from the castle. I decided that nobody was likely to steal our suitcases, but just in case, I calculated which two of the four held the most valuable items, and I pulled those up to the front porch. Still no Michael, though I could hear him shouting down to me, something about how many feet to go.

I brought the remaining suitcases up the back staircase to the terrace, where we would bring them in by the side door (by experience we had learned that this was preferable to pulling suitcases up the interior spiral staircase). Then I noticed that Jean-Louis and Nadine had cleaned off a year's growth of ivy and weeds. They had also cut the terrace lawn, torn out the roots of the stinging weeds the French call *ronces,* and planted *belles de nuit,* which were all closed up in the sunlight but I knew would open exotic scarlet blossoms at evening. This was more impressive to me than the *lauriers,* which I had always assumed would do what *lauriers* do and grow a yard a year. (Michael, never much interested in plant life, had never really trusted the predictions that a row of mere laurel bushes could create a wall of defense between him and the enemy.) In best marital fashion, I pretended to be more astonished than I was at the miracle of the *lauriers*, and then he pretended to be more impressed than he was at the amount of work Jean-Louis and Nadine had done on our behalf in the yard. We both knew that these were two propitious developments. With a natural screen between us and the catapult, Michael's chief irritation with our summer home might be assuaged. And the generous labors that Jean-Louis and Nadine had given to our property spoke volumes about our growing friendship.

The next morning, our house-opening chores took a quarter the usual time, because Jean-Louis and Nadine had turned on the water and electricity, swept the house out, and chased away cobwebs. By noon Michael had the terrace table and chairs washed off and was sitting out there, with his back to the village, gazing admiringly at the *lauriers* and urging them skyward with little tickling motions of his upturned fingers. I had just returned from the grocery store by the river, where I had bought just enough for today's lunch and dinner. (Tomorrow would be the Sarlat outdoor market, and we would get our week's provisions there.) I brought us both up a Perrier with a twist of lemon. We sat in the just-warm-enough sun, in friendly silence. Michael continued to coach the *lauriers* upwards, millimeter by millimeter. I looked down at Mme. Boucher's shuttered house. The garden was still active. I had seen Fernando and Maria working there in the early morning. They had taken over the plot, with permission from Mme. Boucher's granddaughter, who preferred to see the garden tended rather than let it go wild. Still the house looked dead with the shutters closed tight in the middle of the day. And I missed the sight of Mme. Boucher hoeing in her blue dress and apron, or straightening to call up a greeting when she saw us out on our terrace.

I broke the silence to lay out a plan for the weekend ahead. How about doing the Saturday Sarlat market in the morning, bringing home not only provisions but the flowers for our outdoor pots, which had grown over the years to number ten. Then in the afternoon I would pot the flowers and weed the garden beds, while Michael mounted the back wall and tended the *lauriers*.

"Tend—what do you mean? They're growing fine."

It was hard to convince him that it was necessary to prune the *lauriers*—he did not want them to lose an inch. But he relented when I explained that he needn't shorten them, just trim the overhanging sides, so that they would put energy into growing up, not sideways. He had a grand Saturday. While I shopped at the outdoor market, he went to the hardware store and bought a high ladder and the sharpest pruning shears on the market. I reminded him to get fertilizer and antislug pellets (this idea too produced skepticism, but I assured him that he would find slugs eating the laurel leaves, and they could be deterred by just spreading little green pellets on the soil around each bush's trunk). By evening the *lauriers* looked much more like the neat wall they were intended to be, and our terrace seemed like paradise regained.

Though we had a larder full of wonderful sausages, cheeses, and green leaves (lettuces, arugula, chard, basil, flat parsley), we kept our reservation for dinner at l'Esplanade in the *bastide* of Domme. We faced this dilemma each summer. Saturday was the day we went to the farmers market and had the freshest ingredients to cook from. But it was also the night when the fine restaurants were at their best. They too had been to the farmers market. And they were pulling out the stops for the busiest night of the week. Saturday the chef made his most daring dishes. To support him, the staff was alert, the flowers were fresh picked, the diners were elegantly dressed, and the atmosphere was festive. So we often left a full refrigerator to go out to Saturday dinner.

We arrived at Domme early enough to walk along the parapet and view the splendor of the valley at sunset. A red and yellow hot-air balloon in the shape of a lightbulb glided slowly across the pink-tinged sky, carrying some lucky sightseers by castles and cliffs toward a landing field beyond the bend of the river. For a good ten minutes we stood at the railing, watching the balloon flow one way and the river the other. Then it was time to cross once more the threshold of L'Esplanade, the restaurant that had given us so many delightful evenings over the years. From the *patronne's* warm greeting to the last jellied confection, the meal and its ambiance were perfection. In parting, we shook hands with our favorite waitress and the *patronne* herself, thanking them for another wonderful dinner.

It was half past eleven by the time we reentered Castelnaud. This was the first time we had seen the village with the street lamps gone, and the effect was magical. Small lights shaped like gas lamps hung on the loveliest buildings. As we mounted, we saw that one hung to the side of our door. Yesterday we had not even noticed the addition. Apparently the village had eminent domain when it came to placing fixtures. We rather liked it, but we decided not to stop at our doorway. Instead, we continued up to explore the castle grounds at midnight. Strategically placed lamps gave just enough glow to keep us from stumbling on the rocky path. The castle keep, when we reached it, was luminous. As we stole around the castle to the cliffside wall, the sky opened up, and we faced a brilliant moon centered over a valley sparkling with light. Just under the moon glowed the boxlike castle of Marqueyssac. On the other side of the river the chapel of Beynac glimmered dimly, with the castle left in darkness. We could see only its base, with the cliff lit from below. Across the black gulf of the valley, tiny house lights twinkled like stars.

I remembered the first time we had stood at this spot. On that day, Michael asked me if I would buy the house or not. The sunlit valley had convinced me to say yes. Now I was going to test its nighttime allure.

"Well," I asked him, "was the Vancouver fortune cookie right?"

"I was just thinking about that," he said, taking my hand.

The message in the cookie was this: "The way to love anything is to realize that it might be lost."

EPILOGUE

"Let's celebrate," said Michael. "How about a Fourth of July barbecue out on the terrace?" The Fourth was coming up next Saturday. We would have plenty of time to make the invitations and prepare for company. We had just bought a new grill, but whether we could find all the trimmings for this quintessentially American feast was another question.

"No problem," said Michael. "We'll have paper plates and hot dogs on rolls and plenty of mustard and relish, and if we have to make a few compromises, who will notice?"

Since Bastille Day was coming up, too, we proposed a Franglais holiday, a combined *fête nationale*. We invited Pierre and Annie Delechaux, the Lavals, Jean-Louis and Nadine, and M. Meunier to our Franco-American barbecue. In the invitations we joked that the

French and the Americans shared a similar history: while the French had thrown out the English in the fifteenth century, we had followed suit in the eighteenth. As our guests gathered on our terrace, the mood was lighthearted. I was right: it had been difficult to find all the ingredients we needed—but the compromises were successful. For starters we had *Crème d'Avocat sur Canapés*, one of the recipes out of *The Walnut Cookbook*, and then came the main grill. Instead of hamburgers on buns, we had *steak hâché* on *brioches*, and instead of hot dogs on rolls, *merguez* on *baguettes*, with walnut mustard on the side. There was a salad and strawberry shortcake for dessert (strawberries were at their peak just now), plenty of beer and wine to drink, and cola for the kids.

Of course, the "kids" by now were grown. Nicole, lovely and languid at twenty, was training to become a state nursery school teacher and was serious about a boyfriend who lived in the next town. We saw a photo of him dressed in his soccer uniform—a real bruiser. Precocious little Babette was a teenager whizzing through math and science at her lycée and setting her sights on becoming a lawyer. Her ambition was to train in Paris and return to Sarlat to practice. Anne-Marie and Antoine were delighted with these developments, because they presaged that their daughters would find work and husbands in the region and be able to stay near.

All the Lavals appeared to be prospering. Anne-Marie had given up her tourist shop, in fact had rented the space to the gourmet cookie boutique. She was now selling funeral decorations to mortuaries and motoring around the region as a wholesaler of such supplies. I couldn't imagine a more unlikely calling for someone with her joking manner and rippling laughter. For his part, Antoine was complaining that he now had more electrical work than he could handle. With the renovation and second-home industry flourishing, he found he needed an assistant and a bigger truck. Last summer was a madhouse, but he had taken time off in the fall as always for truffle hunting and was just now telling Michael about a remarkable cache that he and his father had bagged.

Annie was bursting with news about Henri and Hélène, who were working hard in Paris at their new *pâtisserie,* and she had big news, too, about her daughter Roxanne, who had just made her a grandmother. The whole family would be coming for a visit in August. Pierre was busy with plans to add a *pigeonnier* to their house with a guest room for visitors. A swimming pool was on the horizon, too, if not this summer, then maybe the next.

"So when you and I go walking, Michael and Pierre can keep each other company at the *piscine,*" Annie offered.

I glanced over at Jean-Louis and Nadine and saw that they needed to be drawn into the conversation, as they were standing off to one side holding their plates and nibbling at the *faux* hamburgers. I went over, and soon we were talking about their latest projects at the press, one a novel of peasant life before the Revolution, and several new cookbooks of regional recipes. Like us, Jean-Louis and Nadine are *périgourdins* by adoption; he was born in Angoulême, she in Paris. The others had lived in the village all their lives. Michael broke the ice by proposing a toast. He stepped into the house and brought out copies of *The Walnut Cookbook* both in French and English.

"Here's to The Truffle Press," he called out, holding up the books.

I added: "and to our colleagues Jean-Louis and Nadine!"

Our guests seconded the toast with enthusiasm, most raising glasses of the beer we had provided instead of their usual wine. The exception was M. Meunier. He had arrived late, carrying his own bottles, and now he was trying to convince Pierre to sample some of the wine. Remembering the last bottle of his we tried, we interceded.

We expressed astonishment that M. Meunier was still making wine now that he spent most of the year in the north, but no, he told us, he had leased his vineyard to a young neighbor, who was responsible for the current vintage. We were delighted to see our old friend in such excellent spirits. There was even a bounce to his step, which gave us a rather different picture than the one we recalled two years ago.

"So, how are things going in Arras?" we asked.

"*Eh, bien, c'est différent,*" he began, and we anticipated the familiar litany about the north. But instead, he thrust out his chin tolerantly, pouted, and said with a nod, "*Ça va.*"

We asked about family: Claire, the grandchildren, and now the great-grandchildren.

"All well," he assured us, and all here in Castelnaud for the summer—we must come down to visit. And suddenly we were immersed in a flow of anecdotes about the little ones. He grew animated as he talked about them, and it soon became clear that M. Meunier had found his niche as the family patriarch. In Arras the children loved to climb up on his lap and listen to stories about the fairyland with a castle far away where Grandpa was born and where he would take them in summer if they were good.

"And M. Pasquet?"

"*Il va bien, aussi.*" The tone was noncommittal.

"*Et ses bêtes?*" Michael couldn't resist asking.

"*Elles ne sont plus.*"

No further details were forthcoming. Either the bugs were dead (decimated perhaps by some environmental disaster affecting tropical insects in northern France), or (more likely) a caretaker had been found to look after them at M. Pasquet's school. Either way, they would come no more to Périgord.

We munched our burgers, drank, and chatted. The talk turned to the castle. Michael pointed out the fine points of the *laurier* defense against small catapults, and we recalled past summers when Éléonore had nearly driven us mad with her music or when the restaurant exhaust fan in the tower spoiled our meals. M. Meunier thought that fiasco was the funniest and reminded us that he had been born in that very tower, which his father, a penniless farmhand, had fixed up for his bride and the birth of their son. Of course, the tower had been smaller then, in a cruder style than the present restoration, and without a *lauze* roof.

"So, what do you think about all these changes at the castle ?" Michael inquired.

He shrugged. "*Ça change,*" he agreed, "*mais, c'est normal.*" People must eat, so there must be restaurants. Buildings fall down, so they must be restored. As for him, he had his memories, and that was enough. "*Ça suffit.*"

It was time now for dessert. And with the strawberry shortcake, Michael brought out some sparklers he had picked up at the hardware store in lieu of fireworks. They were little handheld gizmos. You pumped a plunger with your thumb, and it spun a metal wheel against a whetstone, giving off sparks. They helped create a festive air. Everyone worked one, and we shouted *"Vive l'Amérique! Vive la France!"* Anne-Marie wanted to know how the American national anthem went, and then she wanted me to sing it, but nobody can sing "The Star Spangled Banner," I told her; it wasn't like "La Marseillaise," which has a roaring good melody.

"Well, try it anyhow," she insisted.

I struggled with a few bars but became self-conscious and gave it up. Then Michael came to my rescue.

"I have just the song for this occasion," he declared. "And everyone knows it."

With that, he ducked into the house and emerged in less than a minute with the cassette recorder, clearing a place for it on the picnic table. Everyone gathered around expectantly, holding their drinks. I had already guessed his choice. It was Josephine Baker, of course, with her sweet, high-pitched voice of the 1930s piping over the old scratches of a pre-war recording. She was putting her whole heart into it, crooning her theme song of two loves, for America and France.

*"J'ai deux amours . . . "*

Michael smiled at me and raised his glass. I knew then that we were staying.

With a gesture to include the company, he called out another toast, and in unison the guests returned it: *"À vos désirs!"*

# FOR FURTHER READING

For armchair and actual travelers who would like to learn more about the Dordogne, the following list is a beginning:

Bentley, James. *The Most Beautiful Villages of the Dordogne.* Photography by Hugh Palmer. London: Thames and Hudson, 1996.

This gorgeous coffee-table book devotes four to six pages of color illustrations to each of thirty-eight villages, arranged by the classic geographical divisions of Périgord Vert, Blanc, Noir, and Pourpre. Castelnaud appears on the back cover of the jacket (with our house clearly visible).

Brook, Stephen. *The Dordogne.* Photography by Charlie Waite. Topsfield, Mass.: Salem House, 1987.

Arranged as an introduction to the region, this volume ranges beyond the northern and eastern borders of the Department to territory that both locals and tourists regard as "of the Dordogne," such as the Causse. The text provides guidance for an intelligent tour.

Busselle, Michael, and Freda White. *Three Rivers of France*. New York: Arcade, 1989.

Originally published in 1952, Freda White's elegantly written book on the regions of the Dordogne, the Lot, and the Tarn remains a classic of travel writing. The new edition, updated by Michael Busselle and including photographs of the scenes described by White, is still the richest guide to the region.

Caro, Ina. *The Road from the Past: Traveling through History in France*. San Diego: Harcourt Brace & Company, 1994.

Caro guides the reader on a tour of France organized by history rather than geography. The chapters on the Dordogne and the Hundred Years War are particularly good and include a description of Castelnaud's role in medieval warfare.

Jones, Vicky. *Dordogne Gastronomique*. Photography by Hamish Park. London: Conran Octopus, 1994.

This tribute to the cuisine of the Dordogne focuses on regional ingredients and their sources, as well as on traditional recipes and the restaurants that have perfected them.

Michelin. *Tourist Guide: Dordogne*. Paris: Michelin et Cie, published annually.

Whether you read your "green guide" in French or in English, and whether it's titled "Dordogne (Périgord-Limousin)" or "Périgord/Quercy" (the focus changes in different editions), you'll be getting reliable guidance on motoring routes, site visits, history, and attractions. Thorough, if a bit stiff.

O'Shea, Stephen. *The Perfect Heresy: The Revolutionary Life and Death of the Medieval Cathars.* New York: Walker, 2000.

If you want to know more about the Cathars, this book provides a short, readable history of the sect and the crusades mounted against its members by the Church in the thirteenth century.

Rose, Phyllis. *Jazz Cleopatra: Josephine Baker in Her Time.* New York: Doubleday, 1989.

Rose presents a sympathetic biography of Josephine Baker, covering her years at les Milandes; the book includes photographs.

Sieveking, Ann. *The Cave Artists.* London: Thames and Hudson, 1979.

Readers will find this a good introduction to the prehistoric cave paintings of the Dordogne. The author summarizes a number of theories concerning the paintings' origins. Illustrated.

Toussaint, Jean-Luc. *The Walnut Cookbook.* Trans. and eds. Betsy Draine and Michael Hinden. Berkeley, Calif.: Ten Speed Press, 1998. Originally published as *La Noix dans tous ses états:131 Recettes Gourmands* (Castelnaud-la-Chapelle, France: L'Hydre, 1994).

Both a recipe book and a compilation of lore about walnuts in Périgord, this is the volume we describe in chapter 13.

And here, to conclude, is one of its recipes (reprinted with the kind permission of the publisher):

*Cake aux Pruneaux et aux Noix*

Walnut-Prune Cake

(Serves 6 to 8)

9 tablespoons of unsalted butter, softened

1 1/4 cups sugar

5 eggs

2/3 cup finely ground almonds

Scant 2/3 cup sifted flour

1/2 teaspoon baking powder

2 tablespoons Cognac (or other brandy)

1 cup walnut pieces

1 cup pitted prunes

1. Preheat oven to 350 degrees Fahrenheit. Butter and flour sides and bottom of a 9-inch round cake pan.
2. In a mixing bowl, beat the softened butter. Add the sugar, and beat until creamy. Add the eggs one by one, beating continually. Add the powdered almonds. Sift the flour and baking powder into the batter, beating until smooth. Finally, fold in the brandy.
3. In a food processor, finely chop the walnuts. Cut the pitted prunes into 1/4-inch dice.
4. Add the chopped walnuts and diced prunes to the batter. Pour the batter into the prepared cake pan.
5. Bake for about 45 minutes, or until the top is rounded and golden. Let cool for 10 minutes. Loosen the sides by running a knife around the side of the pan. Turn the cake onto a cooling rack, with a quick jerk. Immediately reverse the cake, and let it cool top side up.
6. Serve slices alone or with a small scoop of walnut ice cream.